PENG

HELL

Hunter S. Thompson's research on the Hell's Angels involved more than a year of close association with the outlaws – riding, loafing, plotting and eventually being stomped. A native of Louisville, Kentucky, he began writing as a sports columnist in Florida. He started his novel while studying at Columbia University in New York City. He later worked on newspapers and magazines in New York, San Juan and Rio de Janeiro. His articles appeared in *Esquire*, *Rolling Stone* magazine and the *San Francisco Chronicle*.

In the early 1960s, while working as a Caribbean stringer for the *New York Herald Tribune*, Mr Thompson began a second novel, *The Rum Diary*, which he finished in Big Sur. Later he became South American correspondent for the *National Observer*, living on Copacabana Beach and travelling extensively throughout that continent. Upon his return to America, suffering from amoebic dysentry and culture shock, he went to hunt elk and breed Doberman pinschers in Woody Creek, Colorado.

His other books include *Fear and Loathing in Las Vegas*, *Fear and Loathing on the Campaign Trail, 1972*, *The Great Shark Hunt*, *Songs of the Doomed*, *Generation of Swine*, *Better Than Sex* and *Fear and Loathing Letters Vol. 1: 1955–67*. Hunter S. Thompson died in 2005.

HUNTER S. THOMPSON

HELL'S ANGELS

PENGUIN BOOKS

PENGUIN BOOKS

Published by the Penguin Group
Penguin Books Ltd, 80 Strand, London WC2R 0RL, England
Penguin Group (USA) Inc., 375 Hudson Street, New York, New York 10014, USA
Penguin Group (Canada), 90 Eglinton Avenue East, Suite 700, Toronto, Ontario, Canada M4P 2Y3
(a division of Pearson Penguin Canada Inc.)
Penguin Ireland, 25 St Stephen's Green, Dublin 2, Ireland (a division of Penguin Books Ltd)
Penguin Group (Australia), 250 Camberwell Road, Camberwell, Victoria 3124, Australia
(a division of Pearson Australia Group Pty Ltd)
Penguin Books India Pvt Ltd, 11 Community Centre, Panchsheel Park, New Delhi – 110 017, India
Penguin Group (NZ), 67 Apollo Drive, Rosedale, North Shore 0632, New Zealand
(a division of Pearson New Zealand Ltd)
Penguin Books (South Africa) (Pty) Ltd, 24 Sturdee Avenue,
Rosebank, Johannesburg 2196, South Africa

Penguin Books Ltd, Registered Offices: 80 Strand, London WC2R 0RL, England

www.penguin.com

First published in the USA by Random House 1966
Published in Great Britain by Penguin Books 1967
Reprinted in Penguin Classics 2003
Reissued in Penguin Books 2009

002

Printed and bound in Great Britain by Clays Ltd, Elcograf S.p.A.

ISBN: 978-0-141-98809-2

www.greenpenguin.co.uk

FSC www.fsc.org MIX Paper from responsible sources FSC™ C018179

Penguin Books is committed to a sustainable
future for our business, our readers and our planet.
This book is made from Forest Stewardship
Council™ certified paper.

To the friends who lent me money and kept me mercifully unemployed. No writer can function without them. Again, thanks.

H.S.T.

In my own country I am in a far-off land
I am strong but have no force or power
I win all yet remain a loser
At break of day I say goodnight
When I lie down I have a great fear
Of falling.

François Villon

Contents

Acknowledgements

THE author wishes to thank the following for permission to reprint material:

Henry Miller and Grove Press for *The World of Sex*, by Henry Miller.

Newsweek for 'California: The Wild Ones'.

Time for 'The Wilder Ones'.

William R. Rodgers and *The Farm Tribune* for 'They Came, They Saw, They Did Not Conquer'.

Mrs Pat Whitright for her letter on page 39.

The New York Times for 'California Takes Steps to Curb Terrorism of Ruffian Cyclists'.

John Allison and Hollis Music, Inc., for 'The Bowery Grenadiers', by John Allison.

Jerry Leiber, Mike Stoller and Quintet Music, Inc., for 'Black Denim Trousers and Motorcycle Boots'.

Birney Jarvis and *Male* for 'The Hell's Angels Scandal – Black Boots, Booze, and Highway Broads'.

Springfield Music Ltd and Chappell & Co., Inc., for 'A World of Our Own'.

Woody Guthrie and Ludlow Music, Inc., for 'Do-Re-Mi'.

William Murray and Curtis Publishing Company for 'Hell's Angels'.

Jerry Cohen and *The Los Angeles Times* for 'Hell's Angels: How They Live and Think'.

Allen Ginsberg and *Liberation* for 'To The Angels', by Allen Ginsberg.

Mr Ralph Barger for his telegram on p. 264.

ROLL EM, BOYS

1

CALIFORNIA, Labour Day weekend . . . early, with ocean fog still in the streets, outlaw motorcyclists wearing chains, shades and greasy Levis roll out from damp garages, all-night diners and cast-off one-night pads in Frisco, Hollywood, Berdoo and East Oakland, heading for the Monterey peninsula, north of Big Sur. . . . The Menace is loose again, the Hell's Angels, the hundred-carat headline, running fast and loud on the early morning freeway, low in the saddle, nobody smiles, jamming crazy through traffic and ninety miles an hour down the centre stripe, missing by inches . . . like Genghis Khan on an iron horse, a monster steed with fiery anus, flat out through the eye of a beer can and up your daughter's leg with no quarter asked and none given; show the squares some class, give 'em a whiff of those kicks they'll never know. . . . Ah, these righteous dudes, they love to screw it on. . . . Little Jesus, the Gimp, Blind Bob, Gut, Buzzard, Zorro, Hambone, Clean Cut, Tiny, Terry the Tramp, Frenchy, Mouldy Marvin, Mother Miles, Dirty Ed, Chuck the Duck, Fat Freddy, Filthy Phil, Charger Charley the Child Molester, Crazy Cross, Puff, Magoo, Animal and at least a hundred more . . . tense for the action, long hair in the wind, beards and bandanas flapping, earrings, armpits, chain whips, swastikas and stripped-down Harleys flashing chrome as traffic on 101 moves over, nervous, to let the formation pass like a burst of dirty thunder . . .

*

> They call themselves Hell's Angels. They ride, rape and raid like marauding cavalry – and they boast that no police force can break up their criminal motorcycle fraternity. – True, *The Man's Magazine* (*August 1965*)

> They're not bad guys, individually. I tell you one thing: I'd rather have a bunch of Hell's Angels on my hands than these civil rights demonstrators. When it comes to making trouble for us, the demonstrators are much worse. – *Jailer, San Francisco City Prison*

Some of them are pure animals. They'd be animals in any society. These guys are outlaw types who should have been born a hundred years ago – then they would have been gunfighters. – *Birney Jarvis, a charter member of the Hell's Angels. who later became a* San Francisco Chronicle *police reporter*

We're the one percenters, man – the one percent that don't fit and don't care. So don't talk to me about your doctor bills and your traffic warrants – I mean you get your woman and your bike and your banjo and I mean you're on your way. We've punched our way out of a hundred rumbles, stayed alive with our boots and our fists. We're royalty among motorcycle outlaws, baby. – *A Hell's Angel speaking for the permanent record*

•

... The run was on, 'outlaws' from all over the state rolled in packs towards Monterey: north from San Bernardino and Los Angeles on 101; south from Sacramento on 50 ... south from Oakland, Hayward and Richmond on 17; and from Frisco on the Coast Highway. The hard core, the outlaw elite, were the Hell's Angels ... wearing the winged death's-head on the back of their sleeveless jackets and packing their 'mamas' behind them on big 'chopped hogs'. They rode with a fine, unwashed arrogance, secure in their reputation as the rottenest motorcycle gang in the whole history of Christendom.

From San Francisco in a separate formation came the Gypsy Jokers, three dozen in all, the number two outlaw club in California, starved for publicity; and with only one chapter, the Jokers could still look down on such as the Presidents, Road Rats, Nightriders and Question Marks, also from the Bay Area, Gomorrah ... with Sodom five hundred miles to the south in the vast mad bowl of Los Angeles, home turf of the Satan's Slaves, number three in the outlaw hierarchy, custom-bike specialists with a taste for the flesh of young dogs, flashy headbands and tender young blondes with lobotomy eyes; the Slaves were the class of Los Angeles, and their women clung tight to the leather backs of these dog-eating, crotch-busting fools as they headed north for their annual party with the Hell's Angels, who even then viewed the 'L.A. bunch' with friendly condescension ... which the Slaves didn't mind, for they could dump with impunity on the other southern clubs – the Coffin Cheaters, Iron Horsemen, Galloping Gooses, Comancheros, Stray Satans and a homeless fringe element of human chancres so foul that not even the outlaw clubs – north or south – would claim them except in a fight when an extra chain or beer bottle might make the crucial difference,

*

> Over and over again I have said that there is no way out of the present impasse. If we were wide awake we would be instantly struck by the horrors which surround us. . . . We would drop our tools, quit our jobs, deny our obligations, pay no taxes, observe no laws, and so on. Could the man or woman who is thoroughly awakened possibly do the crazy things which are now expected of him or her every moment of the day? – *Henry Miller, in* The World of Sex *(1,000 copies printed by J. N. H., for 'friends of Henry Miller', 1941)*

> People will just have to learn to stay out of our way. We'll bust up everyone who gets in our way. – *A Hell's Angel talking to police*

> Better to reign in hell than serve in heaven. – *John Milton,* Paradise Lost

*

On the morning of the Monterey Run, Labour Day 1964, Terry the Tramp woke up naked and hurting all over. The night before he'd been stomped and chain-whipped outside an Oakland bar by nine Diablos, a rival East Bay cycle club. 'I'd hit one of their members earlier,' he explained, 'and they didn't appreciate it. I was with two other Angels, but they left a little bit before me, and as soon as they were gone, these bastard Diablos jumped me outside the bar. They messed me up pretty good, so we spent half the night lookin' for 'em.'

The search was futile, and just before dawn Terry went back to Scraggs's small house in San Leandro, where he was living with his wife and two children. Scraggs, a thirty-seven-year-old ex-pug who once fought Bobo Olson, was the oldest Angel then riding, with a wife and two children of his own. But when Terry came down from Sacramento that summer to look for a job in the Bay Area, Scraggs offered bed and board. The two wives got along, the kids meshed, and Terry found a job on the assembly line at a nearby General Motors plant – in itself a tribute to whatever human flexibility remains at the shop level in the American labour movement for Terry at a glance looks hopelessly unemployable, like a cross between Joe Palooka and the Wandering Jew.

He is six feet two inches tall, 210 pounds heavy, with massive arms, a full beard, shoulder-length black hair and a wild, jabbering demeanour not calculated to soothe the soul of any personnel specialist. Beyond that, in his twenty-seven years he has piled up a tall and ugly police record: a multitude of arrests, from petty theft and battery, to rape, narcotic offences and public cunnilingus – and all this without a single felony conviction, being officially guilty of nothing more than what any spirited citizen might commit in some drunk or violent moment of animal weakness.

'Yeah, but that rap sheet's all bullshit,' he insists. 'Most of those charges are phoney. I've never thought of myself as a criminal. I don't work at it; I'm not greedy enough. Everything I do is natural, because I need to.' And then, after a moment. 'But I guess I'm pushin' my luck, even if I'm not a criminal. Pretty soon they'll nail me for one of these goddamn things, and then it's goodbye, Terry, for a whole lot of years. I think it's about time I cut out, went East, maybe to New York, or Australia. You know, I had a card in Actors' Equity once, I lived in Hollywood. Hell, I can make it anywhere, even if I am a fuck-up.'

On another Saturday he might have slept until two or three in the afternoon, then gone out again, with a dozen or so of the brethren, to find the Diablos and whip them down to jelly. But a Labour Day Run is the biggest event on the Hell's Angels' calendar; it is the annual gathering of the whole outlaw clan, a massive three-day drunk that nearly always results in some wild, free-swinging action and another rude shock for the squares. No Angel would miss it for any reason except jail or crippling injury. The Labour Day Run is the outlaws' answer to New Year's Eve; it is a time for sharing the wine jug, pummelling old friends, random fornication and general full-dress madness. Depending on the weather and how many long-distance calls are made the week before, anywhere from two hundred to a thousand outlaws will show up, half of them already drunk by the time they get there.

By nine o'clock that morning both Terry and Scraggs were on their feet. Vengeance on the Diablos could wait. Today, the run. Terry lit a cigarette, examined the bumps and welts on his body, then pulled on a pair of crusty Levis, heavy black boots, no underwear and a red sweatshirt smelling of old wine and human grease. Scraggs drank a beer while his wife heated water for instant coffee. The children had been put with relatives the night before. The sun was hot outside. Across the Bay, San Francisco was still covered by a late-lifting fog. The bikes were gassed and polished. All that remained was the gathering of any loose money or marijuana that might be lying around, lashing the sleeping-bags to the bikes and donning the infamous 'colours'.

The all-important colours . . . the uniform, as it were, the crucial identity . . . which the Attorney-General of California has described with considerable accuracy in a fuzzy but much-quoted official document titled 'The Hell's Angels Motorcycle Clubs'.

The emblem of the Hell's Angels, termed 'colors', consists of an embroidered patch of a winged skull wearing a motorcycle helmet. Just below the wing of the emblem are the letters 'MC'. Over this is a band bearing the words 'Hell's Angels'. Below the emblem is another patch bearing the local chapter name, which is usually an abbreviation for the city or locality. These patches are sewn on the back of a usually sleeveless denim shirt. In addition, members have been observed wearing various types of *Luftwaffe* insignia and reproductions of German Iron Crosses. Many affect beards and their hair is usually long and unkempt. Some wear a single earring in a pierced ear lobe. Frequently they have been observed to wear belts made of a length of polished motorcycle drive chain which can be unhooked and used as a flexible bludgeon.

The Hell's Angels seem to have a preference for large heavy-duty American-made motorcycles [Harley–Davidsons]. Club members usually use a nickname, designated as their 'legal' name, and are carried on club rolls under that name. Some clubs provide that initiates shall be tattooed, the cost of which is included in the initiation fee. Probably the most universal common denominator in identification of Hell's Angels is their generally filthy condition. Investigating officers consistently report these people, both club members and their female associates, seem badly in need of a bath. Fingerprints are a very effective means of identification because a high percentage of Hell's Angels have criminal records. . . .

Some members of the Hell's Angels as well as members of other 'disreputable' motorcycle clubs belong to what is alleged to be an elite group termed 'One Percenters', which meets monthly at various places in California. The local Hell's Angels clubs usually meet weekly. . . . Requirements for membership or authority to wear the '1%-er' badge are unknown at this time. . . . Another patch worn by some members bears the number '13'. It is reported to represent the thirteenth letter of the alphabet, 'M', which in turn stands for marijuana and indicates the wearer thereof is a user of the drug.

This compact description of rancid, criminal sleeziness is substantially correct except for the hocus-pocus about the one percenters. All Angels wear this patch, as do most other outlaws, and all it means is that they are proud to be part of the alleged one per cent of bike riders whom the American Motorcycle Association refuses to claim. The A.M.A. is the sporting arm of the Motorcycle, Scooter and Allied Trades Association, a fast-growing motorcycle lobby that is seeking desperately to establish a respectable image – an image the Hell's Angels have consistently queered. 'We condemn them,' says an A.M.A. director. 'They'd be condemned if they rode horses, mules, surfboards, bicycles or skateboards. Regretfully, they picked motorcycles.'

The A.M.A. claims to speak for all decent motorcyclists, yet its fifty thousand or so members rode less than five per cent of the 1,500,000 motorcycles registered in the United States in 1965. As one of the trade magazines has noted, that left a lot of outlaws unaccounted for.

Terry and Scraggs left the house about ten, taking it easy on the two mile run through downtown Oakland, keeping the engine noise down, aware of the stares from passing motorists and people on street corners, observing stop signs and speed limits, then suddenly accelerating a half-block from the house of Tommy, vice-president of the local chapter, where the others were waiting. Tommy was living on a quiet, deteriorating residential street in East Oakland . . . an old neighbourhood with small, once-white frame houses sitting close to each other on tiny lots and sparse front lawns worn down by generations of newsboys delivering the

Oakland Tribunal. Now, on this holiday morning, his neighbours were out on front porches or at living-room windows, watching the awful show build up. By eleven about thirty Hell's Angels were there, half blocking the narrow street, shouting, drinking beer, brushing green dye on their beards, gunning their engines, adjusting their costumes and knocking each other around to get the feel of things. The girls stood quietly in a group, wearing tight slacks, kerchiefs and sleeveless blouses or sweaters, with boots and dark glasses, uplift bras, bright lipstick and the blank, wary expressions of half-bright souls turned mean and nervous from too much bitter wisdom in too few years. Like the Angels, the girls were mainly in their twenties – although some were obvious teenagers and a few were ageing whores looking forward to a healthy outdoor weekend.

In any gathering of Hell's Angels, from five to a possible hundred and fifty, there is no doubt who is running the show: Ralph 'Sonny' Barger, the Maximum Leader, a six-foot, 170-pound warehouseman from East Oakland, the coolest head in the lot, and a tough, quick-thinking dealer when any action starts. By turns he is a fanatic, a philosopher, a brawler, a shrewd compromiser and a final arbitrator. To the Oakland Angels he is Ralph. Everybody else calls him Sonny . . . although when the party gets wild and loose he answers to names such as Prez, Papa and Daddy. Barger's word goes unquestioned, although many of the others could take him in two minutes if it ever came to a fight. But it never does. He rarely raises his voice – except in a rumble with outsiders. Any dissenters in the ranks are handled quietly at the regular Friday-night meetings, or they simply fade out of the picture and change their life pattern so as never to cross paths with any group of Angels.

If the gathering at Tommy's was a little disorganized, it was because Sonny was in a rehabilitation centre, serving six months for possession of marijuana. With Sonny in jail, the others were keeping the action to a minimum – even though Tommy, in his quiet, disaffiliated sort of way, was running the show pretty well. At twenty-six he was a year younger than Barger: blond, clean-shaven, with a wife and two children, making $180 a week as a construction worker. He knew he was only filling in for the Prez but he also knew that the Oakland Angels had to make a tough, full-strength appearance at the Labour Day Run. Anything less would forfeit the spiritual leadership back to southern California, to the San Bernardino (or Berdoo) chapter – the founding fathers, as it were – who started the whole thing in 1950 and issued all new charters for nearly fifteen years. But mounting police pressure in the south was causing many Angels to seek refuge in the Bay Area. By 1965, Oakland was on its way to becoming the capital of the Hell's Angels' world.

Prior to their ear-splitting departure, there was a lot of talk about the Diablos and what manner of lunacy or strange drug had caused them to commit such a sure-fatal error as an attack on a lone Angel. Yet this was a routine beef, postponed* and forgotten as they moved on to the freeway for an easy two-hour run to Monterey. By noon it was so hot that many of the riders had taken off their shirts and opened their black vests, so the colours flapped out behind them like capes and the oncoming traffic could view their naked chests, for good or ill. The southbound lanes were crowded with taxpayers heading out for a Labour Day weekend that suddenly seemed tinged with horror as the Angel band swept past . . . this animal crowd on big wheels, going somewhere public, all noise and hair and bust-out raping instincts . . . the temptation for many a motorist was to swing hard left, with no warning, and crush these arrogant scorpions.

At San Jose, an hour south of Oakland, the formation was stopped by two state Highway Patrolmen, causing a traffic jam for forty-five minutes at the junction of 17 and 101. Some people stopped their cars entirely, just to watch. Others slowed to ten or fifteen miles an hour. As traffic piled up, there were vapour locks, boil-overs and minor collisions.

'They wrote tickets for everybody they could,' said Terry. 'Things like seats too low, bars too high, no mirror, no hand hold for the passenger – and like always they checked us for old warrants, citations we never paid and every other goddamn thing they could

* Within a month the Diablos had disbanded – terrorized by a series of stompings, beatings and chain-whippings; the Angels hunted them down one by one and did them in. 'Things like that don't happen very often,' Terry explained later. 'Other clubs don't usually mess with us, because when they do, that's the end of them.'

think of. But the traffic was really piling up, with people staring at us and all, and finally, by God, a Highway Patrol Captain showed up and chewed those bastards good for "creating a hazard" or whatever he called it. We had a big laugh, then we took off again.'

*

> We get treated good here [in Monterey]. Most other places we get thrown out of town. – *Frenchy from Berdoo talking to a reporter not many hours before the Angels were thrown out of town*

*

Between San Jose and the turnoff to Monterey, 101 rolls gracefully through the rich farming foothills of the Santa Cruz Mountains. The Hell's Angels, riding two abreast in each lane, seemed out of place in little towns like Coyote and Gilroy. People ran out of taverns and dry-goods stores to stare at these fabled big-city Huns. Local cops waited nervously at intersections, hoping the Angels would pass quietly and not cause trouble. It was almost as if some far-ranging band of Viet Cong guerrillas had appeared, trotting fast in a tight formation down the middle of Main Street, bound for some bloody rendezvous that nobody in town even cared to know about as long as the dirty buggers kept moving.

The Angels do try to avoid trouble on the road. Even a minor arrest in a country town at the start of a holiday weekend can mean three days in jail, missing the party, and a maximum fine when they finally come to court. They know, too, that in addition to the original charge – usually for a traffic violation or disorderly conduct – they will probably be accused of resisting arrest, which can mean thirty days, a jail haircut and a fine of $150 or so. Now, after many a painful lesson, they approach small towns the same way a travelling salesman from Chicago approaches a known speed trap in Alabama. The idea, after all, is to reach the destination – not to lock horns with hayseed cops along the way.

The destination this time was a big tavern called Nick's, a noisy place on a main drag called Del Monte, near Cannery Row in downtown Monterey. 'We went right through the middle of town,' recalls Terry, 'through the traffic and everything. Most of the guys knew Nick's but not me because I was in jail the other time.

We didn't make it till about three because we had to wait in a gas station on 101 for some of the guys running late. By the time we got there I guess we had about forty or fifty bikes. Berdoo was already in with about seventy-five, and people kept coming all that night. By the next morning there were about three hundred from all over.'

The ostensible purpose of the gathering was the collection of funds to send the body of a former Angel back to his mother in North Carolina. Kenneth 'Country' Beamer, vice-president of the San Bernardino chapter, had been snuffed by a truck a few days earlier in a desert hamlet called Jacumba, near San Diego. Country had died in the best outlaw tradition: homeless, stone broke, and owning nothing in this world but the clothes on his back and a big bright Harley. As the others saw it, the least they could do was send his remains back to the Carolinas, to whatever family or memory of a home might be there. 'It was the thing to do,' Terry said.

The recent demise of a buddy lent the 1964 affair a tone of solemnity that not even the police could scoff at. It was the sort of gesture that cops find irresistible: final honours for a fallen comrade, with a collection for the mother and a bit of the uniformed pageantry to make the show real. In deference to all this, the Monterey police had let it be known that they would receive the Angels in a spirit of armed truce.

It was the first time in years that the outlaws had been faced with even the semblance of civic hospitality – and it turned out to be the last, for when the sun came up on that bright Pacific Saturday the infamous Monterey rape was less than twenty-four hours away from making nationwide headlines. The Hell's Angels would soon be known and feared throughout the land. Their blood, booze and semen-flecked image would be familiar to readers of *The New York Times*, *Newsweek*, *The Nation*, *Time*, *True*, *Esquire* and *The Saturday Evening Post*. Within six months small towns from coast to coast would be arming themselves at the slightest rumour of a Hell's Angels 'invasion'. All three major television networks would be seeking them out with cameras and they would be denounced in the U.S. Senate by George Murphy, the former tap dancer. Weird as it seems, as this gang of costumed hoodlums converged on Monterey that morning they were on the verge of 'making it big', as the showbiz people say, and they would owe most of their success to a curious rape mania that rides on the shoulders of American journalism like some jeering, masturbating raven. Nothing grabs an editor's eye like a good rape. 'We really blew their minds this time,' as one of the Angels explained it. According to the newspapers, at least twenty of these dirty hopheads snatched two teenage girls, aged fourteen and fifteen, away from their terrified dates, and carried them off to the sand dunes to be 'repeatedly assaulted'.

REPEATEDLY . . . ASSAULTED
AGED 14 AND 15 . . .
STINKING, HAIRY THUGS

A deputy sheriff summoned by one of the erstwhile dates said he 'arrived at the beach and saw a huge bonfire surrounded by cyclists of both sexes. Then the two sobbing, near-hysterical girls staggered out of the darkness, begging for help. One was completely nude and the other had on only a torn sweater.'

Here, sweet Jesus, was an image flat guaranteed to boil the public blood and foam the brain of every man with female flesh for kin. Two innocent young girls, American citizens, carried off to the dunes and ravaged like Arab whores. One of the dates told police they tried to rescue the girls but couldn't reach them in the mob scene that erupted once the victims were stripped of their clothing. Out there in the sand, in the blue moonlight, in a circle of leering hoodlums . . . they were penetrated, again and again.

The next morning Terry the Tramp was one of four Angels arrested for forcible rape, which carries a penalty of one to fifty years in the penitentiary. He denied all knowledge of the crime, as did Mother Miles, Mouldy Marvin and Crazy Cross – but several hours later, with bond set at a lowly $1,100 each, they were lodged in the Monterey County Jail in Salinas . . . out there in Steinbeck country, the hot lettuce valley owned in the main by smart second-generation hillbillies who got out of Appalachia while the getting was good, and who now pay other, less-smart hillbillies to supervise the work of Mexican *braceros*, whose natural fitness for stoop labour has been explained by the ubiquitous Senator Murphy: 'They're built low to the ground,' he said, 'so it's easier for them to stoop.'

Indeed. And since Senator Murphy has also called the Hell's Angels 'the lowest form of animals', it presumably follows that they are better constructed for the mindless rape of any prostrate woman they might come across as they scurry about, from one place to another, with their dorks carried low like water wands. Which is not far from the truth, but for different reasons than California's ex-lightfoot senator might have us believe.

Nobody knew, of course, as they gathered that Saturday at Nick's, that the Angels were about to make a publicity breakthrough, by means of rape, on the scale of the Beatles or Bob Dylan. At dusk, with an orange sun falling fast into the ocean just a mile or so away, the main event of the evening was so wholly unplanned that the principal characters – or victims – attracted little attention in the noisy crowd that jammed Nick's barroom and spilled out to the darkening street.

Terry says he noticed the girls and their 'dates' only as part of the overall scene. 'The main reason I remember them is I wondered what that white pregnant girl was doing with a bunch of suede dudes. I figured that was her business, and I wasn't hurtin' for pussy anyway. I had my old lady with me – we're separated now, but then we were doin' okay and she wouldn't have none of me hustlin' anything else while she was around. Besides, hell, when you're seein' old friends you haven't seen in a year or two, you don't have time to pay much attention to strangers.'

The only thing Terry and all the other Angels agree on – in relation to the 'victims'' first appearance – is that 'they sure as hell didn't look no fourteen and fifteen, man; those girls looked every bit of twenty'. (Police later confirmed the girls' ages, but all other information about them – including their names – was withheld in accordance with California's policy of denying Press access to rape victims.)

'I can't even say if those girls were pretty or not,' Terry went on. 'I just don't remember. All I can say for sure is that we didn't have no trouble at Nick's. The cops were there, but only to keep people away. It was the same old story as every place we go: traffic piling up on the street outside, local bad-asses prowling around, young girls looking for kicks, and a bunch of Nick's regular customers just digging the party. The cops did right by staying around.

Everywhere we go there's some local hoods who want to find out how tough we are. If the cops weren't there we'd end up having to hurt somebody. Hell, nobody wants trouble on a run. All we want to do is to have some fun and relax.'

It is said, however, that the Hell's Angels have some offbeat ideas about fun and relaxation. If they are, after all, 'the lowest form of animals', not even Senator Murphy could expect them to gather together in a drunken mass for any such elevated pastimes as ping pong, shuffleboard, and whist. Their picnics have long been noted for certain beastly forms of entertainment, and any young girl who shows up at a Hell's Angels' bonfire camp at two o'clock in the morning is presumed, by the outlaws, to be in a condition of heat. So it was only natural that the two girls attracted more attention when they arrived at the beach than they had earlier in the convivial bedlam at Nick's.

One aspect of the case overlooked in most newspaper accounts had to do with elementary logistics. How did these two young girls happen to be on a deserted midnight beach with several hundred drunken motorcycle thugs? Were they kidnapped from Nick's? And if so, what were they doing there in the first place, aged fourteen and fifteen, circulating all evening in a bar jammed wall to wall with the state's most notorious gang of outlaws? Or were they seized off the street somewhere – perhaps at a stoplight – to be slung over the gas tank of a bored-out Harley and carried off into the night, screaming hysterically, while bystanders gaped in horror?

Police strategists, thinking to isolate the Angels, had reserved them a campsite far out of town, on an empty stretch of dunes between Monterey Bay and Fort Ord, an Army basic-training centre. The reasoning was sound; the beasts were put off in a place where they could whip themselves into any kind of orgiastic frenzy without becoming dangerous to the citizenry – and if things got out of hand, the recruits across the road could be bugled out of bed and issued bayonets. The police posted a guard on the highway, in case the Angels got restless and tried to get back to town, but there was no way to seal off the camp entirely, nor any provision for handling local innocents who might be drawn to the scene out of curiosity or other, darker reasons not mentioned in police training manuals.

The victims told police they had gone to the beach because they 'wanted to look at the cyclists'. They were curious – even after several hours at Nick's, which was so crowded that evening that most of the outlaws took to pissing in the parking lot rather than struggle inside to the bathroom.

'Hell, those broads didn't come out there for any singsong,' said Terry. 'They were loaded and they wanted to get off some leg, but it just got to be too many guys. To start with, it was groovy for 'em. Then more and more guys came piling over the dunes ... "yea, pussy", you know, that kinda thing... and the broads didn't want it. The suede dudes just split; we never saw 'em again. I don't know for sure how it ended. All I knew then was that they had some mamas out there in the dunes, but me and my old lady went and crashed pretty early. I was so wasted I couldn't even make it with her.'

No family newspaper saw fit to quote the Angel version, but six months later, playing pool in a San Francisco bar, Frenchy remembered it this way: 'One girl was white and pregnant, the other was coloured, and they were with five coloured studs. They hung around Nick's about three hours on Saturday night, drinking and talking with our riders, then they came out to the beach with us – them and their five boy friends. Everybody was standing round the fire, drinking wine, and some of the guys were talkin' to them – hustlin' 'em, naturally – and pretty soon somebody asked the two chicks if they wanted to be turned on – you know, did they want to smoke some pot? They said yeah, and then they walked off with some of the guys to the dunes. The spade went with a few guys, and then she wanted to quit, but the pregnant one was really hot to trot; the first four or five guys she was really draggin' into her arms, but after that she cooled off too. By this time, though, one of their boy friends had got scared and gone for the cops – and that's all it was.'

'The next morning,' said Terry, 'I rode in with somebody – I forget who – to some drive-in on the highway, where we got some breakfast. When we got back to the beach they had a roadblock set up with those two broads sittin' there in the cop car, lookin' at everybody. I didn't know what was going on, but then a cop said: "You're one," and they slapped the cuffs on me. Those goddamn girls were gigglin', righteously laughin' ... you know,

"Ha ha, that's one of 'em." So off I went to the bucket, for rape.

'When we got to the jail I said: "Hey, I want to be checked. Let's see a doctor. I ain't had no intercourse in two days." But they wouldn't go for it. Marvin and Miles and Crazy Cross were already there and we figured we were deep in the shit until they told us bail was only eleven hundred dollars. Then we knew they didn't have much of a case.'

Meanwhile, out on Marina Beach, the rest of the Angels were being rounded up and driven north along Highway 156 towards the county line. Laggards were thumped on the shoulders with billy clubs and told to get moving. Side roads were blocked by state troopers while dozens of helmeted deputies – many from neighbouring counties – ran the outlaws through the gauntlet. Traffic was disrupted for miles as the ragged horde moved slowly along the road, gunning their engines and raining curses on everything in sight. The noise was deafening and it is hard to imagine what effect the spectacle must have had on the dozens of out-of-state late-summer tourists who pulled over to let the procession come through. Because of the proximity of an Army base, they undoubtedly thought they were making way for a caravan of tanks, or at least something impressive and military – and then to see an army of hoodlums being driven along the road like a herd of diseased sheep – ah, what a nightmare for the California Chamber of Commerce.

At the county line on U.S. 101 a reporter from *The San Francisco Chronicle* talked with Tommy, and with another Angel, named Tiny, a six-foot-six, 240-pound outlaw with a shoulder-length pigtail who later gained nationwide fame for his attack on a Get Out of Vietnam demonstration at Berkeley.

'We're ordinary guys,' said Tommy. 'Most of us work. About half are married, I guess, and a few own their homes. Just because we like to ride motorcycles, the cops give us trouble everywhere we go. That rape charge is phoney and it won't stick. The whole thing was voluntary.'

'Shit, our bondsman will have those guys out in two hours,' said Tiny. 'Why can't people let us alone, anyway? All we want to do is get together now and then and have some fun – just like the Masons, or any other group.'

But the presses were already rolling and the eight-column headlines said: HELL'S ANGELS GANG RAPE. The Masons haven't had that kind of publicity since the eighteenth century, when Casanova was climbing through windows and giving the brotherhood a bad name. Perhaps the Angels will one day follow the Freemasons into *bourgeois* senility, but by then some other group will be making outrage headlines: a Hovercraft gang, or maybe some once-bland fraternal group tooling up even now for whatever the future might force on them.

What is the trend in Kiwanis? There are rumours in Oakland of a new militancy in that outfit, a radical ferment that could drastically alter the club's image. In the drift and flux of these times it is easy enough to foresee a Sunday morning, ten or twenty years hence, when a group of middle-aged men wearing dark blazers with Hell's Angels crests on the pockets will be pacing their mortgaged living-rooms and muttering sadly at a headline saying: KIWANIS GANG RAPE: FOUR HELD, OTHERS FLEE, RINGLEADERS SOUGHT.

And in some shocked American city a police chief will be saying – as the Monterey chief said in 1964 of the Hell's Angels – 'They will not be welcomed back, because of the atmosphere created.'

THE MAKING OF THE MENACE, 1965

2

The daily press is the evil principle of the modern world, and time will only serve to disclose this fact with greater and greater clearness. The capacity of the newspaper for degeneration is sophistically without limit, since it can always sink lower and lower in its choice of readers. At last it will stir up all those dregs of humanity which no state or government can control. – *Sören Kierkegaard,* The Last Years: *Journals 1853–5*

The best thing about the Angels is that we don't lie to each other. Of course that don't go for outsiders because we have to fight fire with fire. Hell, most people you meet won't tell you the truth about *anything*. – *Zorro, the only Brazilian Hell's Angel*

It was part of the cover story. – *Arthur Schlesinger, Jr, explaining why he wapped the Press with a bogus explanation of the Bay of Pigs invasion*

*

POLITICIANS, like editors and cops, are very keen on outrage stories, and State Senator Fred Farr of Monterey County is no exception. He is a leading light of the Carmel—Pebble Beach set and no friend of hoodlums anywhere, especially gang rapists who invade his constituency. His reaction to the Monterey headlines was quick and loud. Farr demanded an immediate investigation of the Hell's Angels and all others of that breed, whose lack of status caused them to be lumped together as 'other disreputables'. In the cut-off world of big bikes, long runs and classy rumbles, this new, state-sanctioned stratification made the Hell's Angels very big. They were, after all, Number One – like John Dillinger.

Attorney-General Thomas C. Lynch, then new in his job, moved quickly to mount an investigation of sorts. He sent questionnaires to more than a hundred sheriffs, district-attorneys and police chiefs, asking for information on the Hell's Angels and 'other disreputables'. He also asked for suggestions as to how the law might deal with them.

Six months went by before all the replies were condensed into a fifteen-page report that read like a plot synopsis of Mickey Spillane's worst dreams. But in the matter of solutions it was vague. The state was going to centralize information on these thugs, urge more vigorous prosecution, put them all under surveillance whenever possible, etc.

A careful reader got the impression that, even if the Angels were the monsters they seemed to be, there was not much the cops could do – and that indeed Mr Lynch was well aware he'd been put, for political reasons, on a pretty weak scent.

The report was colourful, interesting, heavily biased and consistently alarming – just the sort of thing to make a clanging good item for the national Press. There was plenty of mad action, senseless destruction, orgies, brawls, perversions and a strange parade of innocent victims that, even on paper and in careful police language, was enough to tax the credulity of the dullest police reporter. The demand was so heavy in newspaper and magazine circles that the Attorney-General's office had to order a second printing. Even the Hell's Angels got a copy; one of them stole mine. The heart of the report was a section titled 'Hoodlum Activities', a brief account of outlaw activities dating back for almost a decade. To wit:

On April 2, 1964, a group of eight Hell's Angels invaded the home of an Oakland woman, forcing her male friend out of the house at gunpoint and raping the woman in the presence of her three children. Later that same morning, female companions of the Hell's Angels threatened the victim that if she co-operated with the police she would be cut on the face with a razor. . . .

Early on the morning of June 2, 1964, it was reported that three Hell's Angels had seized a 19-year-old woman in a small bar in the northern part of Sacramento, and while two of them held her down on the barroom floor, the third removed her outer clothing. The victim was menstruating at the time; her sanitary napkin was removed and the third individual committed cunnilingus upon her. . . .

Early on the morning of October 25, 1964, nine Hell's Angels and two of their female companions were arrested by Gardena police and sheriff's officers after a riot call had been received from a Gardena bar.

Police reported the group 'started ripping up the whole place' after someone had splashed a mug of beer over one of the group. The bar was left in shambles, and pool tables covered with beer and urine....

The Lynch report chronicled eighteen such outrages and left hundreds more implied. Newspapers all over the state carried highlights, along with the Attorney-General's assurance that police pressure would soon put an end to the problem. Most California editors gave the story prominent play for a day or so, then let it drop. The Hell's Angels had made headlines before, and the Lynch report – based on a survey of old police files – contained little that was new or startling.

The Angels seemed headed for obscurity once again, but the tide was turned by a *New York Times* correspondent in Los Angeles, who filed a lengthy and lurid commentary on the Lynch report. It appeared in the *Times*, dated 16 March, under a two-column headline – which was all the impetus the story needed: the rumble was on. *Time* followed with a left hook titled 'The Wilder Ones'. *Newsweek* crossed with a right titled 'The Wild Ones'. And by the time the dust had settled, the national news media had a guaranteed grabber on their hands. It was sex, violence, crime, craziness and filth – all in one package. Here is *Newsweek's* 1965 description of a Labour Day Run to Porterville a year and a half earlier:

A roaring swarm of 200 black-jacketed motorcyclists converged on the small, sleepy southern California town of Porterville. They rampaged through local bars, shouting obscenities. They halted cars, opening their doors, trying to paw female passengers. Some of their booted girl friends lay down in the middle of the streets and undulated suggestively. In one bar, half a dozen of them brutally beat a 65-year-old man and tried to abduct the barmaid. Only after 71 policemen from neighbouring cities and the Highway Patrol, police dogs and water hoses were brought into action did the cyclists jump on their Harley–Davidsons and roar out of town.

Both *Newsweek* and *Time* compared the 1963 'invasion' of Porterville with a film called *The Wild One*, based on a similar incident at Hollister, California, in 1947, and starring Marlon Brando . . . which *Time* called a 'slice-of-seedy-life picture about a pack of vicious, swaggering motorcycle hoods called the Black Rebels'. But *The Wild One* passed quickly into oblivion, said *Time*.

because 'the characters were too overdrawn and the violence they wrought was too unrelieved to engage the credulity of its audience'.

Who, after all, could believe that a gang of two-wheeled Huns might invade and terrify a whole Californian town? Not *Time*. At least not in 1947, when the first such incident occurred; and not in 1953, when the film was released; and not even ten years later, when the same thing supposedly happened again, in a different town. But 26 March 1965, eighteen years after the first so-called motorcycle riot in America, *Time* finally came to grips with the story, and the editors of that journal were alarmed. The Huns were real! They'd been holed up somewhere for eighteen years, polishing their motorcycles and greasing their chain whips until California's Attorney-General decided to introduce them to the Press. *Time*'s West Coast legman lost no time in forwarding the terrible news to the Luce fortress, where it was immediately transformed into two columns of supercharged hokum for the National Affairs section: 'Last week it [*The Wild One*] was back – and in real life!'

'Lynch amassed a mountain of evidence about Hell's Angels,' said *Time*, '. . . the thrust of which shows that the group has more than lived up to its sinister moniker. . . . It was a rape case that ignited Lynch's investigation. Last fall, two teenage girls were taken forcibly from their dates and raped by several members of the gang.' This was a flagrant libel, for in fact all charges against Terry, Marvin, Mother Miles and Crazy Cross were dropped less than a month after their arrest. In their eagerness to get at the hair and meat of the story, *Time*'s interpreters apparently skipped page one of the Lynch report, which clearly stated that 'further investigation raised questions as to whether forcible rape had been committed or if the identifications made by the victims were valid. By letter dated September 25, 1964, the District Attorney of Monterey County requested dismissal of charges in the Monterey–Carmel Municipal Court, which request was with the concurrence of the Grand Jury.' Not quoted in the report were the comments of a deputy district attorney for the county: 'A doctor examined the girls and found no evidence to support charges of forcible rape,' he said. 'And besides, one girl refused to testify and the other was given a lie-detector test and found to be wholly unreliable.' This was pretty dull stuff, however, and *Time* couldn't find room for it. The article continued instead in a high-pitched, chattering whine, with a list of phoney statistics:

Founded in 1950 at Fontana, a steel town 50 miles east of Los Angeles, the club now numbers about 450 in California. Their logbook of kicks runs from sexual perversion and drug addiction to simple assault and thievery. Among them they boast 874 felony arrests, 300 felony convictions, 1,682 misdemeanor arrests and 1,023 misdemeanor convictions, only 85 have ever served time in prisons or reform schools.

No act is too degrading for the pack. Their initiation rite, for example, demands that any new member bring a woman or girl (called a 'sheep') who is willing to submit to sexual intercourse with each member of the club. But their favorite activity seems to be terrorizing whole towns. . . .

Time then told the same Porterville invasion story that appeared simultaneously in *Newsweek*. The article continued:

When they are not thus engaged, the Angels – sometimes accompanied by the young children of a member or by the unmarried females who hang out with the club – often rent a dilapidated house on the edge of a town, where they swap girls, drugs and motorcycles with equal abandon. In between drug-induced stupors, the Angels go on motorcycle-stealing forays, even have a panel truck with a special ramp for loading the stolen machines. Afterward, they may ride off again to seek some new nadir in sordid behavior.

There was clearly no room for this sort of thing in the Great Society, and *Time* was emphatic in saying it was about to be brought to a halt. These ruffians were going to be taught a lesson by hard and ready minions of the Establishment. The article ended on a note of triumph:

. . . all local law enforcement agencies have now been supplied with dossiers on each member of the Hell's Angels and on similar gangs, and set up a co-ordinated intelligence service that will try to track down the hoods wherever they appear. 'They will no longer be allowed to threaten the lives, peace and security of honest citizens of our state,' said he [Lynch]. To that, thousands of Californians shuddered a grateful amen.

No doubt there was some shuddering done in California that week, but not all of it was rooted in feelings of gratitude. The Hell's

Angels shuddered with perverse laughter at the incredible swill that had been written about them. Other outlaws shuddered with envy at the Angels' sudden fame. Cops all over California shuddered with nervous glee at the prospect of their next well-publicized run-in with any group of motorcyclists. And some people shuddered at the realization that *Time* had 3,042,902 readers.*

The significant thing about *Time*'s view of the Angels was not its crabwise approach to reality, but its impact. At the beginning of March 1965 the Hell's Angels were virtually non-existent. The club's own head count listed roughly eighty-five, all in California. Routine police harassment had made it impossible for the outlaws to even wear their colours in any city except Oakland. Membership in the San Francisco chapter had dwindled from a one-time high of seventy-five to a mere eleven, with one facing expulsion. The original Berdoo (including Fontana) chapter was reduced to a handful of diehards determined to go down with the ship. In Sacramento a two-man vendetta in the form of Sheriff John Miserly and a patrolman named Leonard Chatoian had made life so difficult that the Angels were already planning the big move to Oakland . . . and even there the heat was on for real. 'Shit, we never knew when they was gonna bust into the El Adobe and line us up against the bar with shotguns,' Sonny Barger recalls. 'We even started drinking at the Sinners Club because it had a back door and a window we could get out of. I mean the heat was on, man. We were hurtin'.'

*

> A good reporter, if he chooses the right approach, can understand a cat or an Arab. The choice is the problem, and if he chooses wrong he will come away scratched or baffled. – *A. J. Liebling*

*

At the time of the report the State of California had admittedly been dealing for fifteen years with a criminal conspiracy of the most vicious kind – yet in the five single-spaced pages devoted to the Hell's Angels' hoodlum activities – most involving anywhere from a dozen to a hundred outlaws – the report mentioned only sixteen

* *Time*'s circulation in its December 1964 report.

specific arrests and two convictions. What was a man to think? Another part of the report stated that of 463 identified Hell's Angels, 151 had felony convictions. This is the kind of statistic that gives taxpayers faith in their law enforcement agencies . . . and it would have been doubly edifying if the 463 Hell's Angels had actually existed when the statistic was committed to print. Unfortunately, there were barely 100. Since 1960 the number of active members has never been more than 200, and easily a third of these are Hell's Angels in name only . . . old grads, gone over the hump to marriage and middle age, but donning the colours once or twice a year for some major event like the Labour Day Run.

The Lynch report mentioned several of these annual affairs, but the descriptions were not entirely objective. For obvious reasons, policemen rarely witness a crime in progress, so they have to rely on others to tell them what happened.

Newsweek's version of the Porterville raid* was lifted almost verbatim from the Lynch report. Another version of that affair had appeared on 5 September 1963, in the *Porterville Farm Tribune*. It was an eye-witness account, written within hours of the action by a *Tribune* reporter named Bill Rodgers. The headline said: THEY CAME, THEY SAW, THEY DID NOT CONQUER.

Porterville police knew by Saturday morning that the motorcycle clan of California might hit Porterville during the weekend.

By late afternoon there were riders beginning to congregate at Main and Olive, with the Eagle Club as their drinking centre. A few riders were in Murry Park. No one that we saw was out of line.

By early evening great numbers had begun to arrive and there was a build-up at Main and Olive. Our phone got hot as people wanted to know what the city was doing about the situation. We were urged to call out the National Guard, to order wholesale arrests, to deputize citizens and arm them with axe handles and shotguns.

Around 6.30 P.M. we checked Main Street. The show was starting. Perhaps 200 of the motorcycle clan, including some women and children, were becoming boisterous; some were crowding out into the street molesting motorists and pedestrians; a hundred or more motorcycles were parked on the east side of Main.

We returned to the police station. Torigian and Searle were handling things there, Porrazzo joined them. There was still no violence, or no

* See page 33.

real reason to make arrests. It was a case of waiting as the situation developed. Decision was made to close Murry Park.

About 8.00 P.M. radio word came that the motorcyle group was pulling out, heading east. It was possible they would stay out of town. But a few minutes later a fight and accident was reported in a club at the city line in Doyle Colony and an ambulance was requested. It was also reported that the clan was moving back into town.

Decision was made at this point to force the motorcycle group out of town. . . .

Throughout the evening the city police switchboard was cluttered by calls, some of them legitimate, but many of them from anonymous people announcing they were citizens, demanding protection, insulting the police.

Traffic was bumper to bumper on Main Street; 1,500 local people stood around at Main and Olive to see what would happen. The motorcycle clan, perhaps 300 strong at this point was living it up drinking, tying up traffic, breaking bottles in the street, using profane and insulting language, putting on what they considered a show.

Police were hampered by the heavy traffic and the mass of spectators. We moved through the area in a loudspeaker-equipped police car asking Porterville people to move out of the area. Result – no one moved, others came in to see what was happening, the motorcycle clan booed.

The Main Street block from Garden to Olive, then from Oak, was closed to traffic; Highway Patrolmen were on the south, city police on the north. The area rapidly cleared of traffic; the clan group figured they had it made, that police were turning a block of Main Street over to them.

By 9.30 P.M. officers of the mutual aid group were assembled at the city police station. Torigian briefed them on plan of action – move south down Main Street in cars; walk the final half block; head the motorcycles south; no one goes north. Highway Patrol units would remain south of Olive and Main. Take no lip or abuse; either they move out or they go to jail.

A city fire engine was placed in position at the Penney Store; the police with night sticks and shotguns moved out, there were no sirens, just flashing red lights. The motorcycle clan massed in the middle of the street, some of them laid down. Torigian led the officers, talking through a bull horn. 'You have five minutes to get out of town. Move.' Defiance faded. Motorcycles started. There was some resistance, a half dozen were arrested. City firemen went down the street and moved the hose in on the clan. One rider tried to go north; he was knocked off his motorcycle with the firehose water.

Many of the riders headed south and kept going. Some stopped at the Sports Center. Police were sent to clean out Murry Park. Night spots were checked by police.

Leaders of the three major clubs represented were taken to police headquarters for questioning, while remaining riders were held at the Sports Center. There were threats from the Hell's Angels.that if their arrested members were not released they would come and get them.

Torigian said the only way to get them was to bail them out. Officers with riot guns were ready if a jail break was attempted.

Around 2.30 A.M. some of the riders headed back toward Porterville. Torigian stopped them at the Main Street bridge. He told them to turn around and get out or they would be arrested and their motorcycles impounded, chained together six at a time, and drug off.

By daylight a few scattered riders were still in the area. But the threat of violence and damage had been met and broken.

*

> A man that should call everything by its right name would hardly pass the streets without being knocked down as a Common Enemy. – *Lord Halifax*

*

A less glaring example of the way police reports tend to overdramatize the Angels is this account of a Fourth of July 1964 run to Willits, a lumbering town of about thirty-five hundred in northern California. The official version follows an account from a San Francisco housewife, Mrs Terry Whitright, whose husband is a native of Willits. The two versions are not contradictory, but the difference in point of view suggests that the Hell's Angels' reality often depends on who describes it.

Here is what Mrs Whitright said in a letter dated 29 March 1965:

Dear Hunter

The first time I had ever seen the Hell's Angels was on the 4th of July celebration in Willits, Calif. Willits is a very small town approximately 100 miles North of S.F. Every 4th of July they have a *Frontier's Day Celebration*, which includes a carnival, parade, dances, etc. We went up for it, and on Willits' Main Street, the Hell's Angels were lined up for a block and a half, coming in and out of a very populated bar. We (Lori, Barbie, Terry & I), were walking down the street and one man, wearing a black leather jacket, boots, dirty black Tee-shirt, etc., grabbed Lori by the hand, and talked to her for awhile, asking her name, & all the time being very gentle and very nice. This was around 2.30 in the afternoon. Later that evening we went to a elderly woman's house where we were staying while we were in town. She has a nephew by the name of Larry Jordon. He is a Wilackey Indian about 27 or 28. He is also a brother to Phil Jordon, a professional basketball player who played for New York Knickerbockers and also the Detroit Pistons. Well, anyhow, to get back to Larry Jordon; about 7.30 that evening a girl came to the door crying and shouting, 'Eileen, Eileen, help me'. I came to the door, and there stood Larry, blood pouring down the side of his neck, and from his temple. Eileen his aunt, completely fell apart, so I had to take him to the bathroom and clean him up. He had been cut severely with either a razor blade or a knife by the Hell's Angels. Now, the reason never was established, why he was jumped by 6 or 7 Hell's Angels, but he's the type of guy who looks like he thinks he's better than anyone. But this isn't the way he is, he holds himself very aloof, never looks for trouble, but never backs away from trouble either. It's rather hard to explain, you'd have to know him, I think. If you know any Indians well, maybe you understand.

Terry came back (he had been to the store) and after some talking and persuading he got Larry into the car and to the hospital. Of course everyone was drinking and they all wanted to get a bunch together and run the Hell's Angels out of town, but they didn't.

One other acquaintance of ours by the name of Fritz Bacchie also got beat up by them. He went home to get a gun, and the local police threw him in jail for the nite.

All in all, there wasn't too much damage done, but an air of uneasiness hung over the town, no one knew what would happen next, and no one could really relax and have any fun or enjoy themselves as they usually do on these celebrations on the 4th of July.

The Attorney General told it this way:

On July Fourth 1965, at the invitation of the same bartender who had previously worked at a Hell's Angels hangout in Rodeo, the Oakland Hell's Angels made a 'run' to Willits. An advance group of 30 entered the city the previous day and by the afternoon of the Fourth there were some 120 motorcyclists and their female companions congregating at a local bar. In addition to those from Oakland, there were Angels from Vallejo and Richmond, as well as the 'Mofo' club from San Francisco. Periodic fighting between the motorcyclists and local citizens broke out with beer bottles, belts made from motorcycle drive chains, and metal beer can openers being used as weapons. It was noted that some members apparently designated as sergeants at arms did not drink, but spent their time watching the group. When police were called, these people would pick up broken bottles, pour beer on any blood remaining on the floor, and move groups in and out of the bar to make police interrogation more difficult. When one local citizen took it upon himself to obtain a shotgun and returned to the bar where the group was congregated, he was arrested. Assistance was obtained from the California Highway Patrol and the Mendocino County sheriff's office. The group was then instructed by the chief of police to move out of town to the city limits. After the move, some fights between Angels themselves occurred, but no local citizenry were involved.

The Lynch–*Newsweek* account of the Porterville incident was hazy in detail, but brutally clear with its image of Hell's Angels swarming over the town and wreaking havoc on the terrified citizenry. By comparison, the eye-witness version was pale and slow . . . like Mrs Whitright's tale of the Willits incident, which lacked all the zip and tension of the colourful police version. There is not much argument about basic facts, but the disparities in emphasis and context are the difference between a headline and a filler in most big-city newspapers. Do the Hell's Angels actually 'take over' a town – as they're often accused of doing – or merely clog a main street and a few local taverns with drunken noise, thus flaying the sensibilities of various locals?

In a larger context, how much of a menace are the Hell's Angels? And how seriously do they threaten the lives and limbs of people in California . . . or in Idaho, Arizona, Michigan, New York, Indiana, New Hampshire, Maryland, Florida, Nevada, Canada and all the other places whose citizens have felt threatened by them at one time or another?

3

Indeed I tremble for my country when I reflect that God is just.
– *Thomas Jefferson*

*

ACCORDING to Attorney-General Lynch's own figures, California's overall crime picture makes the Angels look like a gang of petty jack-rollers. The police counted 463 Hell's Angels: 205 around Los Angeles, 233 in the San Francisco–Oakland area, and the rest scattered wildly around the state. These woeful departures from reality made it hard to accept their other statistics. The dubious package cited Hell's Angels convictions on 1,023 misdemeanour counts and 151 felonies – primarily vehicle theft, burglary and assault. This was for all years and all alleged members including many long since retired.

California's overall figures for 1963 showed 1,116 homicides, 12,448 aggravated assaults, 6,257 sex offences and 24,532 burglaries. In 1962 the state listed 4,121 traffic deaths, up from 3,839 in 1961. Drug-arrest figures for 1964 showed a 101 per cent increase in juvenile marijuana arrests over 1963, and a 1965 back-page story in *The San Francisco Examiner* said: 'The venereal disease rate among [the city's] teenagers from 15 to 19 has more than doubled in the past four years.' Even allowing for the annual population jump, juvenile arrests in all categories are rising by 10 per cent or more each year. Late in 1965 Governor Edmund 'Pat' Brown, a Democrat, was berated by Republicans in the Legislature for 'remaining aloof' to the threat of the rising crime rate, which they said had jumped 70 per cent during his seven years in office.

Against this background, it is hard to see how it would make any difference to the safety and peace of mind of the average Californian if every motorcycle outlaw in the state (all 901, according to the police) were garrotted within twenty-four hours.

If the 'Hell's Angels Saga' proved any one thing, it was the awesome power of the New York Press establishment. The Hell's

Angels as they exist today were virtually created by *Time*, *Newsweek* and *The New York Times*. The *Times* is the heavyweight champion of American journalism. On nine stories out of ten the paper lives up to its reputation. Yet the editors make no claims to infallibility, and now and then they will blow the whole duke. It would be useless to try to list these failures, and besides that the purpose of this harangue is not to nail any one newspaper or magazine – but to point out the potentially massive effect of any story whose basic structure is endorsed and disseminated not only by *Time* and *Newsweek*, but by the hyper-prestigious *New York Times*. The *Times* took the Lynch report at face value and simply reprinted it in very condensed form. The headline said: CALIFORNIA TAKES STEPS TO CURB TERRORISM OF RUFFIAN CYCLISTS. The bulk of the article was straight enough, but the lead was pure fiction: 'A hinterland tavern is invaded by a group of motorcycle hoodlums. They seize a female patron and rape her. Departing, they brandish weapons and threaten bystanders with dire reprisals if they tell what they saw. Authorities have trouble finding a communicative witness, let alone arresting and prosecuting the offenders.'

This incident never occurred. It was created, as a sort of journalistic montage, by the correspondent who distilled the report. But the *Times* is neither written nor edited by fools, and anyone who has worked on a newspaper for more than two months knows how technical safeguards can be built into even the wildest story, without fear of losing reader impact. What they amount to, basically, is the art of printing a story without taking legal responsibility for it. The word 'alleged' is a key to this art. Other keys are 'so-and-so said' (or 'claimed'), 'it was reported' and 'according to'. In fourteen short newspaper paragraphs, the *Times* story contained nine of these qualifiers. The two most crucial had to do with the Hollywood lead and the ' "*alleged* gang rape" last Labor Day of two girls, 14 and 15 years old, by five to ten members of the Hell's Angels gang on the beach at Monterey' (my italics). Nowhere in the story was it either reported or implied that the Monterey charges had long since been dropped – *according to page one of the report quoted*. The result was a piece of slothful, emotionally biased journalism, a bad hack job that wouldn't have raised a ripple had it appeared in most American newspapers . . . but the *Times* is a heavyweight even when it's wrong, and the effect of this article was to put the seal of respectability on a story that was, in fact, a hysterical, politically motivated accident.

Had *Time* and *Newsweek* never touched the story, the New York-based mass media would have jumped on it anyway. A social cancer had been uncovered by the nation's leading newspaper. And then . . . one week later came the *Time–Newsweek* double-barrelled blast that really put the Angels over the top. What followed was an orgy of publicity. The long-dormant Hell's Angels got eighteen years' worth of exposure in six months, and it naturally went to their heads.

Until the Monterey rape they were bush-league hoods known only to California cops and a few thousand cycle buffs. For whatever it was worth, they were the state's biggest and most notorious motorcycle gang. Among outlaws their primacy was undisputed – and nobody else cared.

Then, as a result of the Monterey incident, they made the front page of every daily in California, including the Los Angeles, Sacramento and San Francisco papers – which are scanned and clipped each day by researchers for *Time* and *Newsweek*. Some of the stories said the victims had been roasting weenies on the beach with their *two* dates – who fought like tigers to save them – when an advance party of some four thousand Hell's Angels suddenly surrounded the campfire and said things like: 'Don't worry, kid, we're just going to break the girls in for you.' (And then, according to one account: 'The bearded one pressed his hairy lips to hers. She screamed and struggled. He and another Angel picked her up and hauled her, screaming, into the darkness. A piercing scream was followed by a deep-throated curse. . . .')

HELL'S ANGELS RAPE TEENAGERS
4,000 CYCLISTS INVADE MONTEREY

Yet only two of the eighteen specific outrages cited in the Lynch report occurred after Labour Day of 1964, and both of these were bar brawls. So the story was just as available to the Press on the day after the Monterey rape as it was six months later, when the Attorney-General called a Press conference and handed it out in a neat white package, one to each newshawk. Until then nobody had shown much interest . . . or they hadn't had time, for in the fall of 1964 the Press was putting every available talent on the national-election story. It was, after all, a real humdinger. All manner of crucial issues were said to be hanging in the balance, and somebody had to keep tabs on the national pulse.

Not even Senator Goldwater seized on the Hell's Angels issue. 'Crime in the streets' was a winner for him; millions of people felt threatened by gangs of punks, roaming, on foot, through streets in the immediate vicinity of their homes in urban slums. Democrats called this a racist slur . . . but what would they have said if Goldwater had warned the voters about an army of vicious, doped-up Caucasian hoodlums numbering in the thousands . . . based in California but with chapters proliferating all over the nation and even the globe far faster than a man could keep track of them . . . and so highly mobile with their awesome machines that huge numbers of them might appear almost anywhere, at any moment, to sack and destroy a community?

*

Filthy Huns! Breeding like rats in California and spreading east. Listen for the roar of the Harleys. You will hear it in the distance like thunder. And then, wafting in on the breeze, will come the scent of dried blood, semen and human grease . . . the noise will grow louder and then they will appear, on the west horizon, eyes bugged and bloodshot, foam on their lips, chewing some rooty essence smuggled in from a foreign jungle . . . they will ravish your women, loot your liquor stores and humiliate your mayor on a bench on the village square. . . .

*

Now there was an issue. All that mumbo jumbo about 'crime in the streets' was too vague. What Goldwater needed was an up-to-date concept like 'crime on the highway', motorized crime, with nobody safe from it. And the first time the Democrats challenged him, he could have produced photos of the dirtiest Hell's Angels and read from newspaper accounts of the Monterey rape and other stories: '. . . they hauled her, screaming, into the darkness'; '. . . the bartender, barely conscious, crawled toward the bar while the Angels beat a tattoo on his ribs with their feet. . . .'

Unfortunately, neither candidate picked up the Monterey story and, with no other takers, it quickly slipped from sight. From September 1964 to March of the next year the Hell's Angels fought a quiet, unpublicized series of skirmishes with police in both Los Angeles and the Bay Area. The massive publicity of the Monterey rape had made them so notorious in California that it was no longer any fun to be part of the act. Every minute on the streets was a calculated risk for any man wearing a Hell's Angels jacket. The odds were worse than even – except in Oakland* – and the penalty for getting caught was likely to be expensive. At the peak of the heat a former Frisco Angel told me: 'If I was fired from my job tomorrow and went back to riding with the Angels, I'd lose my driver's licence within a month, be in and out of jail, go way in debt to bondsmen and be hounded by the cops until I left the area.' At the time I pegged him as a hopeless paranoid. Then I bought a big motorcycle and began riding around San Francisco and the East Bay. The bike was a sleek factory-style B.S.A., bearing no aesthetic resemblance to an outlaw Harley, and my primary road garb was a tan sheepherder's jacket, the last thing a Hell's Angel might wear. Yet within three weeks after buying the bike, I was arrested three times and accumulated enough points to lose my California driver's licence – which I retained on a more or less day-to-day basis, only because of a fanatic insistence on posting large amounts of bail money and what seemed like a never-ending involvement with judges, bailiffs, cops and lawyers, who kept telling me the cause was lost. Before buying the motorcycle, I had driven cars for twelve years, in all but four states of the nation, and

* There was a basic difference between the kind of pressure the Angels got in Oakland and the kind they felt elsewhere. In Oakland it was not political, not the result of any high-level pressure or policy decision – but more of a personal thing, like arm-wrestling. Barger and his people get along pretty well with the cops. In most cases, and with a few subtle differences, they operate on the same emotional frequency. Both the cops and the Angels deny this. The very suggestion of a psychic compatibility will be denounced – by both groups – as a form of Communist slander. But the fact of the thing is obvious to anyone who has ever seen a routine confrontation or sat in on a friendly police check at one of the Angel bars. Apart, they curse each other savagely, and the brittle truce is often jangled by high-speed chases and brief, violent clashes that rarely make the papers. Yet behind the sound and fury, they are both playing the same game, and usually by the same rules.

been tagged for only two running violations, both the result of speed traps – one in Pikeville, Kentucky, and the other somewhere near Omaha. So it was a bit of a shock to suddenly face loss of my licence for violations incurred in a period of three weeks.

The heat was so obvious that even respectable motorcyclists were complaining of undue police harassment. The cops denied it officially, but shortly before Christmas of that year a San Francisco policeman told a reporter: 'We're going to get these guys. It's war.'

'Who do you mean?' asked the reporter.

'You know who I mean,' the policeman said. 'The Hell's Angels, those motorcycle hoods.'

'You mean everybody on a motorcycle?' said the reporter.

'The innocent will have to suffer along with the guilty,' the policeman replied.

'When I finished the story,' the reporter recalls, 'I showed it to a cop I ran into on the street outside the Hall of Justice. He laughed and called another cop over. "Look at this," he said, "— stepped on his prick again."'

The only significant Press breakthrough during this crack-down winter of 1964–5 was a tongue-in-cheek series in *The San Francisco Chronicle*, based on some Angel parties at the Frisco chapter's new clubhouse – which was raided and closed down almost immediately after the series appeared. Meanwhile, the Oakland Angels fattened steadily on the tide of refugees. From Berdoo, Hayward, Sacramento, the Angels were moving into the few remaining sanctuaries. By December, Barger's chapter was so swollen and starved for enemies that they began crossing the bridge and attacking the Frisco Angels. Barger felt that Frisco, by allowing the membership to shrink to eleven, had so dishonoured the Hell's Angels' tradition that they should forfeit their colours. Accordingly, he declared the Frisco chapter void and sent his people over to collect the jackets. The Frisco Angels refused, but they were badly unnerved by the mad-dog raids from Oakland. 'Man, we'd be sitting over there in the bar,' said one, 'just coolin' it around the pool table with a few beers – and all of a goddamn sudden the door would bust open and there they'd be, chains and all.

'We finally got back at 'em, though. We went over to their

hangout and set fire to one of their bikes. You should of seen it – we burned it right in the middle of the street, man, then we went into their pad and wiped 'em out. What a blast! Man, I tell you we had some real beefs.'

That was in December. Two more quiet months followed . . . and then came the Attorney-General's report, coast-to-coast infamy and a raft of new possibilities. The whole scene changed in a flash. One day they were a gang of bums, scratching for any hard dollar . . . and twenty-four hours later they were dealing with reporters, photographers, free-lance writers and all kinds of showbiz hustlers talking big money. By the middle of 1965 they were firmly established as all-American bogeymen.

Besides appearing in hundreds of wire-serviced newspapers and a half-dozen magazines, they posed for television cameramen and answered questions on radio call-in shows. They issued statements to the Press, appeared at various rallies and bargained with Hollywood narks and magazine editors. They were sought out by mystics and poets, cheered on by student rebels and invited to parties given by liberals and intellectuals. The whole thing was very weird, and it had a profound effect on the handful of Angels still wearing the colours. They developed a *prima-donna* complex, demanding cash contributions (to confound the Internal Revenue Service) in return for photos and interviews. *The New York Times* was hard hit by these developments, and a dispatch from Los Angeles on 2 July 1965, said: 'A man representing himself as a "public relations man" for . . . [the Hell's Angels] has approached news media offering to sell photographic coverage of this weekend's "rumble" for sums ranging from $500 to $1,000. He also offered to arrange interviews with club members for $100 apiece, or more if pictures were taken. The representative told reporters it would be "dangerous" to go to the San Bernardino bar where the group regularly congregates without paying the money for "protection". One magazine, he said, paid $1,000 for permission to have a photographer accompany the group this weekend.'

The report was a combination of truth and absurdity, compounded by the fact that the *Times*'s Los Angeles correspondent had by this time developed a serious aversion to anything connected with the Hell's Angels. His reasons were excellent; they had threatened him with a beating if he attempted to get a story on the Angels without first contributing to the club's coffers. No journalist likes to be held up for cash payoffs in the line of duty, and the normal reaction – or at least the mythical reaction – is a quick decision to clamp down on the story like a bulldog and write it at all costs.

The *Times*'s reaction was more subtle. They tried to de-emphasize the Angels, hoping they would go away. Which is exactly the opposite of what happened. The story was already snowballing, and the monsters which the *Times* had helped to create came back, with a Press agent, to haunt them. Here was a handful of hoodlums, without status even in San Bernardino, demanding $1,000 from any journalist who wanted to hang around them for a single weekend. Most of the Angels saw the humour in it, but even at that stage of the game, there were a few who felt they were asking a fair price for their act . . . and their faith was justified when 'one magazine' came through with either $1.000 (according to the *Times*) or $1,200 (according to the Angels). The question of this contribution is very touchy, for even if the editors would admit such a payoff, the writer and/or photographer who required it would do everything possible to avoid being labelled as one who has to buy his stories. The Angels talked freely about the money at first, but later denied it, after Sonny Barger passed the word that such talk could get them in tax trouble. It is a fact, however, that a *Life*-assigned photographer spent quite a bit of time with the Angels, working on a photofeature that was never published.

An interesting sidelight on the demand for protection money is that the Angels got the idea from a man who makes more than $100,000 a year by capitalizing on various fads. This is the public relations man referred to by the *Times*. His involvement with the Angels began in Berdoo with the dragster set, but he was never their public relations man – only a noisy contact, a phone number and an unhired hustler with a penchant for bugging the Press. (By the summer of 1965 he was marketing Hell's Angels Fan Club T-shirts, which sold fairly well until the Angels announced they would burn every one they saw, even if they had to rip them off people's backs.)

In the long run he queered the Berdoo Angels' whole stance by demanding big money from anybody who wanted to see them.

And because nobody (except 'one magazine') was willing to pay, and also because nobody called his bluff, he was able to pass for almost half a year as the well-connected front man for a thing that had long since gone down the tube. The Berdoo Angels made the classic Dick Nixon mistake of 'peaking' too early. Publicity from the Monterey rape and two subsequent local brawls had brought such relentless heat that those few who insisted on wearing the colours were forced to act more like refugees than outlaws, and the chapter's reputation withered accordingly. By the middle of August 1965 – while the action in Oakland was booming – *The Los Angeles Times* assayed the Berdoo situation: HELL'S ANGELS FADE IN VALLEY, POLICE PRESSURE TAMES OUTLAW CLUBS. The lead paragraph said: 'Whatever outlaw motorcyclists there are in the [San Fernando] Valley have filtered underground, police say. They are lying low and causing very little trouble and no uproar.'

'If a couple of them stick their heads up and appear on the streets now,' said a police sergeant, 'the first patrol car that sees them stops them for questioning. If we can't find anything else, we can almost always learn that they have traffic warrants outstanding against them. That's enough to get them off the street, and it really bugs them.*

'We maintain a checkpoint at Gorman on the Ridge Route to stop and discourage them when groups from northern California – where they are more active – try to move into Los Angeles. We have other checkpoints along the Pacific Coast Highway, especially near Malibu.

'They have become a very fluid branch. We have a list of twenty-five hundred [*sic*] names of members in the various clubs, but we don't even bother to try to keep addresses. They move constantly. They change their addresses, they change their names, they even change the colour of their hair.'

* This tactic quickly became popular with police in other parts of the state and in situations having nothing to do with the Hell's Angels. It is an especially effective means of crowd control and by the middle of 1966 was standard procedure for dealing with peace marchers in Berkeley. Police began seizing people at random and running radio checks on their driving records. Moments later the word would come back from headquarters, and if the person being detained had even one unpaid traffic or parking citation he would be 'taken off the street' – a police euphemism meaning 'put in jail'.

In Fontana, heartland of the Berdoo chapter's turf, the Angels don't raise much hell in public and they are not often rousted. 'Four or five of them together, that's all right,' said Police Inspector Larry Wallace. 'A whole bunch of 'em, ten or twelve or more, and we bust it up.'

In his private office Wallace keeps a souvenir to remind himself of what the Angels mean to him. It's a two-by-four framed reproduction of a Modigliani woman he confiscated out of an Angel pad. The lady is sleepy-looking, long-necked, with a prim little mouth. An Iron Cross has been scrawled over her head, and the word 'help' is entwined in her hair. Around her neck hangs a Star of David with a swastika stamped into it, and there's a bullet hole in her throat, with a drawing of the bullet emerging from the back of her head. Scattered here and there are Angel maxims of the day:

Dope Forever
Forever Loaded

Honest officer, had I known my
health stood in jeprody I
would never have lit one.

The Angels survived in Berdoo, but they never regained their status of the late fifties and early sixties. When fame finally beckoned, they had little to offer but a hideous reputation and a shrewd Press agent. Otto, president of the chapter, couldn't get a handle anywhere. Sal Mineo was talking about a $3,000 fee to cover outlaw participation in a movie, but the Angels couldn't muster a quorum: some were in jail, others had quit and many of his best specimens had gone north to Oakland – or 'God's Country', as some of them called it – where Sonny Barger called the shots and there was no talk at all of the Hell's Angels fading away. But Otto wanted some of the action too, and he still had a handful of loyalists to back him up. Between them they managed to pull off one last coup – a full-dress show for a writer from *The Saturday Evening Post*.

The *Post* article appeared in November 1965, and although the view it expressed was critical, the Angels were far more impressed with the quantity of such coverage than the quality. Its total effect on them was considerable. They had, after all, made the cover of

The Saturday Evening Post – in colour and along with Princess Margaret. They were *bona-fide* celebrities, with no worlds left to conquer. Their only gripe was that they weren't getting rich. ('All these mothers are using us and making a scene,' Barger told the *Post* reporter, 'and we ain't getting a damn cent out of it.') It was true that the Oakland Angels had been cut out of the Los Angeles bargaining, but they eventually got nearly $500 for the photos they sold to the *Post*, so it was difficult to view them as a wholly exploited minority.

*

We're a gallant bunch of heroes,
We've been organized ten years,
We're known about the city
as the Bowery Grenadiers . . .
We're good old stock
with a Cobble rock,
and a length of gaspipe too.
We can lick the Brooklyn Guards
if they only show their cards,
We can run like the devil
when the ground is level
For about four hundred yards.
And the girls, the little dears,
they're in love up to their ears,
When they see the style
and smell the hair oil,
of the Bowery Grenadiers

– From 'The Bowery Grenadiers', by John Allison

*

My dealings with the Angels lasted about a year, and never really ended. I came to know some of them well and most of them well enough to relax with. But at first – due to numerous warnings – I was nervous about even drinking. I met a half-dozen Frisco Angels one fine afternoon in the bar of a sleazy dive called the DePau Hotel, located in the south industrial section of the San Francisco waterfront and on the fringe of the Hunter's Point Ghetto. My contact was Frenchy,* one of the smallest and shrewdest of the outlaws

* Frenchy from Frisco, not Frenchy from Berdoo.

who was then part-owner of a transmission-repairs garage called the Box Shop, across Evans Avenue from the degraded premises of the DePau. Frenchy is twenty-nine, a skilled mechanic and an ex-submariner in the Navy. He is five foot five and weighs 135 pounds, but the Angels say he is absolutely fearless and will fight anybody. His wife is a willowy, quiet young blonde whose taste runs more to folk music than to brawls and wild parties. Frenchy plays the guitar, the banjo and the tiple.

The Box Shop is always full of cars, but not all of them belong to paying customers. Frenchy and a rotating staff of three or four other Angels run the place, working anywhere from four to twelve hours a day most of the time, but occasionally taking off for a bike trip, an extended party or a run down the coast on a sailboat.

I talked to Frenchy on the phone and met him the next day at the DePau, where he was taking his customary afternoon break. When I got there he was playing pool with Okie Ray, Crazy Rock and a young Chinaman called Ping-Pong. Immediately upon entering the bar, I took off my Palm Beach sports coat in deference to the starkly egalitarian atmosphere which the customers seemed to prefer.

Frenchy ignored me long enough to make things uncomfortable, then nodded a faint smile and rapped a shot towards one of the corner pockets. I bought a glass of beer and watched. Not much was going on. Ping-Pong was doing most of the talking and I wasn't sure what to make of him. He wasn't wearing any colours and I'd never heard of a Chinese Hell's Angel, but he talked like a veteran. (Later I was told that Ping-Pong had an obsession about getting into the club and spent most of his time hanging around the Box Shop and the DePau. He had no bike, but he tried to compensate by carrying a snub-nosed ·357 Magnum revolver in his hip pocket. The Angels were not impressed. They already had one Chinese member, a mechanic at the local Harley–Davidson shop, but he was a quiet, dependable type and nothing like Ping-Pong, who made the outlaws nervous. They knew he was determined to impress them and they feared his inordinate zeal. He was so anxious to show class, they said, that he was likely to get them all busted.)

When the pool game ended, Frenchy sat down at the bar and

asked what I wanted to know. We talked for more than an hour, but his style of conversation made me nervous. He would pause now and then, letting a question hang, and fix me with a sad little smile . . . an allusion to some private joke that he was sure I understood. The atmosphere was heavy with hostility, like smoke in an airless room, and for a while I assumed it was all focused on me – which most of it was when I made my initial appearance, but the focus dissolved very quickly. The sense of menace remained; it is part of the atmosphere the Hell's Angels breathe. Their collective personality is so rife with hostility that they don't even recognize it. They are deliberately hard on most strangers, but they get bad reactions even when they try to be friendly. I have seen them try to amuse an outsider by telling stories which they consider very funny – but which generate fear and queasiness in a listener whose sense of humour has a different kind of filter.

Some of the outlaws understand this communications gap, but most are puzzled and insulted to hear that 'normal people' consider them horrible. They get angry when they read about how filthy they are, but instead of shoplifting some deodorant, they strive to become even filthier. Only a few cultivate a noticeable body odour. Those with wives and steady girl friends bathe as often as most half-employed people, and make up for it by fouling their clothes more often.* This kind of exaggeration is the backbone of their style. The powerful stench they are said to exude is not so much body odour as the smell of old grease in their crusty uniforms. Every Angel recruit comes to his initiation wearing a new pair of Levis and a matching jacket with the sleeves cut off and a spotless emblem on the back. The ceremony varies from one chapter to another but the main feature is always the defiling of the initiate's new uniform. A bucket of dung and urine will be collected during the meeting, then poured on the newcomer's head in a solemn baptismal. Or he will take off his clothes and stand naked while the bucket of slop is poured over them and the others stomp it in.

* The Angels' old ladies are generally opposed to B.O. 'My old man went for two months once without taking a shower,' a girl from Richmond recalls. 'He wanted to see what it would be like to live up to the reputation people gave us. . . . I've got sinus and I can't smell that good anyhow, but it finally got so bad I sez: "Go pull out the other mattress – I ain't gonna sleep with you till you shower."'

These are his 'originals', to be worn every day until they rot. The Levis are dipped in oil, then hung out to dry in the sun – or left under the motorcycle at night to absorb the crankcase drippings. When they become too ragged to be functional, they are worn over other newer Levis. Many of the jackets are so dirty that the colours are barely visible, but they aren't discarded until they literally fall apart. The condition of the originals is a sign of status. It takes a year or two before they get ripe enough to make a man feel he has really made the grade.

Frenchy and the other Angels at the DePau wanted to know if I'd located them by following the smell. Later that night, at the weekly meeting, I noticed that several were wearing expensive wool shirts and ski jackets under their colours. When the bars closed at two, five of the outlaws came over to my apartment for an all-night drinking bout. The next day I learned that one was an infamous carrier of vermin, a walking crab farm. I went over my living-room carefully for signs of body lice and other small animals but found nothing. I waited nervously for about ten days, thinking he might have dropped eggs that were still incubating, but no vermin appeared. We played a lot of Bob Dylan music that night, and for a long time afterwards I thought about crabs every time I heard his voice.

That was in early spring of 1965. By the middle of summer I had become so involved in the outlaw scene that I was no longer sure whether I was doing research on the Hell's Angels or being slowly absorbed by them. I found myself spending two or three days each week in Angel Bars, in their homes, and on runs and parties. In the beginning I kept them out of my own world, but after several months my friends grew accustomed to finding Hell's Angels in my apartment at any hour of the day or night. Their arrivals and departures caused periodic alarums in the neighbourhood and sometimes drew crowds on the sidewalk. When word of this reached my Chinese landlord he sent emissaries to find out the nature of my work. One morning I had Terry the Tramp answer the doorbell to fend off a rent collection, but his act was cut short by the arrival of a prowl car summoned by the woman next door. She was very polite while the Angels moved their bikes out of her driveway, but the next day she asked me whether 'those boys' were my friends. I said yes, and four days later I received an eviction notice. The appearance of the rape omen was a clear and present danger to property values; the block had to be purified. It was not until much later after I'd moved, that I realized the woman had been thoroughly frightened. She'd seen groups of Angels going in and out of my apartment now and then, but once she got a look at them and heard the terrible sound of their machines, she felt a burning in her nerves every time she heard a motorcycle. They menaced her day and night – whirring and booming below her window – and it never crossed her mind that the occasional blast of the outlaw chopper was any different from the high-pitched wailing of the little bikes at the dental fraternity a half-block away. In the afternoon she would stand on her front steps, watering the sidewalk with a garden hose and glaring at every Honda that came over the hill from the nearby medical centre. At times the whole street seemed alive with Hell's Angels. It was more than any taxpaying property owner should have to bear. Actually, their visits were marked by nothing more sinister than loud music, a few bikes on the sidewalk, and an occasional shot out the back window. Most of the bad action came on nights when there were no Angels around: one of my most respectable visitors, an advertising executive from New York, became hungry after a long night of drink and stole a ham from the refrigerator in a nearby apartment; another guest set my mattress afire with a flare and we had to throw it out the back window; another ran wild on the street with a high-powered Falcon air horn normally carried on boats for use as a distress signal; people cursed him from at least twenty windows and he narrowly escaped injury when a man in pyjamas rushed out of a doorway and swung at him with a long white club.

On another night a local attorney drove his car across the sidewalk and over the ledge of my entranceway, where he leaned on his horn and tried to knock down the door with his bumper. A visiting poet hurled a garbage can under the wheels of a passing bus, causing a noise like a bad accident. My upstairs neighbour said it sounded like a Volkswagen being crushed. 'It jolted me right out of bed,' he said. 'But when I looked out of the window all I could see was the bus. I thought the car must have hit it head on and gone underneath. There was an awful dragging sound. I thought people were mashed down there in the wreckage.'

One of the worst incidents of that era caused no complaints at all: this was a sort of good-natured firepower demonstration, which occurred one Sunday morning about three-thirty. For reasons that were never made clear, I blew out my back windows with five blasts of a 12-gauge shotgun, followed moments later by six rounds from a ·44 Magnum. It was a prolonged outburst of heavy firing, drunken laughter and crashing glass. Yet the neighbours reacted with total silence. For a while I assumed that some freakish wind pocket had absorbed all the sound and carried it out to sea, but after my eviction I learned otherwise. Every one of the shots had been duly recorded on the gossip log. Another tenant in the building told me the landlord was convinced, by all the tales he'd heard, that the interior of my apartment was reduced to rubble by orgies, brawls, fire and wanton shooting. He had even heard stories about motorcycles being driven in and out the front door.

No arrests resulted from these incidents, but according to neighbourhood rumour they were all linked to the Hell's Angels, operating out of my apartment. Probably this is why the police were so rarely summoned; nobody wanted to be croaked by an Angel revenge party.

Shortly before I moved out, a clutch of the landlord's Mandarin-speaking relatives came to inspect the place, apparently for the purpose of compiling a bill of damages. They seemed puzzled, but hugely relieved, to find no grave destruction. There were no signs of a Hell's Angel's presence, and the only motorcycle in sight was on the sidewalk. When they left they stopped to look at it, chattering rapidly in their own tongue. I was a little worried that they might be talking about seizing my bike in lieu of back rent, but the one member of the group who spoke English assured me that they were admiring its 'elegance'.

The landlord himself had only a dim understanding of the Hell's Angels' threat to his property. All complaints had to be translated into Chinese, and I suspect he found them inscrutable. With a personal frame of reference unfazed by the English-speaking mass media, he could have no way of knowing why my neighbours were so agitated. The people he sent to hustle me when the rent was overdue were similarly blank on the subject of outlaw motorcyclists. They were terrified of my Doberman pup, but they didn't blink an eye that morning when they rang the doorbell and came face to face with Terry the Tramp.

He had been up all night and was groggy from pills and wine. It was a cold wet day, and on the way to my place he had stopped at a Salvation Army store and bought the shaggy remains of a fur coat for thirty-nine cents. It looked like something Marlene Dietrich might have worn in the twenties. The ragged hem flapped around his knees, and the sleeves were like trunks of matted hair growing out of the armholes of his Hell's Angels vest. With the coat wrapped around him, he appeared to weigh about three hundred pounds . . . something primitive and demented, wearing boots, a beard, and round black glasses like a blind man.

Letting him answer the doorbell seemed like a final solution to the rent problem. As he stomped down the hallway we opened a new round of beers and waited to hear the terrified cries and the sound of running feet. But all we heard was a quick mumbled conversation, and seconds later Terry was back in the living-room. 'Hell, they never even flinched,' he said. 'To them I'm just another American. The two old ladies just grinned at me, and the little guy that spoke English was so polite I got shook up. I said you were gone and I didn't know when you'd be back, but they said they'd wait.'

He'd been back in the room about thirty seconds when we heard a commotion in the street. The police had come for the bikes, and Terry hurried outside. The ensuing debate drew a crowd of about two dozen, but the Chinese paid no attention. They had come to talk about money, and they were not about to be lured off the scent by a senseless squabble between cops and something that looked like it had burrowed straight through the earth from Mongolia.

Most people who stopped to watch the argument had recognized the emblem on Terry's back, so they were able to view the scene from many different levels of involvement – although the only real question was whether Terry and Mouldy Marvin (who stayed inside) would be fined $15 each for blocking a driveway or the law might opt for mercy and allow the bikes to be moved ten feet up the hill to a legal parking space.

The cops were obviously enjoying the whole thing. A routine parking complaint had led to a dramatic confrontation (before a good crowd) with one of the most notorious of the Hell's Angels. The worst they could do was write two citations totalling $30, but it required twenty minutes to make the fateful decision. Finally, the cop who'd grabbed the initiative in the first moments of the drama brought it all to an end by abruptly pocketing his citation book and turning his back on Terry with a sigh of weary contempt. 'All right, all right,' he snapped. 'Just get the goddamn things out of the way, will ya? Christ, I should have 'em both towed in, but . . .' The cop was young, but he had a fine stage presence. It was like watching Bing Crosby shame the Amboy Dukes by refusing to press charges against one of their warlords accused of spitting on the bells of St Mary's.

4

They're the Wild Bill Hickoks, the Billy the Kids – they're the last American heroes we have, man. – *Ed 'Big Daddy' Roth*

Go get those punks. – *Newsweek (March 1965)*

*

NOT all the outlaws were happy to be celebrities. The Frisco Angels had been severely burned after a series of articles in the *Chronicle* and viewed reporters as pilot fish for disaster. Across the Bay in Oakland the reaction was more varied. After seven years of being virtually ignored by the Press, the East Bay outlaws were more curious than wary – except among the newer arrivals, especially those from Berdoo. They had come up to Oakland for refuge, not publicity, and the last thing they needed was a Press photographer. Several were wanted in southern California on charges of theft, assault and non-support. Even a chance photo or a name shouted carelessly across a parking lot might set off a chain of events that would land them in jail; a photograph taken in Oakland, or an interview mentioning names, could be picked up by a wire service and published in San Bernardino the next morning. After that it would only be a matter of hours before the hounds found the trail again.

The publicity also had a bad effect on their employment picture. At the end of 1964 perhaps two thirds of the outlaws were working, but a year later the figure was down to about one third. Terry was summarily fired from his assembly-line job at General Motors a few days after the *True* article appeared.* 'They just told me to move on,' he said with a shrug. 'They didn't give no reason, but the guys I worked with told me the foreman was all shook up about that article. He asked one guy if he'd ever seen me take dope and if I ever talked about gang rapes – that kind of bullshit. The union says they're gonna fight it, but what the hell – I got other ways to get bread.'

* August 1965.

Motorcycle outlaws are not much in demand on the labour market. With a few exceptions, even those with saleable skills prefer to draw unemployment insurance . . . which gives them their leisure to sleep late, spend plenty of time on their bikes, and free-lance for extra cash whenever they feel the need. Some practise burglary, and others strip cars, steal motorcycles or work erratically as pimps. Many are supported by working wives and girl friends, who earn good salaries as secretaries, waitresses and night-club dancers. A few of the younger outlaws still live with their parents, but they don't like to talk about it and only go home when they have to – either to sleep off a drunk, clean out the refrigerator, or cadge a few bucks from the family cookie jar. Those Angels who work usually do it part time or drift from one job to another, making good money one week and nothing at all the next.

They are longshoremen, warehousemen, truck drivers, mechanics, clerks and casual labourers at any work that pays quick wages and requires no allegiance. Perhaps one in ten has a steady job or a decent income. Skip from Oakland is a final inspector on a General Motors assembly line, making around $200 a week; he owns his own home and even dabbles in the stock market. Tiny, the Oakland chapter's sergeant at arms and chief head-knocker, is a 'credit supervisor' for a local TV appliance chain. He owns a Cadillac and gets $150 a week for hustling people who get behind on their payments.* 'We get a lot of deadbeats in this business,' he says. 'Usually I call 'em up first. I come on real businesslike until I'm sure I have the right guy. Then I tell him: "Listen, motherfucker, I'm givin' you twenty-four hours to get down here with that money." This usually scares the shit out of 'em and they pay up quick. If they don't then I drive out to the house and kick on the door until somebody answers. Once in a while I get a wise-ass trying to give me the run-around . . . then I pick up a couple of guys, lay a few bucks on 'em for the help, and we go out to see the punk. That always does it. I never had to stomp anybody yet.'

There are others with steady incomes, but most of the Angels work sporadically at the kind of jobs that will soon be taken over

* Numerous court appearances crippled Tiny's income towards the end of 1965, and in June of 1966 he was forced to take an indefinite leave of absence to attend his own trial on a charge of forcible rape.

by machines. It is hard enough to get unskilled work while wearing shoulder-length hair and a gold earring . . . it takes an employer who is either desperate or unusually tolerant . . . but to apply for work as a member of a nationally known 'criminal motorcycle conspiracy' is a handicap that can only be overcome by very special talents, which few Angels possess. Most are unskilled and uneducated, with no social or economic credentials beyond a colourful police record and a fine knowledge of motorcycles.*

So there is more to their stance than a wistful yearning for acceptance in a world they never made. Their real motivation is an instinctive certainty as to what the score really is. They are out of the ballgame and they know it. Unlike the campus rebels, who with a minimum amount of effort will emerge from their struggle with a validated ticket to status, the outlaw motorcyclist views the future with the baleful eye of a man with no upward mobility at all. In a world increasingly geared to specialists, technicians and fantastically complicated machinery the Hell's Angels are obvious losers, and it bugs them. But instead of submitting quietly to their collective fate, they have made it the basis of a full-time social vendetta. They don't expect to win anything, but on the other hand, they have nothing to lose.

If one drawback to being a public figure was the inability to get a job, another was the disappointment in discovering that fame can come without money. Shortly after the news magazines made them celebrities they began to talk about 'getting rich from it all', and their fear of being wiped out soon gave way to a brooding resentment over being 'used' to sell newspapers and magazines. They weren't sure how the riches would come, or why, or even if they deserved them . . . but they seemed pretty certain that the balance of payments was about to tip their way. This feeling reached its zenith when an Angel made the *Post* cover, and for a few weeks after that it was hard to talk to them about anything but money. They had all kinds of deals working, numerous offers that had to be juggled and judged . . . whether to go fast and hard for bundles

* By the middle of 1966 the war in Vietnam had put several of the Angels back in the money. The volume of military shipping through the Oakland Army Terminal caused such a demand for handlers and loaders that Hell's Angels were hired almost in spite of themselves.

of short-term cash or try to stay cool and set up a schedule of royalties to be doled out in perpetuity.

None of them realized what an empty bag they were holding until their deals began to collapse. The Angels weren't quick to see the trend, because they were still celebrities. But one day the phone stopped ringing and the game was all over. They were still talking money, but the talk would soon go sour. Cash was all around, but they couldn't get their hands on it. What they needed was a good agent or a money-mad nark, but they couldn't get that either. There was nobody to hustle Sal Mineo for the $3,000 they wanted for helping him make his movie. And nobody to coax $2,000 out of the producers of the Merv Griffin show, who had also talked about a film. (God knows I tried, and the Angels still blame me for blowing that two grand they wanted, but the sad truth is that Merv's people just wouldn't pay . . . perhaps because they knew Les Crane had already scheduled a Hell's Angels bit.) There were others who tried to put the outlaws on to some loot: a San Francisco journalist who knew the Angels was contacted by a man from one of the TV networks who wanted to be on hand with a camera crew the next time the outlaws ripped up a town. But the deal fell through when the Angels offered, for $100 apiece, to terrorize any town the TV people selected. It must have been tempting, a flat guarantee of some hair-raising footage . . . and its a measure of the television industry's concern for public welfare that the offer was turned down.

The Angels were extremely proud of their *Post* exposure, though the cover featured one of the most obscure and least typical members. Given a chance to present their 6,670,000* readers with a really unnerving tableau, the *Post* chose instead to go with Skip Von Bugening, a former rock-'n'-roll musician and supermarket clerk who looks and talks like everybody's idea of the ideal Job Corps candidate. Skip is a good lad, but to foist him off on the public as a typical Hell's Angel is like reshooting *The Wild One* with Sal Mineo playing the lead instead of Marlon Brando. Less than six months after he made the *Post* cover, Skip was stripped of his colours and kicked out of the club. 'He never

* Circulation figure at the end of 1965, according to the *Post* circulation department.

was Angel material,' said one. 'He was just a goddamn show-off.'

As the outlaws got more and more publicity their reaction to it became increasingly ambiguous. At first, when nearly everything written about them was taken from the Lynch report, they were outraged that responsible journalists could be so sloppy and biased. They spoke of editors and reporters as so much human garbage, hopelessly corrupt and not worth talking to under any circumstances. Every unfavourable article produced outbursts of bitterness, but they enjoyed being interviewed and photographed, and instead of withdrawing into angry silence, they kept trying to even the score by giving new interviews to set the record straight.

Only once did they become seriously hostile to everything connected with the news media. This was immediately after the *Time* and *Newsweek* articles. I recall trying to show the *Time* article to Crazy Rock, then working as a night custodian at the San Francisco Hilton. He glanced at the clipping and tossed it aside. I'd go nuts if I started reading that stuff,' he said. 'It doesn't make any sense. It's all bullshit.' The Frisco Angels wanted to give me a chain-whipping on general principles. Later, when I met the Oakland Angels, there was talk of setting me on fire because of what *Newsweek* had done. It was not until my article on motorcycles appeared in *The Nation* that they really believed I hadn't been conning them all along.

Yet later in the year, and especially after they made their political debut – in a clash with the Berkeley peace marchers – the Angels stopped laughing at their Press clippings. The tone of the coverage was changing, notably in Hearst's *San Francisco Examiner* and William Knowland's *Oakland Tribune*. Even in *The San Francisco Chronicle*, a paper that had never done anything but laugh at the Angels, the late Lucius Beebe devoted one of his Sunday columns to sneering at the Berkeley marchers and ended it by saying: 'The Hell's Angels would appear to be possessed of a sense of fitness and realism that is lacking elsewhere on the East Bay scene.'

At this point it was a toss-up as to whether the Angels were bamboozling the Press or vice-versa. Impartial observers and newspaper buffs found the truth very strange. Here was *Examiner*, which had always viewed the Angels with fear and loathing, suddenly presenting them as misunderstood patriots. The *Examiner* has fallen on hard times recently, but it remains influential among those who fear King George III might still be alive in Argentina. The *Tribune* is the same kind of newspaper, but free of the confusing deviations that have come to characterize the *Examiner*. In 1964, for instance, the Hearst empire forsook Goldwater, while the *Tribune* held the line. As it happened, Mr Knowland had managed the senator's successful California primary campaign, so there was not much doubt where the *Tribune* stood – without much company – in November. In some circles the *Tribune* is seen as a classic example of what anthropologists call an 'atavistic endeavour'.*

Lucius Beebe was in a class by himself, and his opinions have not been a factor in any meaningful issue since the introduction of barbed wire to the prairies . . . but every now and then he would come up with a really classic screed, and for some reason the *Chronicle* continued to print them even after his death, in early 1966. In three years of reading the paper I had never encountered anyone who took Beebe seriously until several of the Hell's Angels quoted his column to me – with straight faces and a certain amount of pride. When I laughed they got huffy. He'd compared them favourably to the Texas Rangers – and with the kind of Press they were used to, that amounted to a gold-star break-through. I tried to explain that Lucius was a quack, but they would have none of it. 'Shit, this is the first time I ever read anything good about us,' said one, 'and you try to tell me the guy's an asshole . . . hell, it's better than anything *you* ever wrote about us.'

Which was true, and I felt rotten about it. It had never occurred to me to compare Tiny to Bat Masterson. Or Terry to Billy the Kid. Or Sonny to Buffalo Bill. Even after Big Daddy put it all in a nut I still missed the connection . . . and then came Beebe, with his Texas Rangers linkage, which the Angels recognized immediately.

* It also turns a profit, unlike the *Examiner* – which in 1965 finally threw in the towel and merged with the *Chronicle*, now the only morning daily in San Francisco. Rather than fold altogether, the *Examiner* switched to afternoon publication.

Would ye deny the public prints? – *Anglo-Saxon motto*

*

Whatever else might be said about the Angels, nobody has ever accused them of modesty, and this new kind of Press was pure balm to their long-abused egos. The Angels were beginning to view their sudden fame as a confirmation of what they had always suspected: they were rare, fascinating creatures ('Wake up and dig it, man, we're the Texas Rangers'). It was a shock of recognition, long overdue, and although they never understood the timing, they were generally pleased with the result. At the same time they revised their traditional view of the Press: not *all* reporters were congenital liars – there were exceptions, here and there, with the guts and keen understanding to write the real stuff.

5

He wore black denim trousers and motorcycle boots
And a black leather jacket with an eagle on the back.
He had a hopped-up cycle that took off like a gun,
That fool was the terror of Highway 101. –
Juke box hit of the late 1950s

*

THE Californian climate is perfect for bikes as well as surfboards, convertibles, swimming pools and abulia. Most cyclists are harmless weekend types, no more dangerous than skiers or skin-divers. But ever since the end of the Second World War the West Coast has been plagued by gangs of young wild men on motorcycles, roaming the highways in groups of ten to thirty and stopping whenever they get thirsty or road-cramped to suck up some beer and make noise. The hellbroth of publicity in 1965 made the phenomena seem brand new, but even in the ranks of the Hell's Angels there are those who insist that the outlaw scene went over the hump in the mid-fifties when the original faces began drifting off to marriage and mortgages and time payments.

The whole thing was born, they say, in the late 1940s, when most ex-GIs wanted to get back to an orderly pattern: college, marriage, a job, children – all the peaceful extras that come with a sense of security. But not everybody felt that way. Like the drifters who rode west after Appomattox, there were thousands of veterans in 1945 who flatly rejected the idea of going back to their pre-war pattern. They didn't want order, but privacy – and time to figure things out. It was a nervous, downhill feeling, a mean kind of *Angst* that always comes out of wars . . . a compressed sense of time on the outer limits of fatalism. They wanted more action, and one of the ways to look for it was on a big motorcycle. By 1947 the state was alive with bikes, nearly all of them powerful American made irons from Harley–Davidson and Indian.*

* Now defunct.

Two dozen gleaming, stripped-down Harleys filled the parking lot of a bar called the El Adobe. The Angels were shouting, laughing and drinking beer – paying no attention to two teen-aged boys who stood on the fringe of the crowd, looking scared. Finally one of the boys spoke to a lean, bearded outlaw named Gut: 'We like your bikes, man. They're really sharp.' Gut glanced at him, then at the bikes. 'I'm glad you like them,' he said. 'They're all we have.' *September 1965*

*

The Hell's Angels of the sixties are not keenly interested in their origins or spiritual ancestors. 'Those guys aren't around any more,' Barger told me. But some were – although in 1965 it wasn't easy to locate them. Some were dead, others were in prison and those who'd gone straight were inclined to avoid publicity. One of the few I managed to locate was Preetam Bobo. I found him on a Saturday afternoon in the Sausalito Yacht Harbour, across the Bay from San Francisco, getting his forty-foot sloop in shape for a one-way cruise to the Caribbean. His crew for the trip, he said, would consist of his sixteen-year-old son, two seaworthy Hell's Angels and his striking blonde British girl friend, who was stretched out on the deck in a blue bikini. Preetam is one of only two lifetime members of the Frisco Angels chapter. The other, Frank, retired from the outlaw world after seven years as Frisco president and is now surfing in the South Pacific. Frank is the George Washington of Angeldom; his name is mentioned with reverence, among the other chapters as well as Frisco. 'He was the best president we ever had,' they say. 'He held us together and he was good for us.' Frank had class, and he set many styles – from the gold earring to the purple-dyed beard to the clip-on nose ring that he wore whenever he had the right audience. All during his reign, from 1955 to 1962, he held a steady job as a respected cameraman, but he needed more action than any job could provide. For this he had the Angels, a vehicle for his humour and fantasies, a sop for any aggressions and an occasional chance to bust out of the workaday murk like some kind of sabre-rattling golem and lay at least a small jolt on people he had no other way of reaching. Frank was so completely hip that he went down to Hollywood and bought the blue-and-yellow striped sweatshirt that Lee Marvin wore in *The Wild One*.

Frank wore it ragged, and not only for runs and parties. When he felt the Angels were being persecuted beyond the norm he would make an appearance in the police chief's office, wearing his Hollywood sweatshirt and demanding justice. If that didn't get results, he would go to the American Civil Liberties Union – a step that Oakland's Barger has flatly ruled out because of its 'Communist' implications. Unlike Barger, Frank had a wry sense of humour and a very sophisticated instinct for self-preservation. In seven years at the head of what was the biggest and wildest of all the Hell's Angels chapters, then and now, he was never arrested and never had an intramural fight. Even the Angels find his record amazing. Preetam had to win his vice-presidency by fighting seven Angels in the space of one week – three in one night – and whipping them all to sore pulps. But that was Bobo's gig; before the Hell's Angels came into his life he was one of San Francisco's more promising middleweight boxers, and it was no feat for him to put down a half-dozen unsuspecting tavern brawlers. Later, when he became a karate expert, he happily destroyed a new generation of challengers.

The Angels considered him a valuable hatchet man. 'A punch-out artist is good to have around,' said one, 'but he has to cool it around his buddies. Some guys get boozed up and just start teeing off on people.'

Until his departure Bobo was the horned toad of waterfront literary bars. His colleagues were not eager to drink with him, and for good reason. He was not a comfortable man to get drunk with. Once, in a fit of pique, he lashed out with a karate chop and cracked a four-inch-thick marble bench in the Hall of Justice. Even the police were leery of him. He ran a karate schoool and enjoyed 'death battles', a karate version of the no-limit, bare-knuckle boxing matches of the John L. Sullivan era. It is not necessary for one of the combatants to die, but the fight will continue until one of them can't stand up, for whatever reason . . . and if the reason happens to be death, then the prearranged understanding, among both fighters and carefully screened spectators, is that the death is accidental.* Unfortunately, Bobo accepted a spur of the

* Deaths are extremely rare. The combat usually ends when the backers of either man decide the cause is lost.

moment death challenge from a visiting Jap on a night when a San Francisco society columnist and several of her friends had come to see him about the possibility of an off-beat feature. The result was a nightmare of blood, fierce screaming and panic in the gallery. Nobody was killed, but it was a very crude show, and soon afterwards Preetam Bobo's name was removed from the rolls of licensed karate instructors.

It was only then, after exhausting all other means of demoralizing the public, that he turned seriously to writing. Several years earlier he had given up bikes 'because of the stigma'. After a long stint as a motorcycle messenger he stumbled on the *Rubáiyát* of Omar Khayyám and thought it necessary to publish his own views. He could, however, only on the condition that he move through the streets of the world in conventional fashion. 'I felt like a whore,' he says, 'but I told the editor I'd play it straight. Hell, I didn't want to spend the rest of my life as a delivery boy.'

Preetam Bobo is a study in something, but I was never sure what to call it. He is a walking monument to everything the Hell's Angels would like to stand for, but which few of them do. Preetam is the Compleat Outlaw, and he somehow makes it work. Like Frank, he went through his whole activist period without ever being arrested. 'All it takes is the sense to be quiet around cops,' he says. 'Whenever we had trouble with the law I just drifted off to the side and kept my mouth shut. If a cop ever asked me a question I'd answer politely and say "sir". In those situations, man, a cop appreciates somebody calling him "sir". It's the smart thing to do, that's all. And besides, it's a hell of a lot cheaper than going to jail.'

Bobo was a motorcyclist long before he was a Hell's Angel. He remembers one night when he passed the corner of Leavenworth and Market in downtown San Francisco and saw a bunch of bikes outside a pool hall called Antones. He stopped to say hello, and soon afterwards he was part of a loosely knit group of riders who called themselves, half jokingly, the Market Street Commandos. Motorcycles were comparatively rare in the early 1950s, and people who rode them were happy to find company. 'You could go by there any hour of the day or night,' Preetam recalls, 'and there'd always be at least ten bikes out in front. Sometimes on weekends there'd be fifty or sixty. It was a police problem even then. Businessmen were complaining that the bikes kept customers from parking in front of their stores.'

The Market Street Commandos drifted on, without much action, for about a year. Then, in early 1954, *The Wild One* came to town, and things changed. 'We went up to the Fox Theatre on Market Street,' said Preetam. 'There were about fifty of us, with jugs of wine and our black leather jackets. . . . We sat up there in the balcony and smoked cigars and drank wine and cheered like bastards. We could all see ourselves right there on the screen. We were all Marlon Brando. I guess I must have seen it four or five times.'

The Commandos were still in the grip of *The Wild One* when the second new wave hit – in the person of the wild prophet Rocky, the messiah, bringing the Word from the Southland. Ten years later Birney Jarvis, a *San Francisco Chronicle* police reporter and former Hell's Angel, described the moment of truth in an article:*

> One hot summer day in 1954, a swarthily handsome devil, sporting a pointed beard and a derby, broadslid his Harley–Davidson to a screeching halt at a motorcycle hangout in San Francisco.
>
> His faded blue Levi jacket, the sleeves roughly hacked off with a knife, was emblazoned with the leering winged death's-head that has become so well known to California lawmen.
>
> You could see the sweat-stained armpits of his checkered shirt as he wrestled the four-foot-high handlebars into position. With a flick of his wrist he blasted the afternoon quiet of a Sunday on Market Street.
>
> He laid his bike over on the kickstand, polished the glistening chrome of his 'X.A.' spring forks – four inches longer than stock – with a ragged handkerchief. He looked around him, nonchalantly wiping his greasy hands on his oil-crusted jeans.
>
> This was Rocky. Nobody cared what his last name was because he was 'classical' and he was a Hell's Angel from down Berdoo way.
>
> Thirty cyclists with polished boots and neatly barbered hair had watched his arrival, not without suspicion because he was, at that time, a stranger and all of them had been riding pals for a long time. . . . The welcoming committee was prime for membership in the Hell's Angels. Although completely square compared to the latter-day Angels, the street corner gang had had constant brushes with the law. . . . Rocky

* For *Male* magazine.

was elected president of the new branch of the Hell's Angels because he could really ride and because he had style.

'He could spin donuts on that hog with his feet on the pegs, and man, he was a wiggy cat,' a member of the Angels recalled. The cyclists found a seamstress who could duplicate Rocky's sinister emblem and it wasn't long before nearly 40 Angels were roaring out of San Francisco. The neat 'Hell's Angels – Frisco' surrounding the grinning skull with wings cost $7.50 and was ordinarily sewn on a Levi jacket. The white background of the red lettering soon became spotted with grime – and blood – from the many barroom battles that ensued.

'Listen, man, those beefs ain't our fault,' said a battle-scarred veteran of beer-hall punchouts. 'We'd go into a bar and someone'd mouth off or try to move in on our chicks and then we'd fight. What else could you do?'

Police reports kept pouring in as the Angels were forced to move from one hangout to another. A hangout – usually an all-night restaurant or a pool hall – would last about a week, until complaints of noisy or rowdy behavior brought the law.

'We chased those bike bums off Market Street because they were having drag races right through the traffic. A lot of them were stealing motorcycles and we'd check them all out,' said Terrible Ted, a motorcycle policeman who once called several of the Hell's Angels his friends.

'We called that bike heat Terrible Ted because he really was bad, man. Why, he'd ride like a nut to catch us and then he'd throw the book at us.'*

'It got so I had to go to work just so's I could pay off my tickets and stay out of the slammer,' said an Angel who lost his license to drive four times because of his driving record.

One humorous incident connected with the Hell's Angels insignia several years ago is still a source of amusement to the hard-riding cycle gang.

An Angel known as 'the Mute' was stopped for speeding by a policeman near the beach in Santa Cruz one Sunday afternoon. The Mute was proudly displaying his colours on a ragged Levi jacket. 'Take that off,' the patrolman jotted down on a notepad politely offered by the Mute, who was deaf and dumb.

The Mute stripped off his Levi jacket, exposing another Angel decal

* In 1966 Terrible Ted ran a red light in an unmarked police car and collided with a Greyhound bus. The crash killed his wife, destroyed the car and critically injured the patrolman.

on his leather jacket. 'Take that off, too,' the irate patrolman ordered, again using the Mute's notepad and pencil. And under the leather jacket was a wool shirt – also emblazoned with the club colours. 'Off with it,' the officer scribbled angrily. Under the shirt was an undershirt. It too had been stencilled with the club insignia. 'Okay, wise guy, take that off too,' the nonplussed patrolman wrote.

With a smirk the Mute removed his undershirt, and puffing out his chest, brought into full view the Hell's Angels' grinning death's-head, which had been tattooed on his body. The policeman threw up his hands in disgust, handed the Mute a ticket and sped off in his patrol car. But the Mute had the last laugh. He was prepared to go all the way. His trousers and shorts were also stenciled.

'He was a way-out mother,' the Mute's friends agree.

*

> People are already down on us because we're Hell's Angels. That's why we like to blow their minds. It just more or less burns em, that's all. – *Jimmy from Oakland*

*

Many of the Angels are graduates of other outlaw clubs . . . some of which, like the Booze Fighters, were as numerous and fearsome in their time as the Angels are today. It was the Booze Fighters, not the Hell's Angels, who kicked off the Hollister riot which led to the filming of *The Wild One*. That was in 1947, when the average Hell's Angel of the 1960s was less than ten years old.

Hollister at that time was a town of about four thousand, a farming community an hour's fast drive south of Oakland, off in the foothills of the Diablo mountain range. Its only claim to fame in 1947 was as the producer of seventy-four per cent of all the garlic consumed in the United States. Hollister was – and remains, to some extent – the kind of town that Hollywood showed the world in the film version of *East of Eden*, a place where the commander of the local American Legion post is by definition a civic leader.

And so it came to pass, on the Fourth of July of that year, that the citizens of Hollister gathered together for the annual celebration. The traditional Independence Day rites – flags, bands, baton virgins, etc. – were scheduled to precede a more contemporary event, the annual motorcycle hill climb and speed tests, which the previous year had drawn contestants from miles around . . . valley boys, farmers, small-town mechanics, veterans, just a crowd of decent fellas who happened to ride motorcycles.

The 1947 Hollister hill climb and races also drew contestants from miles around . . . many miles, and many contestants. When the sun rose out of the Diablos on the Fourth of July morning the seven-man local police force was nervously sipping coffee after a sleepless night attempting to control something like 3,000 motorcyclists. (The police say 4,000; veteran cyclists say 2,000 – so 3,000 is probably about right.) It has been established beyond doubt, however, that Hollister filled up with so many bikes that 1,000 more or less didn't make much difference. The mob grew more and more unmanageable; by dusk the whole downtown area was littered with empty, broken beer bottles, and the cyclists were staging drag races up and down Main Street. Drunken fist fights developed into full-scale brawls. Legend has it that the cyclists literally took over the town, defied the police, man-handled local women, looted the taverns and stomped anyone who got in their way. The madness of that weekend got enough headlines to interest an obscure producer named Stanley Kramer and a young actor named Brando. Shortly before her death, in 1966, Hollywood gossip columnist Hedda Hopper took note of the Hell's Angels menace and traced its origins back through the years to *The Wild One*. This led her to blame the whole outlaw phenomenon on Kramer, Brando and everyone else in any way connected with the movie. The truth is that *The Wild One* – despite an admittedly fictional treatment – was an inspired piece of film journalism. Instead of institutionalizing common knowledge, in the style of *Time*, it told a story that was only beginning to happen and which was inevitably influenced by the film. It gave the outlaws a lasting romance-glazed image of themselves, a coherent reflection that only a few had been able to find in a mirror, and it quickly became the bike rider's answer to *The Sun also Rises*. The image is not valid, but its wide acceptance can hardly be blamed on the movie. *The Wild One* was careful to distinguish between 'good outlaws' and 'bad outlaws', but the people who were most influenced chose to identify with Brando instead of Lee Marvin, whose role as the villain was a lot more true to life than Brando's portrayal of the confused hero. They saw themselves as modern Robin Hoods . . . virile, inarticulate brutes whose good instincts got warped somewhere in the struggle for self-expression and who spent the rest of their violent lives seeking revenge on a world that done them wrong when they were young and defenceless.

Another of Hollywood's contributions to the Hell's Angels lore is the name. The Angels say they are named after a famous First World War bomber squadron that was stationed near Los Angeles and whose personnel raced around the area on motorcycles when they weren't airborne. There are others who say the Angels got their name from a 1930 Jean Harlow movie based on some scriptwriter's idea of an Army Air Corps that may or may not have existed at the time of the First World War. It was called *Hell's Angels* and no doubt was still being shown in 1950, when the restless veterans who founded the first Angel chapter at Fontana were still trying to decide what to do with themselves. While the name might have originated before any Hell's Angel was born, it was lost in the history of some obscure southern California military base until Hollywood made it famous and also created the image of wild men on motorcycles – an image that was later adopted and drastically modified by a new breed of outcasts that not even Hollywood could conceive of until they appeared, in the flesh, on California highways.

The concept of the 'motorcycle outlaw' was as uniquely American as jazz. Nothing like them had ever existed. In some ways they appeared to be a kind of half-breed anachronism, a human hangover from the era of the Wild West. Yet in other ways they were as new as television. There was absolutely no precedent, in the years after the Second World War, for large gangs of hoodlums on motorcycles, revelling in violence, worshipping mobility and thinking nothing of riding five hundred miles on a weekend . . . to whoop it up with other gangs of cyclists in some country hamlet entirely unprepared to handle even a dozen peaceful tourists. Many picturesque, outback villages got their first taste of tourism not from families driving Fords or Chevrolets, but from clusters of boozing 'city boys' on motorcycles.

In retrospect, eye-witness accounts of the Hollister riot seem timid compared to the film. A more accurate comment on the nature of the Hollister 'riot' is the fact that a hastily assembled force of only twenty-nine cops had the whole show under control by noon of 5 July. By nightfall the main body of cyclists had roared out of town, in the best *Time* style, to seek new nadirs in sordid behaviour. Those who stayed behind did so at the request of the police; their punishment ranged from $25 traffic fines to ninety days in jail for indecent exposure. Of the 6,000 to 8,000 people supposedly involved in the fracas, a total of 50 were treated for injuries at the local hospital. (For a better perspective on motorcycle riots it helps to keep in mind that more than 450,000 Americans die each year as the result of automobile accidents.)

Nobody has ever accused the Hell's Angels of wanton killing, at least not in court . . . but it boggles the nerves to consider what might happen if the outlaws were ever deemed legally responsible for even three or four human deaths, by accident or otherwise. Probably every motorcycle rider in California would be jerked off the streets and ground into hamburger.

For a lot of reasons that are often contradictory, the sight and sound of a man on a motorcycle has an unpleasant effect on the vast majority of Americans who drive cars. At one point in the wake of the Hell's Angels uproar a reporter for *The New York Herald Tribune** did a long article on the motorcycle scene and decided in the course of his research that 'there is something about the sight of a passing motorcyclist that tempts many automobile drivers to commit murder.'

Nearly everyone who has ridden a bike for any length of time will agree. The highways are crowded with people who drive as if their sole purpose in getting behind the wheel is to avenge every wrong ever done them by man, beast or fate. The only thing that keeps them in line is their own fear of death, jail and lawsuits . . . which are much less likely if they can find a motorcycle to challenge instead of another two-thousand-pound-car or a concrete abutment. A motorcyclist has to drive as if everybody else on the road is out to kill him. A few of them are, and many of those who aren't are just as dangerous – because the only thing that can alter their careless, ingrained driving habits is a threat of punishment, either legal or physical, and there is nothing about a motorcycle to

*** Now defunct.**

threaten any man in a car.* A bike is totally vulnerable; its only defence is manoeuvrability, and every accident situation is potentially fatal – especially on a freeway, where there is no room to fall without being run over almost instantly. Despite these hazards, California – where freeways are a way of life – is by long odds the nation's biggest motorcycle market.

* Preetam Bobo tells a story about a man in a 'big new car' who forced him off the road on Highway 40 one Sunday afternoon in the 1950s. 'The dirty little bastard kept running up on my taillight,' said Preetam, 'until finally I just pulled over and stopped. The other guys had seen it, so we decided to teach the bastard a lesson. Man, we swarmed all over him. . . . We whipped on his hood with chains, tore off his aerial and smashed every window we could reach . . . all this at about seventy miles an hour, man. He didn't even slow down. He was terrified.'

6

We began to see that the Hell's Angels were assuming a mythical character. They had become folk heroes – vicarious exemplars of behavior most youth could only fantasize (unless swept away in mob activity), and legendary champions who would come to the rescue of the oppressed and persecuted. An old motorcyclist, witnessing police harassments of his fellows at a town outside Prince George's County, was heard to remark, 'Just wait till the Angels hear about this when they come in tomorrow – they'll tear this place apart.' – *From an article in* TransAction (*August 1966*), *written by two psychologists who worked with Maryland police to avert rioting in a town preparing to host national motorcycle races*

I smashed his face. He got wise. He called me a punk. He must have been stupid. – *A Hell's Angel explaining to a stranger*

*

Of all their habits and predilections that society finds alarming, the outlaws' disregard for the time-honoured concept of an eye for an eye is the one that frightens people most. The Hell's Angels try not to do anything halfway, and outcasts who deal in extremes are bound to cause trouble, whether they mean to or not. This, along with a belief in total retaliation for any offence or insult, is what makes the Angels such a problem for police and so morbidly fascinating to the general public. Their claims that they don't start trouble is probably true more often than not, but their idea of provocation is dangerously broad, and one of their main difficulties is that almost nobody else seems to understand it. Yet they have a very simple rule of thumb: in any argument a fellow Angel is *always right*. To disagree with a Hell's Angel is to be *wrong* – and to persist in being wrong is an open challenge.

Despite everything psychiatrists and Freudian castrators have to say about the Angels, they are tough, mean and potentially dangerous as packs of wild boar. The moment a fight begins, any leather fetishes or inadequacy feelings are entirely beside the point, as anyone who has ever tangled with them will sadly testify. When you get in an argument with a group of outlaw motorcyclists, your chances of emerging unmaimed depend on the number of heavy-handed allies you can muster in the time it takes to smash a beer bottle. In this league, sportsmanship is for old liberals and young fools.

Many of their 'assault victims' are people who have seen too many Western movies; they are victims of the John Wayne complex, which causes them to start swinging the moment they sense any insult. This is relatively safe in some areas of society, but in saloons frequented by outlaw motorcyclists it is the worst kind of folly. 'They're always looking for somebody to challenge them,' said a San Francisco policeman. 'And once you're involved with them, it's all or nothing. A stranger who doesn't want anything to do with them, if one of the bums says something to his woman, he can't take offence or he'll have to fight four or five Angels, not just the one. People should understand this.'

One of the Frisco Angels explained it without any frills: 'Our motto, man, is "All on One and One on All". You mess with an Angel and you've got twenty-five of them on your neck. I mean, they'll break you but good, baby.'

The outlaws take the 'all on one' concept so seriously that it is written into the club charter as Bylaw Number 10: 'When an Angel punches a non-Angel, all other Angels will participate.'

The outlaws never know, from one moment to the next, when they might have to grapple with some foe bent on humiliating the colours. Here is a hazy, yet fairly instructive account of a clash with an ex-Angel named Phil and his XKE Jaguar. For several hours prior to the incident, Phil had been drinking and arguing in a roadhouse with a half-dozen members of the Oakland chapter. Finally they told him to leave or be stomped. Phil went outside, backed his car off about fifty yards from the row of bikes at the curb, then ploughed into them like a bulldozer, breaking the leg of one Angel who tried to get his bike out of the way. This is how the Lynch report told it:

On November 4, 1961, a San Francisco resident driving through

Rodeo, possibly under the influence of alcohol, struck a motorcycle belonging to a Hell's Angel parked outside a bar. A group of Angels pursued the vehicle, pulled the driver from the car and attempted to demolish the rather expensive vehicle. The bartender claimed he had seen nothing, but a cocktail waitress in the bar furnished identification to the officers concerning some of those responsible for the assault. The next day it was reported to the officers that a member of the Hell's Angels gang had threatened the life of this waitress as well as another woman waitress. A male witness who definitely identified five participants in the assault, including the president of the Vallejo Hell's Angels and the Vallejo 'Road Rats' [since absorbed by Angels], advised officers that because of his fear of retaliation by club members he would refuse to testify to the facts he had previously furnished.

Motorcycles are knocked over by cars every day all over the nation, but when the incident involves outlaw motorcyclists it's something else again. Instead of settling the thing with an exchange of insurance information or, at the very worse, an argument with a few blows, the Hell's Angels stomped the driver (a former member) and 'attempted to demolish the vehicle'. I asked one of them whether the police exaggerated this aspect, and he said no, they had done the natural thing: smashed headlights, kicked in doors, broken windows and torn various components off the engine.

Another instructive clash occurred soon after the Monterey incident, when the outlaws were still feeling tough. It began as an everyday act of revenge, but it didn't come off. Perhaps for this reason, the police report was unusually restrained:

On September 19, 1964, a large group of Hell's Angels and Satan's Slaves converged on a bar in South Gate (Los Angeles County), parking their motorcycles and cars in the street in such a fashion as to block one half of the roadway. They told officers that three members of the club had recently been asked to stay out of the bar and that they had come to tear it down. Upon their approach the bar owner locked the doors and turned off the lights and no entrance was made, but the group did demolish a cement block fence. On arrival of the police, members of the clubs were lying on the sidewalk and in the street. They were asked to leave the city, which they did reluctantly. As they left, several were heard to say that they would be back and tear down the bar.

In all, it was a pretty quiet outrage, and except for the demolition of a fence, it went into the books as a routine victory for law and order. It was also a good example of the total-retaliation ethic: when you're asked to stay out of a bar you don't just punch the owner – you come back with your army and tear the place down, destroy the whole edifice and everything it stands for. No compromise. If a man gets wise, mash his face. If a woman snubs you, rape her. This is the thinking, if not the reality, behind the whole Hell's Angels act. It is also the aspect of the story that gets to the editors of news magazines. The combined testimony of 104 police departments is proof enough that the outlaws are unable to enforce their savage codes on any level of society but their own . . . and yet the white-collar, button-down world is obviously alarmed to hear that these codes exist at all. Which they do, and they are also adhered to, as noted in the concluding paragraphs of the California Attorney-General's report:

> The group seeks to exploit the so-called 'gangsters' code' of group loyalty and threats to persons who might appear in court against them. There have been instances of Hell's Angels punishing witnesses by physical assault. In the event the witness or victim is female, the women associates of the Angels seem willing to participate in threats to discourage testimony. A practical problem seen in various cases is that both victims and witnesses generally exist in the same environment as do the Hell's Angels. While gang rapes and forced sex perversions may have occurred, the victims and witnesses frequently are not of the higher social strata and thus are vulnerable to the mores of 'saloon society'. It is believed that the only feasible approach to the solution of this problem is for investigating officers to recognize it and take all steps possible to protect witnesses both before and after trial.

Not many members of saloon society will find consolation in these words. The Angels and their allies bear grudges much longer than police feel it's necessary to protect witnesses, and cops have a tendency to lose interest in a prosecution witness about five minutes after the jury comes in with a verdict. No bartender who has caused the arrest of an Angel will ever feel anything but panic at the sound of motorcycle engines in the street and the clumping of leather boot heels coming towards his door. The Angels don't wilfully trace their enemies from one place to another, but they spend so much of their time in bars that they are likely to turn up thirsty almost anywhere. And once an enemy is located, the word goes out fast on the network. It takes only two or three Angels, and no more than five minutes, to wreck a bar and put a man in the hospital. Chances are they won't be arrested . . . but even if they are, the damage is already done.

An intended victim – such as the bar owner in South Gate, who suffered only the loss of a fence in the first attack – will always know that his place has a certain distinction: it is marked, and as long as the Hell's Angels or Satan's Slaves exist, there is a chance that some of them will come back to finish the job.

The outlaw hierarchy is alway in flux, but the spirit is no different now than in 1950, when the first Angel chapter was formed in the long shadow of the Booze Fighters. The root definition remains the same: a dangerous hoodlum on a big, fast motorcycle. And California has been breeding them for years. Many are independents, indistinguishable from any Hell's Angel except for the lettering on their backs – 'No Club' or 'Lone Wolf' or sometimes just 'Fuck You'. Perhaps five hundred or so, definitely less than a thousand, belong to clubs like Gypsy Jokers, Nightriders, Commancheros, Presidents and Satan's Slaves. About a hundred and fifty – as of 1966 – form the outlaw elite, the Hell's Angels.

The only difference between the Hell's Angels and the other outlaw clubs is that the Angels are more extreme. Most of the others are part-time outlaws, but the Angels play the role seven days a week: they wear their colours at home, on the street and sometimes even to work; they ride their bikes to the neighbourhood grocery for a quart of milk. An Angel without his colours feels naked and vulnerable – like a knight without his armour.

A Sacramento cop once asked a five-foot-five, 135-pound Angel: 'What's the big attraction?'

'Nobody bugs me as long as I'm flying the colours,' he replied.

The dividing line between outlaws and the square majority is subject to change at any moment, and many respectable clubs have queered their image overnight. All it takes is a noisy fracas, a police report and a little publicity . . . and suddenly they're outlaws. In most cases this leads to the break-up of the club, with a majority of the erstwhile members feeling hurt and scandalized that such a thing could happen. But those few responsible for the trouble will no longer be welcome in respectable circles. Technically, they become 'independents', but that term is a misnomer because any rider who applies it to himself is already an outlaw anyway. All he lacks is a club to join, and he will sooner or later find one. The motorcycle fraternity is very tight – on both sides of the law – and the most extreme viewpoints are represented by the American Motorcycle Association and the Hell's Angels. There is no status in the middle, and people who are serious enough about motorcycles to join an A.M.A. club will not take rejection lightly. Like converts to Communism or Catholicism, Hell's Angels who were once A.M.A. members take their outlaw role more seriously than the others.

The Angels are too personally disorganized to have any clear perspective on the world, but they admire intelligence, and some of their leaders are surprisingly articulate. Chapter presidents have no set term of office, and a strong one, like Barger, will remain unchallenged until he goes to jail, gets killed or finds his own reasons for hanging up the colours. The outlaws are very respectful of power, even if they have to create their own image of it. Despite the anarchic possibilities of the machines they ride and worship, they insist that their main concern in life is 'to be a righteous Angel', which requires a loud obedience to the party line. They are intensely aware of *belonging*, of being able to depend on each other. Because of this, they look down on independents, who usually feel so wretched – once they've adopted the outlaw frame of reference – that they will do almost anything to get in a club.

'I don't know why,' said an ex-Angel, 'but you almost have to join a club. If you don't, you'll never be accepted anywhere. If you don't wear any colours, you're sort of in between – and you're nothing.'

This desperate sense of unity is crucial to the outlaw mystique. If the Hell's Angels are outcasts from society, as they freely admit, then it is all the more necessary that they defend each other from attack by 'the others' – mean squares, enemy gangs or armed agents of the Main Cop. When somebody punches a lone Angel every one of them feels threatend. They are so wrapped up in their own image that they can't conceive of anybody challenging the colours without being fully prepared to take on the whole army.

*

For many are called, but few are chosen. – *St Matthew*

*

Since the revelations of the Lynch report the Angels have rejected so many membership bids that one of them said it was 'like a plague of locusts'. The majority of would-be Angels are independents who suddenly feel the need for fellowship and status ... but in one case the Angels deigned to absorb a whole club: the Question Marks, from Hayward, which became the Hayward chapter of the Hell's Angels. Other charter applications came from as far away as Indiana, Pennsylvania, New York, Michigan and even Quebec ... and when the charters were not forthcoming, a few cycle clubs in the East simply created their own insignia and began calling themselves Hell's Angels.*

As of 1966, the Hell's Angels proper were still confined to California, but if the general response to their publicity is any indicator, they are going to have to expand whether they want to or not. The name isn't copyrighted, but even if it were, the threat of a lawsuit wouldn't be much of a deterrent to any gang of riders who wanted to appropriate it. The Angels' only hope for controlling their image lies in selective expansion, chartering only the biggest and meanest clubs who apply, but only on the condition that they terrorize anybody else in their area who tries to use the name.

* A club called the Detroit Renegades decided to hang on to their identity and go the Angels one better. In January 1966 forty-four of them were arrested when a police raid on their storefront clubhouse netted eighteen pistols. The raid was prompted by neighbours' complaints that the Renegades' presence cast a pall of fear on the neighbourhood. 'They came from out of a clear blue sky,' said a tenant in a nearby building. 'And they drink down there. When they get too much, the women in the neighbourhood are scared.' Police said most of the outlaws were factory workers and filling-station attendants, ranging in age from eighteen to thirty-three. Despite the elegance of the Renegade uniform – black leather jackets and satin shirts – a neighbour described them as 'crummy-looking people'. Later in 1966 an unofficial Hell's Angels chapter appeared in Detroit. After several well-publicized mass arrests, the leaders appealed to Barger for a national charter.

The Angels won't have any trouble exporting their name to the East,* but the day-to-day realities of being an outlaw motorcyclist in California are not easily transplantable. Bikes are a sunshine thing; they are dangerous and uncomfortable in rain and snow. A gang of riders in New York, Chicago or Boston could only operate in the far-ranging Hell's Angels style for a few months of the year, while in California the outlaws can move around – except in the mountains – any time they get the urge. This factor is reflected in nationwide motorcycle sales: in 1964 New York registered 23,000 bikes, while California had 203,420 – a roughly 9-to-1 ratio. On the other hand, there were more than twice as many motorcycles in New York in 1964 as there were in 1961, when only 10,000 were registered.†

Using the A.M.A.'s one-percenter gimmick, a sociologist could deduce from these figures that by 1970 New York alone will have some 500 potential Hell's Angels – about five times the size of the group that managed to blitz the national Press in 1965 – and by 1970 every Angel chapter will have a Press agent. According to the motorcycle industry, there were nearly 1,500,000 motorcycles registered in the United States in 1965, with an average of 4·1 riders to each licensed bike. (This is a wholly unrealistic figure; 1·5 would be more like it.) By the industry's count, however, it adds up to slightly over 6,000,000 riders, with more than 1,000,000 of these in California. (This too is questionable; not only is it based on the specious figure of 4·1 riders per bike, but by using the word 'motorcycle' without any qualifiers, it conjures up the image of California freeways swarming with huge high-powered bikes.)

In context the figures are not so menacing. According to the magazine *Cycle World* and *The Los Angeles Times*, 'Accelerated growth of the motorcycle market is centred on the lightweight division which represents 90 per cent of the total.' What the industry calls a lighweight is a very different animal from a 'chopped

* In August 1966 the Angels officially changed their patch to read 'Hell's Angels' on top of the skull, 'California' underneath. New chapters in the East and Midwest were expected to be operative by 1967. They would be allowed to wear the traditional patch, but with the name of their own state.

† Pennsylvania more than doubled its motorcycle registrations between 1964 (35,196) and 1965 (72,055). Other leading bike states are Florida and Illinois, with more than 50,000 each in 1965, including outlaws.

hog', or Harley 74, and the majority of the little bikes, says *Cycle World*, 'are used for fun, school transportation and trail and desert jaunts by sportsmen'. In other words, the formula for sales in today's motorcycle market is: 'Less weight and little engine equals "fun" and respectability.' And on this basis the industry predicts (at 4·1 per bike) a hard core of 8,894,000 motorcyclists in the United States by 1967. Again, the industry's figures are inflated, but considering the booming popularity of two-wheeled transportation, a figure of say, 6,000,000 for 1967 wouldn't be out of line . . . and that of course would mean 60,000 Huns, or the end of the civilized world.

In terms of pure money, the motorcycle industry is a gold mine. One of my recurring nightmares harks back to 1958 . . . *I have just arrived in New York with a $1,000 cushion, and one crisp afternoon in October, I emerge from the subway station in Times Square. . . . I dodge several panhandlers, a cluster of junkies, two transvestites and a Jehovah's Witness who talks like Elmer Fudd . . . and then, on a narrow part of the sidewalk next to the U.S. Army Recruiting Centre, I am buttonholed by an unkempt young Japanese who claims to be one of the Honda brothers . . . he is broke and desperate, needing funds for a plane ticket back to Tokyo, and for $894 he offers me his share of the business signed over, witnessed and wrapped up tight in the presence of any lawyer I care to name . . . he shows me his passport and a crumpled batch of motorcycle blueprints; no doubt he is one of the Honda boys. . . . I listen, smile knowingly and buy my way past him with one silver quarter and a subway token, rejecting my luck with a stupid finality and rushing off to some worthless job interview.*

Even now any man with the sense to pour piss out of a boot should take all the money he might spend on a new motorcycle and instead buy Honda stock – or any one of about thirty others, including Harley–Davidson, which despite a stone-age concept of management and technology is still the only American manufacturer of motorcycles.

The story of Harley–Davidson and the domestic motorcycle market is one of the gloomiest chapters in the history of American free enterprise. At the end of the Second World War there were less than 200,000 motorcycles registered in the United States, very few of them imports. During the 1950s, while H–D was consolidating its monopoly, bike sales doubled and then tripled. Harley had a gold mine on its hands – until 1962–3 when the import blitz began. By 1964 registrations had jumped to nearly 1,000,000 and lightweight Hondas were selling as fast as Japanese freighters could bring them over the ocean. The H–D brain trust was still pondering this Oriental duplicity when they were zapped on the opposite flank by Birmingham Small Arms Ltd of England. B.S.A. (which also makes Triumphs) decided to challenge Harley on its own turf and in its own class, despite the price-boosting handicap of a huge protective tariff. By 1965, with registrations already up fifty per cent over the previous year, the H–D monopoly was sorely beset on two fronts. The only buyers they could count on were cops and outlaws, while the Japanese were mopping up in the low-price field and B.S.A was giving them hell on the race track. By 1966, with the bike boom still growing, Harley was down to less than ten per cent of the domestic market and fighting to hold even that.

With all its machinery and thinking geared to 1,200-cubic-inch engines, the company has little hope of competing on the light and middleweight markets until at least 1970 . . . but they still have plenty of muscle in the heavyweight class, and in 1966 Harleys were winning as many big races as B.S.A.s or Triumphs. This hazy equality has not been maintained, however, in the market place. Most H–D racers are custom-built originals, made to order for some of the best riders in America and with much larger engines than their British competitors. Harley has yet to come up with a production model that can compete with Japanese or European imports – on the street, the track or in dirt – in terms of weight, price, handling ability or engine size.

There is surely some powerful lesson in the failure of Harley–Davidson to keep pace with a market they once controlled entirely. It is impossible to conceive of a similar situation in the automobile market. What if Ford, for instance, had been the only American manufacturer of autos at the end of the Second World War? Could they have lost more than ninety per cent of the market by 1965? A monopoly with a strong protective tariff should be in a commanding position even on the Yo-Yo market. How would the Yo-Yo king feel if he were stripped, in less than a decade, of all his customers except Hell's Angels and cops?

7

In a prosperous democracy that is also a society of winners and losers, any man without an equalizer or at least the illusion of one is by definition underprivileged. – *Sr Cazador, a sporting type of sorts, with a knowledge of triggers and a good eye for the openings*

They're a bunch of mean-hair fairies, that's all. They're enough to make anyone sick. – *San Francisco drag queen*

A Hell's Angel who lived on Thirty-seventh Street in Sacramento was continually being complained about for making suggestive comments to women who passed by his house. . . . 'Let's make it, baby', or 'Hey, beautiful, come sit on Papa's face'. A patrolman, checking on one of these complaints, first threatened the outlaw with jail and then asked him contemptuously if he couldn't find 'something better to do'. The Angel thought for a moment and then replied: 'Not unless it was to be fucking a cop.' – *From a conversation with a Sacramento policeman*

*

THE current boom in lightweight bikes relates to outlaw motorcycles the same way the bogus Hell's Angels Fan Club T-shirts relate to the real Hell's Angels. The little bikes are fun, handy and relatively safe . . . while the big ones are two-wheeled bombs, and the outlaws who ride them would rather walk than be seen on a Honda, Yamaha or Suzuki. Safety and respectability are the last things they want; their machines are dangerous, temperamental and expensive in every way;* there has never been an outlaw who saw his bike as anything but a King Kong equalizer, and there has never been one, either, who had anything but contempt for the idea of good clean fun . . . which is one of the reasons they shun even the minimum safety measures that most cyclists take for

* In 1966 a California licence tag for a year-old Harley 74 cost $48.

granted. You will never see a Hell's Angel wearing a crash helmet. Nor do they wear the Brando-Dylan-style 'silver studded phantom' leather jackets, commonly associated with motorcycle hoodlums and 'leather fetish cults'. This viewpoint is limited to people who know nothing about motorcycles. Heavy leather jackets are standard even for New York's Madison Avenue Motorcycle Club, an executive-level gang whose members include a dentist, a film producer, a psychiatrist and a United Nations official. Ted Develet, the film producer, has lamented the image problem that he and the others run into with their leather jackets. 'But if you're practical you have to dress that way,' he explained. 'If you take a skid, it's a lot cheaper to shred that leather than to scrape off your own skin.'

It is also a lot less painful. An eight-inch circle of raw flesh on your back is awkward to live with and slow to heal. Professional motorcycle racers, who have learned the hard way, wear helmets, gloves and full-length leather suits.

But not the Hell's Angels. Anything safe, they want no part of. They'll stoop to wearing shades or weird goggles on the road, but more for show than protection. The Angels don't want anybody to think they're hedging their bets. The leather jackets were in vogue until the mid-fifties, and many of the outlaws sewed their colours on them. But as their reputation grew and the police began closing in, one of the Frisco Angels came up with the idea of removable colours, to be snatched off and hidden in times of stress. This marked the era of the sleeveless denim vest. In the beginning most outlaws wore the colours on top of leather jackets, but in southern California it was too hot for that, so the Berdoo chapter pioneered the idea of wind in the armpits, no jackets at all – only colours. The next step, logically, will be the dropping of the Levis, and then the image will be complete – nothing but boots, beards, vests and bizarre decorations of the genitalia. A few of the older outlaws still wear leather jackets, especially around the Bay area, where the winters are cold, but they are definitely not the style, and any independent making a pitch for Angel membership would be rejected as 'corny and chickenshit' if he showed up in leather.

A mass of Hell's Angels on the road is a sight that no one who ever sees it will forget. Their arrival at a gas station causes panic among attendants. There is simply no way to cope with a caravan of nationally known thugs rolling in, each demanding a gallon or two of gas. One Saturday morning near Oakland I pulled into a service station on Highway 50 and was talking amiably with the attendant about the broiling heat and the general perfidy of machinery . . . when the station suddenly filled up with outlaw motorcyclists gunning their engines, yelling and darting back and forth between the pumps. 'Holy Jesus!' said the attendant. His manner became distracted. He forgot how much money I owed him and left me to fill my own radiator while he kept a terrified eye on the outlaws. It was a big, brand-new station, with four attendants, but the combined Hell's Angel–Gypsy Joker contingent was completely in command from the moment they arrived. They pumped their own gas, tossed beer cans back and forth and rummaged through the racks, looking for fifty-weight motorcycle oil. The five or six motorists at the pumps simply sat in their cars and watched. The attendants moved around cautiously, hoping that none of the outlaws would try to steal something in front of their eyes. Overt theft would call for action, and nobody wanted it. Anyone who has ever dealt with the Angels in a mass will agree that this is one of the worst aspects: at what point do you start protesting minor theft, insult or damage . . . at the risk of starting an argument that might end in a bloody fight? Is it cheaper to let a hoodlum caravan get off with ten quarts of oil and five tanks of gasoline unpaid for – or should a man risk his teeth and his plate-glass windows by insisting that the outlaws pay, to the last penny, for everything they leave with? The dilemma is especially bad for an employee. A filling-station attendant faced with a gang of Hell's Angels is like a salaried bank teller faced with an armed holdup man. Should a pump jockey risk a beating any more than a teller should risk his or her life to save a bank's insured money?

If the Angels had good sense they would only patronize gas stations operated on a lease basis by absentee owners. The difference is easily discernible, in less than a minute's time, to anyone who has ever pumped gas for a living, and many of the outlaws have. But as a group they scorn foresight and rely on a colourful, wilful ignorance that brings them now and then to pick on a gas station whose owner works twelve hours a day on the premises, has his life savings tied up in the franchise, and whose body bloats with adrenalin at the prospect of being victimized by a gang of punks. People like this keep revolvers in the cash register, in the tool-rack and even – in rough or robbery-type neighbourhoods – in shoulder holsters under their friendly service jackets. Most of the Angels' gas-station incidents involve proprietors who panic or go into a rage at the very sight of them.

Some people can make the tough act work, but others will blow it badly. The Angels fear these 'nuts', as they call them, because they are just as likely to shoot for no reason at all as for the very best of reasons. But God's mercy on a man who pulls a gun on a group of Hell's Angels and then has it taken away. There are some awful stories about this, and in every case the victims could have saved themselves by shooting first and later pleading self-defence. On the Angel scale of values the only thing worse than a fink with a loose or frightened mouth is a loud antagonist who can't follow through. People like this get the full measure of retribution – the natural attack on any human obstacle, plus the hyped-up heel-grinding contempt for a man who tries and fails to deal with them on their own terms . . . or at least what seems to be their own terms, if only by default.

The odd truth is that the Angels have only a wavering respect for their own terms – or again, what seems to be their own terms – and they are generally receptive, in any action beyond their own turf, to people who haven't prejudged them to the extent of assuming they have to be dealt with violently. They are so much aware of their mad-dog reputation that they take a perverse kind of pleasure in being quiet and friendly.

A filling-station owner near the Sierra town of Angels Camp (site of Mark Twain's story *The Celebrated Jumping Frog of Calaveras County*) recalls his first confrontation with the Hell's Angels in tones of fear and wonderment:

'About thirty of them soared into my station one night. They said they needed a place to work on their bikes. I took one look at them and told them the place was theirs, and got the hell out of there in a hurry.'

It was a normal enough reaction for a man running a no-help station at night in the mountains – for even a decision to fight to the death wouldn't have accomplished much against thirty hoodlums. 'After an hour or so I finally summoned the courage to go back to see if my place was still standing.' he said. 'The Angels were just finishing up. I was never so surprised in my whole life. The place was spotless. They had washed every tool they used with gasoline and hung it back exactly where they found it. They even swept the floor. The place was actually cleaner than when they first came in.'

Stories like this are common, even among cops. There is the testimony of the bar owner in Porterville: 'Sure, they rode their motorcycles into my place, even tore up the tile doing it. But before they left they paid for every bit of damage, every broken glass. And I never sold so much beer in my life. They're welcome here any time.'

Many a grovelling merchant has made a buck off the Hell's Angels. All they ask is tribute, and naked fear is a very pure form of it. Any man who tacitly admits to being terrified is safe from them unless he overdoes it . . . and this happens, often with covert homosexuals long gone on booze or drugs and unable to control themselves in the presence of so much 'rough trade'. The outlaws will nearly always give a flip-out a bad time. I recall a party one night when they decided to set an offending Berkeley student on fire. Then, when the host protested, they looped a rope around the victim's ankles and said they were going to drag him away behind a motorcycle. This also caused protests, so they settled for hanging him by one arm from a living-room rafter. After a half-hour or so they relented and cut him down, shaking their heads at his stony silence. The wretch hadn't uttered a word throughout the ordeal. He seemed in a daze; there was no sign of pain and I had a fleeting impression that he'd planned the whole thing. Afterwards he went outside and sat on a stump for several hours, saying nothing at all, but trembling now and then like a man coming down from some indescribable peak.

The Angels are great favourites on the sado-masochism circuit, and although motorcycle hoods as a group are consistently accused of deviate leanings, I suspect the issue was stripped to the bony truth one afternoon by a Frisco Angel who said: 'Hell, yes, I'll take a blow-job any day for ten bucks. Just the other night in some bar downtown I had a queer come up to me with a big tenner

. . . he laid it on me and said what did I want to drink? I said: 'A double Jack Daniels, baby," so he told the bartender: "Two of those for me and my friend," and then he sat down there on the bar rail and gave me a hell of a blow-job, man, and all I had to do was smile at the bartender and keep cool.' He laughed. 'Hell, and me with four kids and a broad up front dancing the wig or the wag or something like that with some spade. Shit, man, the day they can call me a queer is when I let one of these faggots suck on me for less than a tenner. . . . Man, I'd go underwater and fuck fish for that kind of money, you just tell me who's payin'.'

To whatever extent the Hell's Angels may or may not be latent sado-masochists or repressed homosexuals is to me – after nearly a year in the constant company of outlaw motorcyclists – almost entirely irrelevant.

There are literary critics who insist that Ernest Hemingway was a tortured queer and that Mark Twain was haunted to the end of his days by a penchant for inter-racial buggery. It is a good way to stir up a tempest in the academic quarterlies, but it won't change a word of what either man wrote, nor alter the impact of their work on the world they were writing about. Perhaps Manolete was a hoof fetishist, or suffered from terrible haemorrhoids as a result of long nights in Spanish horn parlours . . . but he was a great matador, and it is hard to see how any amount of Freudian theorizing can have the slightest effect on the reality of the thing he did best.

For the same reason, the behaviour of the Hell's Angels would not be changed or subdued for a moment if every newspaper in the land denounced them as brutal homosexuals – even if they were. Significantly, I have never heard anyone who had any personal dealings with them endorse the Freudian viewpoint – probably because anyone who spends any time with the Angels knows the difference between outlaw motorcyclists and homosexual leather cults. At any bar full of Hell's Angels there will be a row of sleek bikes lined up on the curb outside. At a leather bar there are surrealistic renderings of motorcycles on the wall and perhaps, but not always, one or two huge, accessory-laden Harleys parked outside – complete with windshields, radios and red plastic saddle-bags. The difference is as basic as between a professional football player and a rabid fan. One is a performer in a harsh, unique corner of reality; the other is a cultist, a passive worshipper, and occasionally a sloppy emulator of a style that fascinates him because he is so hopelessly remote from the reality he wakes up to every morning.

According to the Lynch report: 'While homosexuals seem to be attracted to Hell's Angels, no information received indicates that the Hell's Angels as a group are homosexuals. They seem primarily concerned with heterosexual contacts. Some heterosexual perversions figure in the police reports, but taken in context, they appear to be means of attracting attention, "being different", and performed primarily for the shock impact on others. These and other attention-attracting actions are characterized by the Angels as "showing class".'

Certainly the Lynch report is not the last word on the Angels, but the nature and bias of the document is such that any available evidence of their homosexual action would have been prominently mentioned. The report makes so many references to cunnilingus that the word *fellatio* is conspicuous by its absence. No doubt there are Freudian ramifications even in this omission – but again, I think they are mainly beside the point. Any attempt to explain the Hell's Angels as an essentially homosexual phenomenon would be a cop-out, a self-satisfied dismissal of a reality that is as complex and potentially malignant as anything in American society.

*

> The motorcycle is obviously a sexual symbol. It's what's called a phallic locomotor symbol. It's an extension of one's body, a power between one's legs. – *Dr Bernard Diamond, University of California criminologist*, 1965

*

The best-known public link between outlaw cyclists and homosexuality is a film titled *Scorpio Rising*. It is an underground classic of sorts, created in the early 1960s by a young San Francisco film-maker named Kenneth Anger. He never claimed that *Scorpio* had anything to do with the Hell's Angels, and most of it was filmed in Brooklyn, with the cooperation of a group of motorcycle buffs so loosely organized that they hadn't even bothered to name themselves. Unlike *The Wild One*, Anger's creation had no journalistic or documentary intent. It was an art film with a rock-'n'-roll score, a bizarre little comment on twentieth-century America, using motorcycles, swastikas and aggressive homosexuality as a new culture trilogy. By the time the Hell's Angels joined the cultural mainstream Anger had made several other films with a strongly homosexual basis, and he seemed offended at the notion that he might be so far behind the times as to turn out anything so banal as a topical documentary.

Nevertheless, *Scorpio Rising* played in San Francisco in 1964 at a North Beach theatre called The Movie, where Anger was living at the time, upstairs, which advertised the film with a sidewalk montage of Hell's Angels newspaper clippings. The implication was so obvious that even the San Francisco Angels made a pilgrimage to check it out. It didn't groove them at all. They weren't angry, but genuinely offended. Their name they felt, had been put to fraudulent commercial use. 'Hell, I liked the film,' said Frenchy. 'But it didn't have anything to do with us. We all enjoyed it. But then we came outside and saw all those clippings about us, pasted up like advertisements. Man, it was a bummer, it wasn't right. A lot of people got conned, and now we have to listen to all this crap about us being queers. Shit, did you see the way those punks were dressed? And those silly goddam junk-wagon bikes? Man, don't tell me that has any connection with us. You know it doesn't.'

Anger seemed to agree, but quietly. There was no need to spoil a new boom for the film . . . and besides, one of the keenest talents in the homosexual repertoire is the ability to recognize homosexuality in others, very nearly without exception. So the phenomenon emerged: the Angels provided the realism that *Scorpio* lacked. The secret-queer factor gave the Press an element of strange whimsy to mix in with the rape reports, and the outlaws themselves were relegated to new nadirs of sordid fascination. More than ever before, they were wreathed in an aura of violent and erotic mystery . . . brawling satyrs, ready to attempt congress with any living thing, and in any orifice.

8

These punks with their cycles and their Nazi trappings have it in for the world – and for everyone in it. They're a menace, a damned serious menace that's growing bigger every year. – *Florida police official quoted in Man's Peril (February 1966)*

They worship their motorcycles. They take them inside their homes at night. They sleep on grease-caked beds, but their bikes are spotless. – *Los Angeles cop, 1965*

*

THE farther the Angels roam from their own turf, the more likely they are to cause panic. A group of them seen on a highway for the first time is offensive to every normal notion of what is supposed to be happening in America; it is bizarre to the point of seeming like a bad hallucination . . . and this is the context in which the term 'outlaw' makes real sense. To see a lone Angel screaming through traffic – defying all rules, limits and patterns – is to understand the motorcycle as an instrument of anarchy, a tool of defiance and even a weapon. A Hell's Angel on foot can look pretty foolish. Their sloppy histrionics and inane conversations can be interesting for a few hours, but beyond the initial strangeness, their everyday scene is as tedious and depressing as a costume ball for demented children. There is something pathetic about a bunch of men gathering every night in the same bar, taking themselves very seriously in their ratty uniforms, with nothing to look forward to but the chance of a fight or a round of head jobs from some drunken charwoman.

But there is nothing pathetic about the sight of an Angel on his bike. The whole – man and machine together – is far more than the sum of its parts. His motorcycle is the one thing in life he has absolutely mastered. It is his only valid status symbol, his equalizer, and he pampers it the same way a busty Hollywood starlet pampers her body. Without it, he is no better than a punk on a street corner.

And he knows it. The Angels are not articulate about many things but they bring a lover's inspiration to the subject of bikes. Sonny Barger, a man not given to sentimental rambling, once defined the word 'love' as 'the feelin' you get when you like somethin' as much as your motorcycle. Yeah, I guess you could say that was love.'

The fact that many Angels have virtually created their bikes out of stolen, bartered or custom-made parts only half explains the intense attachment they have for them. You've got to see an outlaw straddle his hog and start jumping on the starter pedal to fully appreciate what it means. It is like seeing a thirsty man find water. His face changes; his whole bearing radiates confidence and authority. He sits there for a moment with the big machine rumbling between his legs and then he blasts off... sometimes in a cool, muted kind of way, and sometimes with a roaring wheel-stand that rattles nearby windows – but always with style, with *élan*. And by cutting out in the grand manner at the end of each barroom night, he leaves the others with the best possible image of himself. Each Angel is a mirror in the mutual admiration society. They reflect and reassure each other, in strength and weakness, folly and triumph . . . and each night at closing time they cut out with a flourish: the juke box wails a Norman Luboff tune, the bar lights dim, and Shane thunders off drunkenly into the moonlight.

Whether the Hell's Angels are real motorcycle artists or not is hard to say. With the exception of a few drag meets, the outlaws are barred from all sanctioned competition, so there are no performance charts to go on.* Their bikes are entirely different from racing and scrambles machines, and even from other road bikes. The Angels tell tales of wiping out professionals in impromptu showdowns... but there are also stories about outlaws on souped-up hogs being humiliated by lightweight Ducatis.

Perhaps the stories are true, perhaps not – but either way the

* This is a matter of mutual exclusion. An Angel in mufti could enter any A.M.A. event for the price of a two-dollar Sportsman's Card. This would make him eligible to compete, but it would also make him an applicant for membership in the A.M.A. – which his outlaw brethren would never tolerate. The Hell's Angel charter is very explicit on conflict-of-interest situations. No Angel can be a member of any other motorcycle club or organization. It would be worth a man's colours to hold a card in the A.M.A.

argument is still moot. Motorcycles are designed for specific purposes: crosscountry, racing, cruising or just hopping around the neighbourhood. They will all run . . . and so will dogs and horses, but nobody breeds horses to hunt possums, or enters dogs in the Kentucky Derby. Bike manufacturers have been trying for decades to make a genuine all-purpose model, but so far nobody has.

There is no valid comparison between riding in dirt or competition, and riding a bike in traffic, day in and day out, on city streets and highways. Different skills are involved, and different kinds of reflexes. Some of the fastest racing bikes have no brakes, which would mean instant death in traffic – yet many professional riders say highways are far more dangerous than any race track.

Dirt riders feel the same way: few even bother to license their bikes for the street. Don McGuire, a veteran scrambles rider and full-time motorcycle mechanic in Richmond, insists that only a madman or a masochist would ride a bike in traffic. 'Look at it this way,' he says. 'In any kind of race we're all going the same way and we all know what we're doing. Nobody has to worry about nuts or drunks or old ladies coming out of blind alleys. It makes a hell of a difference; you can concentrate on your own motor and keep it under control. We get injuries now and then, but broken bones are about the worst of it, and damn few people get killed.

'But the highways! Christ, here you are, moving along in traffic about sixty-five, right there at the speed limit, and it's all you can do to keep out of people's way. If the road's a little wet – even damp from the fog – you're in trouble no matter what happens. Slow down, and they'll come up on your tail or muscle you out of the lane. Speed up to get some room, and some geek hits his brakes right in front of you – God knows why, but they do it all the time.

'One little thing like that and you're into the meat grinder. The minute you hit the brakes you'll start losing it; bikes don't drift like cars. And once you go down, you'll be lucky if you only get run over twice.'

During 1965 more than a thousand people died in the United States as a result of motorcycle accidents. Automobiles killed nearly fifty times that many, but the growing number of bike deaths caused the American Medical Association to label motorcycles 'a serious health hazard in our communities'. The Hell's

Angels lose an average of four members a year on the road, but considering the way most of them ride, a four per cent annual mortality rate is a towering tribute to their skill. A Harley 74 is probably the only motorcycle that can cause real damage to a car, and a hard-running Angel can intimidate traffic as severely as a speeding torpedo. The outlaws are experts with hogs, and in their own narrow world, on their own terms, they can outride just about anybody.

In the late 1950s, before the Angels became so notorious, Pete, from the Frisco chapter, was one of the top drag racers in northern California. He was sponsored by the local Harley–Davidson dealer and collected a roomful of trophies. Not only did he wear his Hell's Angels colours in the races, but he rode his competition bike to the track, packing his pretty blonde wife on the fender pad behind him. Other dragsters brought their bikes on trailers, handling them like Ming vases.

'Pete could really make a bike go,' one of the Angels recalls. 'It was really classy the way he'd go out and win. When he got to the track, man, he'd just change his spark plugs and go out – high handlebars and all – and wipe out them drag irons.'

In the early sixties Pete retired from the Angels, feeling he'd had enough. Shortly after his thirtieth birthday he moved his wife and two children to a small town in the Sierras, where he tried to settle down as a peaceful country mechanic. His retirement lasted about two years and might have been longer if the Angels had not become famous. But the lure of publicity and new action was too much. By early 1965 Pete was back in town, toasting his old buddies, shedding his family and hustling around for parts to build a new bike.

Like most of the other Angels, he regards the factory product only in terms of potential – a bundle of good raw material, but hardly a machine that any man with class would want to call his own.*

The outlaws tend to see their bikes as personal monuments, created in their own image, however abstract, and they develop an affection for them that is hard for outsiders to understand. It seems

* The bike he finally built turned 108 in the quarter mile, in twelve seconds flat.

like a pose, or even a perversion – and maybe it is, but to bike freaks it is very real. Anybody who has ever owned one of the beasts will always be a little bit queer for them. Not the little bikes, but the big expensive temperamental bastards, the ones that respond to the accelerator like a bucking horse to a whip, that will stand up in the air and run fifteen yards on one wheel, scorching the pavement with a fiery blast from the chrome tailpipes. The little bikes may be fun, like the industry people say, but Volkswagens are fun too, and so are BB guns. Big bikes, Ferraris and ·44 Magnum revolvers are something beyond fun; they are man-made machines so powerful and efficient in their own realms that they challenge a man's ability to control them, to push them to the limits of their design and possibilities. This is one of the pillars of the Big Bike mystique that looms so large in the life of every Hell's Angel. Or as they say: 'That's where it's at, man. That's where it lives.'

Not everyone is comfortable with this concept. I had owned a big motorcycle before, and two motor scooters, but only because they'd been cheap and available when I had some money to buy something. There is no place in the mystique for this kind of sloppy pragmatism, and when I told the Angels I was thinking of buying a bike of my own they were eager to help out. The main thing, of course, was to get a Harley–Davidson. They had several to sell, but the newer ones were all hot . . . they were also cheap: a $1,500 bike for $400 is hard to turn down, but to ride a stolen bike, you have to know how to explain to a cop why your frame or engine numbers bear no resemblance to the numbers on your licence registration. There are ways to carry this off, but the penalty for failure is jail time, and I didn't feel up to it. I tried unsuccessfully to have the Angels find me a cheap, second-hand – and legal – Harley 74, customized in the latest outlaw fashion. Then, like some of the outlaw *avant-garde*, I decided on the lighter, hotter Harley Sportster. After pressure from the respectable camp, I tried the Triumph Bonneville and even the staid B.M.W. In the end I narrowed it down to the Sportster, the Bonneville and the B.S.A. Lightning Rocket. All three will run circles around a stock Harley 74, and even the Angel version of the hog – which is anything but stock – can't run with the newest and best production models without extensive alterations and a very savvy rider. That

I eventually bought the B.S.A. is immaterial; the point is that it took me four weeks of hard asking and thinking, with $1,500 in the balance, to realize that stripped-down Harleys weren't basically superior machines. Later, after riding a few months, I understood that the difference between a Hell's Angel on a hog and a white-collar bike buff on a race-tuned Triumph is not all in the engine. The Angels push their luck to the limit. They take drastic risks with no thought at all. As individuals they have been busted, excluded and defeated in so many ways that they are not about to be polite or careful in the one area where they have an edge.

The special relationship between an Angel and his bike is obvious even to people who know nothing at all about motorcycles. While gathering data for his *Saturday Evening Post* article, Bill Murray watched a half-hour television documentary made by a Los Angeles station with the hazy cooperation of the Berdoo Angels. One of the four specimens was, in Murray's words, 'an almost inarticulate brute behind glass-bottom eyeglasses who was known as Blind Bob. (He spoke fiercely of what would happen to anybody who tried to mess with *his* girl. "If she's with me, she's with me," he said, grinding his jaw.)'

Murray's view of the Angels was wholly contemptuous but he was very much taken with the sight of at least one of the brutes on a hog. 'The most vivid moment of the television programme,' he said, 'came when Blind Bob, an inarticulate earthbound slob during the interview, had been shown riding his cycle down the highway. He handled that big powerful machine with consummate ease, steering it casually with one hand, like Valenzuela bringing Kelso to the starting gate, the wind blowing hard into his face, and his mouth set in a tight grin of pure enjoyment. Planted on the back of his hog, this oaf had acquired instant grace. . . .'

With rare exceptions, the outlaw bike is a Harley 74, a giant of a motorcycle that comes out of the Milwaukee factory weighing seven hundred pounds, but which the Angels strip down to about five hundred. In the argot of the cycle world the Harley is a 'hog', and the outlaw bike is a 'chopped hog'. Basically it is the same machine all motorcycle cops use, but the police bike is an accessory-loaded elephant compared to the lean, customized dynamos the Hell's Angels ride. The resemblance is about the same as that of a factory-equipped Cadillac to a dragster's stripped-down essence of the same car. The Angels refer to standard 74s as 'garbage wagons' and Bylaw Number 11 of the charter is a put-down in the grand manner: 'An Angel cannot wear the colours while riding on a garbage wagon with a non-Angel.' A chopped hog, or 'chopper', is little more than a heavy frame, a tiny seat and a massive 1,200-cubic-centimetre (or 74-cubic-inch) engine. This is nearly twice the size of the engines in the Triumph Bonneville or the B.S.A. Lightning Rocket, both 650-cubic-centimetre machines capable of 120 to 130 miles an hour. The Honda Super Hawk has a 305-cubic-centimetre engine and a top speed of just under 100. A columnist for *The Los Angeles Times* once described hogs as 'the kind of cycle the German couriers used to run down dogs and chickens – and people – in World War II: low brutish machines, with drivers to match'.

There is nothing on the road – with the exception of a few sports or racing cars – that can catch an artfully hopped-up outlaw 74 as long as there's room to 'jam it', or 'screw it on', and take advantage of the huge engine. Because of its size and basic engineering differences, however, a normally equipped Harley 74 can barely outrun a 305-cubic-centimetre Honda, much less a dual-carburettor Triumph or a B.S.A. It is not unusual for people who ride these limey bikes to seek opportunities to humiliate a cop on a Harley. But motorcycle cops are wise – they know. Even the California Highway Patrol, in their souped-up Dodges, view a big British bike or an outlaw chopper as an affront to their king-of-the-road image. I was once stopped for speeding by a Highway Patrol car that raced up to within a few feet of my rear fender before I realized I was being followed. The driver hit his siren at the last moment, and naturally I pulled over, somewhat shaken. When I asked him why he'd run up so close behind me, he said: 'I thought you might try to swing off at that exit and get away.'

I said it had never occurred to me – which was true at the time, although it would now. 'Well, it's a good thing you didn't try it,' he replied. 'The last motorcycle punk who tried to run from me got killed. I kept on his tail until he made a mistake, then I ran right over him.'

For $1,300 to $1,400 anybody with a yen for death-racing with police cars can buy a motorcycle that will do 120 miles per hour right off the showroom floor. But to get that kind of performance out of a 74 requires considerable effort and skill. The first step is a drastic alteration of the weight-to-power ratio. The Angels strip their hogs down to the bare essentials, even to the extent of removing the front-wheel brake. The stripping alone makes a big difference, but most outlaw bikes are also power-jumped with hot cams, larger valves and increased bore and stroke. The only extras they carry are the ones required by law; a tail-light, rear-view mirror and a hand hold for the passenger. A fanatic can satisfy the mirror requirement by using a tiny dentist's mirror, which is technically legal.

Other modifications include a half-size, custom-designed gas tank, no front fender and a shortened or 'bobbed' rear fender that ends at the top of the wheel; very high handlebars and a little seat so low that it looks like a leather pad on top of the engine; extended front forks to lengthen the wheelbase and raise the front end; a foot, or 'suicide' clutch (so-called because it necessitates split-second timing while shifting and braking, both done with the left foot) and a variety of such personal touches as long high-raked mufflers, tiny dual headlights, a bicycle-thin front wheel, tall dagger-designed chrome rails (called 'sissy bars') for a passenger hand hold – and every conceivable kind of chrome and flame-paint trim.

A chopper is often a work of art, costing as much as $3,000 to build, not counting labour. From the polished chrome spokes to the perfectly balanced super-light flywheel and the twelve coats of special paint on the gas tank, it is a beautiful, graceful machine and so nearly perfect mechanically that it is hard to conceive of it screaming along some midnight highway in the hands of a drunken hoodlum only moments away from a high-speed crash into a tree or a steel guardrail. This is one of many paradoxes in the Hell's Angels lore. Whatever they lack in personal grooming, they make up for in spades with their bikes... yet any one of them might take a bike he has worked on for six months and destroy it in seconds with a maniacal top-speed run at a curve that's a guaranteed bust-out at anything over fifty.

This is called 'going over the high side', a nasty experience which one Angel supposedly described like this: 'We've all been over the high side, baby. You know what that is? It's when your bike starts sliding when you steam into a curve at seventy or eighty. . . . She slides towards the high side of the curve, baby, until she hits a curb or a rail or a soft shoulder or whatever's there, and then she flips. . . . That's what you call making a classic get-off, baby.'

One night in the winter of 1965 I took my own bike – and a passenger – over the high side on a rain-slick road just north of Oakland. I went into an obviously dangerous curve at about seventy, the top of my second gear. The wet road prevented leaning it over enough to compensate for the tremendous inertia, and somewhere in the middle of the curve I realized that the rear wheel was no longer following the front one. The bike was going sideways towards a bank of railroad trucks and there was nothing I could do except hang on. For an instant it was very peaceful . . . and then it was like being shot off the road by a bazooka, but with no noise. Neither a deer on a hillside nor a man on a battlefield ever hears the shot that kills him, and a man going over the high side on a motorcycle hears the same kind of high-speed silence. There are sparks, as the chromed steel grinds down on the road, an awful jerk when your body starts cartwheeling on the first impact . . . and after that, if you're lucky, there is nothing at all until you wake up in some hospital emergency ward with your scalp hanging down in your eyes and a blood-soaked shirt sticking to your chest while official-looking people stare down at you and assure each other that 'these crazy bastards won't learn'.

There is nothing romantic about a bad crash, and the only solace is the deadening shock that comes with most injuries. My passenger left the bike in a long arc that ended on the railroad tracks and splintered his thigh bone, driving the sharp edges through muscle and flesh and all the way out to the wet gravel. In the hospital they had to wash the dirt off the bone ends before they put his leg back together . . . but he said it didn't hurt until the next day, not even when he was lying in the rain and wondering if anybody on the road would call an ambulance to pick us up.

There is not a Hell's Angel riding who hasn't made the emergency-ward scene, and one of the natural results is that their fear of accidents is well tempered by a cavalier kind of disdain for physical injury. Outsiders might call it madness or other, more esoteric names . . . but the Angels inhabit a world in which violence is as common as spilled beer, and they live with it as easily as ski bums live with the risk of broken legs. This casual acceptance of blood-letting is a key to the terror they inspire in the square. Even a small, inept street-fighter has a tremendous advantage over the average middle-class American, who hasn't had a fight since puberty. It is a simple matter of accumulated experience, of having been hit or stomped often enough to forget the ugly panic that nice people associate with a serious fight. A man who has had his nose smashed three times in brawls will risk it again with hardly a thought. No amount of instruction in any lethal art can teach this – not unless the instructor is a sadist, and even then it would be difficult because the student's experience would be artificially warped and limited.

San Francisco is a big karate town: in 1965 there were roughly seven thousand full-time fee-paying karate students roaming around the Bay Area . . . but in any active bar you can hear a story about a bartender who 'busted up a guy who tried to pull some karate stuff'. It hardly matters how many of the stories are true. The point is valid: the difference between survival and wipe-out in a physical crisis is nearly always a matter of conditioned reflexes. A bartender with scar tissue all over his knuckles will hit faster and harder than a karate-trained novice who has never been bloodied. For the same reason, a Hell's Angel who has been over the high side often enough to joke about it will ride a motorcycle with a style and abandon that comes only with painful experience.*

After being around the Angels for a while, I became so accustomed to seeing casts, bandages, slings and lumpy faces that I took them for granted and stopped asking what happened. The good bust-up stories were always common topics anyway, and the bad ones were as dull and predictable as the punchouts on any Late Show. Most of their fights are with outsiders who don't realize what they're getting into. People who know them are keenly aware of the 'all on one' ethic, which is not covered by any statute of

* Five Hell's Angels died in fights or crashes in 1964, and three in 1965 – three so far in 1966, along with one shot seriously in the stomach and another permanently paralysed from the neck down, also from a bullet.

limitations. An Angel on his own turf is as secure as a Mafia runner in a tough Italian neighbourhood.

In spite of this sinister immunity, they occasionally overextend themselves and get badly worked over by people who either don't know the score or choose to disregard it. Even Barger, now in hls eighth year as president of the Oakland chapter, admits to having had his nose broken, his jaw busted and his teeth punched out.

But a single bike accident can break a man worse than a dozen disastrous fights. Funny Sonny from Berdoo has a steel plate in his head, a steel rod in one arm, a plastic ankle and a deep scar on his face – all from crackups. He got his nickname when the other Angels decided the steel plate was having a strange effect on his brain. When the Berdoo Angels made a run to Santa Ana in October 1964, Funny Sonny was a big hit with the citizens. Large crowds gathered to hear his street-corner diatribes against cops, courts and the social structure in general. He was later jailed for a large number of outstanding traffic citations.

THE HOODLUM CIRCUS
AND
THE STATUTORY RAPE OF
BASS LAKE

9

How did the Angels grow to be such disliked hell-raisers? The answer is that it wasn't easy. They worked overtime at being crafty, cruel and cowardly. – True Detective *magazine (August 1965)*

I went through all that school and family jazz. It's all crap. Boy, am I glad the Angels took me in! I don't ever want to be anything but an Angel and that's it! – *Reply to a question*

*

BY midsummer of 1965 the Hell's Angels were already the subject of at least two scholarly theses, and no doubt there were others in the works. Yet all over California there were people whose real or imagined dealings with outlaw motorcyclists had been much too personal to allow for any abstract, sociological perspective on the menace. For every one who'd ever seen a Hell's Angel in the flesh, there were half a thousand more who'd been frightened silly by the whooping of the news media. So it came as no surprise when a certain amount of public tension built up as the Fourth of July approached.

On the Friday night before the Fourth, I called the Box Shop. I'd never been on a holiday run and since this one had the making of a real boomer, I decided to go along. Frenchy wanted to make sure I wasn't planning to bring anyone with me before he confirmed the site: 'Yeah, it's Bass Lake,' he said. 'About two hundred miles east from here. I'm a little worried about going. There might be trouble. We're hoping we can just get together and have a good time, but with all this publicity I'm afraid every cop in the state will be there.'

There was good reason to expect a police presence: the Press had been sounding the alarm for weeks.

On 24 June a United Press International bulletin out of Los Angeles said: COPS WORRY ABOUT HELL'S ANGELS' JULY 4 BREAKOUT. It quoted Attorney-General Lynch to the effect that his office had received 'various reports' on what the Hell's Angels had in mind for their annual midsummer picnic. (One of these 'reports' stemmed from the futile attempt to sell coverage of a July Fourth rumble to *The New York Times* and other interested parties. The rumble rumour spread quickly and even got a plug on N.B.C. Monitor newscasts from New York.)

Then, in late June, a motorcycle riot in Laconia, New Hampshire made front-page news all over the nation. The California Press gave it prominent play because the mayor of Laconia blamed the whole thing on the Hell's Angels. The 2 July issue of *Life* carried a big Laconia story, with pictures of a burning car, National Guardsmen with fixed bayonets, and a collection of confiscated weapons including hatchets, crowbars, machetes, brass knuckles, chains and bull-whips. Some fifteen thousand motorcyclists were said to have run wild in the little New England resort, battling police and setting fire to various buildings while the Hell's Angels egged them on. The warning to California was clear. If a handful of Hell's Angels could cause that much trouble three thousand miles from home, it was dreadful to contemplate what the whole clan might do in their own West Coast backyard.

Bass Lake is a tiny resort near Yosemite National Park in the Sierra Nevada. The Angels made a half-hearted attempt to keep the destination a secret, but the vanity of the many swamped the discretion of the few, and once the word leaked out, there was no stopping it. The police got the fix from 'unnamed sources', the Press picked it up from the police, and by the time it reached the air waves it sounded like an Orson Welles radio drama. Early newscasts on Saturday, 3 July, gave the impression that the citizens of Bass Lake were about to make a last-ditch stand against hopeless odds and a fate too vile for description.

But not even the radio newscasters seemed certain of the outlaws' destination. They were careful to attribute their information to police reports, which also said – according to the newspapers that morning – that the Hell's Angels were expected to strike just about everywhere between Tijuana and the Oregon state line. *The Los Angeles Times* speculated that nearby Malibu beach might be the scene of a latter-day version of *The Wild One*, but this time with real blood and without Marlon Brando. *The San Francisco Examiner* reported a Hell's Angels plot to terrorize the annual

Lions' Club bean feed in suburban Marin County, just north of the Golden Gate. And the *Chronicle* uncovered a heart-wrenching Hell's Angels plan to 'bust up' a charity benefit for the Guide Dogs for the Blind, also in Marin County.

HELL'S ANGELS MASSING

At least a dozen communities all over the state were said to be 'braced for invasion'. It added real zest to the holiday atmosphere. Here were all these weekend mountaineers, solid nine-to-five types with a yen to cut loose, bugging off for distant camp-sites with cars full of hot-dogs and charcoal and badminton rackets . . . and all of them wondering if they would get through the weekend without being traumatized or chain-whipped.

Prior to the Bass Lake Run all the outlaws' publicity had been after the fact, lurid tales from police blotters, victims and by-standers. Now, for the first time, it was possible to actually attend a Hell's Angels rally. All you had to do was sift through the grab-bag of rumours and choose the right location.*

The California Highway Patrol had announced the existence of a new and elaborate tracking network, a radio communications system designed to pinpoint any gathering of motorcycle outlaws and broadcast their movements to police all over the state so that no community would be taken by surprise. But there was no announcement of any plans to neutralize the threat. A widespread misapprehension about the Hell's Angels is that they are *prima facie* illegal, and that every one of their potentially explosive runs could be nipped in the bud by simply arresting the whole gang the moment they appeared on the highway. This would set up an interesting legal situation, for the arresting officers would be hard pressed to find a valid charge to book them on. There is nothing illegal about riding a motorcycle from one town to another; a thousand Hell's Angels could ride from New York to Los Angeles without risking arrest until they violated at least one law of local statute. The Angels are well aware of this, and before setting out on a run, they go over their route on a map and exchange information about which towns along the way might be dangerous . . .

* Or call the Box Shop. . . .

because of abnormally tight speed limits, lack of signs, unusual laws, or anything else that could get them hung up. Most have been riding motorcycles all over California for years and they know from experience which towns are likely to be unfriendly. About thirty miles south of San Francisco, for instance, is a village called Half Moon Bay, where motorcycle outlaws are arrested on sight. The Angels know this and try to avoid the place. If they wanted to make an issue of such an obvious harassment policy they could almost certainly get any arrest thrown out of court – but to do that would take time and money, and Half Moon Bay isn't that important to them. It is not much of a party town.

Reno is in a different category. For many years the Angels made their Fourth July Run to Reno, but after a dozen Angels destroyed a tavern in 1960, the 'Biggest Little City in the World' passed a law making it illegal for more than two motorcyclists to ride together inside the city limits. There are no signs proclaiming this along the many approaches to town, and the law would surely be knocked down in court if a trio of touring cyclists from the East was ever clapped in jail for simply riding together through the city, but that isn't likely. The law was designed to give Reno police a legal weapon against the Hell's Angels. And even the Angels could probably beat it in court if any one of them were willing to (1) spend a holiday weekend in jail, (2) post a minimum of $100 in bail money, (3) return to Reno several weeks later, with a lawyer, to plead not guilty and be advised of a trial date, (4) make another trip to Reno, again with a lawyer, to argue the case in court, and (5) in all likelihood return for a third appearance in either Reno or nearby Carson City to appeal the conviction in a higher court, and (6) come up with enough money to pay a lawyer for the time and effort it would take to prepare a brief with enough impact to convince a Nevada state court that one of Reno's local statutes is unconstitutional, irrational and discriminatory.*

* The Angels understand the popular bias against them well enough to avoid court appearances whenever possible. An outlaw faced with a jury trial knows he will have to chop off his hair, shave his beard and borrow a necktie somewhere. Experience has taught them to play it straight in court. A Frisco Angel once beat an assault charge because the arresting officer couldn't identify him at the trial. Without his hair and his colours, he looked like ten thousand other people.

Justice is not cheap in this country, and people who insist on it are usually either desperate or possessed by some private determination bordering on monomania. The Hell's Angels are not of this persuasion – not even when it means giving up the pleasures of Reno. They try to avoid places where the odds are stacked against them, legally or otherwise . . . and they are usually pretty shrewd about knowing what the odds really are. Runs are primarily parties, not war games, and small-town jails are dull.

Consider the alternatives available to a chief of police in a remote town of twenty thousand – with a police force of twenty-five men – when he gets word that anywhere from three hundred to five hundred motorcycle outlaws are due to converge on him in a matter of hours. The worst thing he's had to contend with in nine years was a bank hold-up involving an exchange of a dozen shots with two hoods from Los Angeles. But that was a long time ago, and since then his job has been placid . . . highway accidents, teenage rowdies and weekend drunk fights in some of the local bars. Nothing in his experience has prepared him to face an army of half-human hoodlums, a modern-day James gang . . . infamous thugs who would just as soon stomp on a cop as they would on a toad, and once they get out of hand, the only way to handle them is with brute force.

Even if he has emergency legal powers and a jail big enough to hold them all, there is still the problem of forcing them into submission. Two of his men are sick, two are on vacation, so that leaves twenty-one. He jots down some figures on a desk pad: twenty-one men, each with a pump-action shotgun (five shots) and a revolver (six shots), gives him an outside chance, in a carefully staged ambush, of taking out two hundred of the enemy – leaving hundreds more suddenly gone wild with fear and rage. They could do incredible damage, and an ambush is out of the question anyway because of the nightmarish publicity. What would the Governor of the nation's most progressive state have to say about the deliberate massacre of two hundred citizens by a backwoods police force on Independence Day?

The alternative is to let the outlaws enter the town and try to keep them under control, at least until they start something . . . but that might lead to a close-quarters struggle without warning:

the enemy would have time to get doped up and drunk, time to unlimber his weaponry and choose his terrain. With an all-night effort, some fifty or seventy-five reinforcements might be rallied from neighbouring towns and counties ... but on a holiday weekend no police force has many men to spare, and even these would be subject to instant recall in case the outlaw pack suddenly veered off course and stopped for a beer break at some unexpected place. The whole battle plan would have to be changed on the spur of the moment.

The Angels have never fought a pitched battle with the forces of law and order, but they have attacked individual cops or as many as three and four so often that police in most towns either treat them gently or confront them with as much force as possible. The outlaws don't share the middle-class respect for authority and have no reverence for 'the badge'. They measure a cop's authority by his power to enforce it. Some of the stories from the original Hollister fracas, in 1947, tell of local police being locked in their own jail by rampaging cyclists who then 'took over the town'. But the only Hell's Angel now riding who was actually present at Hollister discounts most of the tales that have grown up over the years. 'We were just there for a party,' he explains. 'As far as punching on the citizens and stuff like that, we didn't do it. Sure, we made a lot of noise, and we chased some people who started throwing rocks at us. When the cops got panicky we put a couple of them in garbage cans and stacked their bikes on top of them, that's all.'

In 1948, a year after Hollister, a thousand or so motorcyclists had a party in Riverside, near Los Angeles. They raced through the streets, hurled firecrackers at the cops and generally terrorized the citizenry. One grinning pack halted the car of an Air Force officer in the middle of town. When the airman honked his horn the cyclists jumped on the hood of his car, and caved it in, smashed every window, slugged the driver and pawed his terror-stricken wife before letting them go with a warning not to honk at pedestrians. Sheriff Cary Rayburn cornered one bunch of invaders and ordered them out of town, but they contemptuously slapped him around, ripped off his badge and tore his uniform. When the sheriff called for reinforcements the outlaws fled.

Long before the era of mutual-assistance pacts between neighbouring police forces, the embryo wild ones had better sense than to fight seriously with armed cops. Even now they will only challenge police if the situation obviously calls for restraint on the part of the law . . . a riot in the making, a roust in front of TV cameras, or any confrontation that draws a crowd and makes shooting out of the question.* Because of this, a pack of Hell's Angels on a run to a resort area is a hellish thing for rural cops to deal with. The trick is to control them without any provocation, but outlaws are very easily provoked. Once a showdown gets out of control, there are bound to be injuries, bad publicity, and the chance of a career-tarnishing reprimand for any cop who loses his head and takes extreme measures, like shooting into a mêlée and hitting the wrong person.

American law enforcement procedures have never been designed to control large groups of citizens in rebellion, but to protect the social structure against specifically criminal acts, or persons. The underlying assumption has always been that the police and the citizenry form a natural alliance against evil and dangerous crooks, who should certainly be arrested on sight and shot if they resist.

There are indications, however, that this 'natural alliance' might be going the way of the Maginot Line. More and more often the police are finding themselves in conflict with whole *blocs* of the citizenry, none of them criminals in the traditional sense of the word, but many as potentially dangerous – to the police – as any armed felon. This is particularly true in situations involving

* In August 1966 three Angels were jailed for attacking police who broke up a Hell's Angel's funeral wake in south San Francisco. 'Your conduct can't be tolerated,' said Judge W. Howard Hartley as he pronounced sentence. 'This business of "let's get the cops" cannot go unpunished. You have acted like parasites. You show no respect for the public or yourselves. Your hostility to the law is beyond comprehension.' The three Angels had pleaded guilty to what was then a new law making it a felony to injure a law enforcement officer . . . so instead of copping a minor resisting-arrest plea, they laid themselves open to new and stiffer penalties. One – Lew Roseberry, twenty-two, of Hayward – got a year in jail and five years' probation. Ray Hutchins III, also twenty-two, was granted mercy because of his honourable discharge from the Air Force; he received only six months in jail and three years' probation. Twenty-two-year-old Ken Krake cited his record as a former Explorer Scout and got off with ninety days in jail.

groups of Negroes and teenagers. The Watts riot in Los Angeles in 1966 was a classic example of this new alignment. A whole community turned on the police with such a vengeance that the National Guard had to be called in. Yet few of the rioters were criminals – at least not until the riot began. It may be that America is developing a whole new category of essentially social criminals ... persons who threaten the police and the traditional social structure even when they are breaking no law ... because they view The Law with contempt and the police with distrust, and this abiding resentment can explode without warning at the slightest provocation.

Some of the Hell's Angels' most spectacular crimes are technically misdemeanours, such as 'lewd and lascivious behaviour' and 'disturbing the peace'. These are routine offences, generally appearing on police blotters as 'vag lewd'. Thousands of people are booked every year for obscenity in public places, for fighting in bars, and racing vehicles in populous areas. But when five hundred delegates from some apparently subhuman species converge on a peaceful community and begin pissing in the streets, hurling beer cans at each other and racing loud motorcycles around the village square ... the shock effect on the citizenry is more severe than a Dillinger-style machine-gun assault on the local bank – which is, after all, insured. Few men will break down and weep at the prospect of the Federal Deposit Insurance Corporation having to pay off a claim ... but reports of a hundred filthy thugs *en route* to a mountain resort can throw the whole population into armed panic.

This was the situation on 3 July 1965. Bass Lake had been tense for days. Copies of the 2 July *Life*, featuring Laconia, were prominently displayed on racks at the village markets. The locals were expecting the worst. Judging from all the publicity, the most optimistic forecast called for drunken brawling and property damage, civic fear, and possible injury at any moment. It was also probable that the outlaws would buy up the town's entire beer supply, as is their wont. And if the brutes lived up to their reputation there was every reason to expect a holocaust of arson, looting, and rape. As the weekend began, the atmosphere at Bass Lake was reminiscent of a Kansas hamlet preparing for a tornado.

10

Man, when you were fifteen or sixteen years old did you ever think you'd end up as a Hell's Angel? How did I get screwed up with you guys anyway? . . . Christ, I got out of the Army and came back to Richmond, started ridin' a bike around, wearing my chinos and clean sports shirts, even a crash helmet. . . . And then I met you guys. I started gettin' grubbier and grubbier, dirtier and dirtier, I couldn't believe it. . . . Then I lost my job, started spending all my time either going on a run or gettin' ready for one – Christ, I still can't believe it. – *Fat D., a Richmond Hell's Angel*

Whaddeyou mean by that word 'right'? The only thing we're concerned about is what's right for us. We got our own definition of 'right'. – *A Hell's Angel sunk in Philosophy*

*

ACCORDING to Frenchy, the run would take off at 8 A.M. from the El Adobe, a tavern on East Fourteenth Street in Oakland. (Until the autumn of 1965 the El Adobe was the unofficial headquarters of the Oakland chapter and a focal point for all Hell's Angels activity in northern California – but in October it was demolished to make way for a parking lot, and the Angels moved back to the Sinners Club.)

Early weather forecasts said the whole state would be blazing hot that day, but dawn in San Francisco was typically foggy. I overslept, and in the rush to get moving I forgot my camera. There was no time for breakfast but I ate a peanut-butter sandwich while loading the car . . . sleeping-bag and beer cooler in back, tape recorder in front, and under the driver's seat an unloaded Luger. I kept the clip in my pocket, thinking it might be useful if things got out of hand. Press cards are nice things to have, but in riot situations a pistol is the best kind of safe-conduct pass.

By the time I left my apartment it was almost eight, and

somewhere on the fog-shrouded Bay Bridge between San Francisco and Oakland, I heard the first radio bulletin:

> The Sierra community of Bass Lake is bracing this morning for a reported invasion of the notorious Hell's Angels motorcycle gang. Heavily armed police and sheriff's deputies are stationed on all roads leading to Bass Lake. Madera County sheriff, Marlin Young, reports helicopters and other emergency forces standing by. Neighbouring law enforcement agencies, including the Kern County sheriff's Canine Patrol have been alerted and are ready to move. Recent reports say the Hell's Angels are massing in Oakland and San Bernardino. Stay tuned for further details.

Among those who made a point of staying tuned that morning were several thousand unarmed taxpayers *en route* to spend the holiday in the vicinity of Bass Lake and Yosemite. They had just got underway, most of them still irritable and sleepy from last-minute packing and hurrying the children through breakfast . . . when their car radios crackled a warning that they were headed right into the vortex of what might soon be a combat zone. They had read about Laconia and other Hell's Angels outbursts, but in print the menace had always seemed distant – terrifying, to be sure, and real in its way, but with none of that sour-stomach fright that comes with the realization that this time, it's *you.* Tomorrow's newspapers won't be talking about people being beaten and terrorized three thousand miles away, but right exactly where you and your family are planning to spend the weekend.

*

The Hell's Angels . . . blood, gang rape . . . glance over at your wife, your children in the back seat, could you protect them against a gang of young toughs gone wild on booze and drugs? . . . remember those pictures? Big ugly street-fighters not even afraid of police, loving a fight, swinging chains and big wrenches, knives – no mercy at all.

*

The bridge was crowded with vacationers getting an early start. I was running late by twenty or thirty minutes, and when I got to the toll plaza at the Oakland end of the bridge I asked the gate-keeper if any Hell's Angels had passed through before me. 'The dirty sonsa-bitches are right over there,' he said with a wave of his hand.

I didn't know what he was talking about until some two hundred yards past the gate, when I suddenly passed a large cluster of people and motorcycles grouped around a grey pickup truck with a swastika painted on the side. They seemed to materialize out of the fog, and the sight was having a bad effect on traffic. There are seventeen eastbound toll gates on the bridge, and traffic coming out of them is funnelled into only three exits, with everyone scrambling for position in a short, high-speed run between the toll plaza and the traffic dividers about a half-mile away. This stretch is hazardous on a clear afternoon, but in the fog of a holiday morning and with a Dread Spectacle suddenly looming beside the road the scramble was worse than usual. Horns sounded all around me as cars swerved and slowed down; heads snapped to the right; it was the same kind of traffic disruption that occurs near a serious accident, and many a driver went off on the wrong ramp that morning after staring too long at the monster rally that – if he'd been listening to his radio – he'd been warned about just moments before. And now here it was, in the stinking, tattooed flesh . . . the Menace.

I was close enough to recognize the Gypsy Jokers, about twenty of them, milling around the truck while they waited for late-running stragglers. They were paying no attention to the traffic but their appearance alone was enough to give anyone pause. Except for the colours they looked exactly like any band of Hell's Angels: long hair, beards, black sleeveless vests . . . and the inevitable low-slung motorcycles, many with sleeping-bags lashed to the handlebars and girls sitting lazily on the little pillion seats.

It was eight-fifteen when I got to the El Adobe. The parking lot was full of bikes. I'd stopped at a diner in downtown Oakland to fill my canteen with coffee and to let the outlaws get mustered. It was the Gypsy Jokers who made up the bulk of the crowd in the El Adobe parking lot when I arrived. A group of fifty or sixty Angels had already left for Bass Lake.

I introduced myself and drew a dead blank. Word had gone out that this was going to be a head-knocking run anyway, and the idea of having a writer in tow didn't groove anybody . . . which was understandable, but I hadn't asked the Jokers if I'd be welcome on the run in the first place and I didn't expect them to bother me if they thought I was with the Angels. Buck, a huge Indian on a purple Harley, told me later that they'd pegged me for a cop.

The hostility was obvious but muted. I decided to stay with the Jokers until they got underway, then try to catch up with the others. They were running a few minutes ahead and I knew they'd be holding to the speed limit. A handful of Angels trying to catch up with a run will often wail through traffic at eighty-five or ninety, using all three lanes of the freeway or running straight down the centreline if there's no other way to pass . . . because they know all the cops are up ahead, watching the big formation. But when the outlaws move in a mass, under the watchful eye of the Highway Patrol, they maintain a legal pace that would do pride to a U.S. Army convoy.

For most of the year the Hell's Angels are pretty quiet. Around home, on their own turf, they cultivate a kind of forced coexistence with the local police. But on almost any summer weekend one of the half-dozen chapters might decide to roam on its own, twenty or thirty strong, booming along the roads to some small town with a token police force, to descend like a gang of pirates on some hapless tavern owner whose only solace is a soaring beer profit that might be wiped out at any moment by the violent destruction of his premises. With luck, he'll get off with nothing more than a few fights, broken glasses or a loud and public sex rally involving anything from indecent exposure to a gang-bang in one of the booths.

These independent forays often make news, but it is on their two major runs – Labour Day and the Fourth – that the hell and headlines break loose, At least twice a year outlaws from all parts of the state gather somewhere in California for a king-size brain-bender.

A run is a lot of things to the Angels: a party, an exhibition and an exercise in solidarity. 'You never know how many Angels there are until you go on a big run,' says Zorro. 'Some get snuffed, some drop out, some go to the slammer and there's always new guys who've joined. That's why the runs are important – you find out who's on your side.'

It takes a strong leader like Barger to maintain the discipline necessary to get a large group of Hell's Angels to the run's destination. Trouble can break out almost anywhere. (The Angels won't admit it, but one of the main kicks they get on a run comes from spooking and jangling citizens along the way.) They'd have no problem getting from the Bay Area to Bass Lake if they wanted to travel incognito, dressed like other weekenders and riding in Fords or Chevrolets. But this is out of the question. They wear their party clothes, making themselves as conspicuous as possible.

'People are already down on us because we're Hell's Angels,' Zorro explained. 'This is why we like to blow their minds. It just more or less burns 'em, that's all. They hate anything that's not right for their way of living.'

Anybody who has ever seen the Angels on a run will agree that rural Californians are likely to reject the spectacle as not right for their way of living. It is a human zoo on wheels. An outlaw whose normal, day-to-day appearance is enough to disrupt traffic will appear on a run with his beard dyed green or bright red, his eyes hidden behind orange goggles, and a brass ring in his nose. Others wear capes and Apache headbands, or oversize sunglasses and peaked Prussian helmets. Earrings, *Wehrmacht* headgear and German Iron Crosses are virtually part of the uniform – like the grease-caked Levis, the sleeveless vests and all those fine tattoos: 'Mother', 'Dolly', 'Hitler', 'Jack the Ripper', swastikas, daggers, skulls, 'LSD', 'Love', 'Rape' and the inevitable Hell's Angels insignia.

Many wear other, more esoteric decorations – symbols, numbers, letters and cryptic mottoes – but few of these had any public meaning until the outlaws began talking to reporters. Among the first to be exposed was the numeral '13' (indicating a marijuana smoker). This one is almost as common as the one-percenter badge. Others, like the patch saying 'DFFL' (Dope Forever, Forever Loaded) and the *Playboy* Rabbit (mocking birth control), were exposed by *True* magazine, which also explained the vari-coloured pilots' wings: red wings indicating that the wearer has committed cunnilingus on a menstruating woman, black wings for the same act on a Negress, and brown wings for buggery.

California has laws against 'outraging the public decency', but for some reason they are rarely applied to the Hell's Angels, whose very existence is a mockery of all public decency.

'When you walk into a place where people can see you, you want to look as repulsive and repugnant as possible,' said one. 'We are complete social outcasts – outsiders against society. And that's the way we want to be. Anything good, we laugh at. We're bastards to the world and they're bastards to us.'

'I don't really care if people think we're bad,' said another. 'I think this is what really keeps us going. We fight society and society fights us. It doesn't bother me.'

There are very few Angels who won't go far out of their way to lay a bad jolt on the squares – preferably to the extent of unbalancing their metabolism and causing them to shriek in their sleep for days afterwards – but there is also a certain amount of humour involved. Funny Sonny once explained the Angels' bizarre garb as 'a kind of a joke – you know, like a giant masquerade'.

Which is true to some extent, but not everybody digs the Angels' sense of humour . . . which can range all the way from belly laughs at Jackie Gleason jokes to quiet giggling at the sight of a man's face being shredded with a broken beer bottle.

*

A Weird Haul at Gang's Hideout

SAN DIEGO, July 18 (UPI) – Four coffins, two grave markers and Nazi emblems were found Saturday in the headquarters of a motorcycle gang where three members were arrested on narcotics charges.

The residence also contained a throne chair five feet tall, a stuffed owl, an Oriental beheading sword and assorted motorcycle trophies, police said.

*

I don't recall any laughter that morning at the El Adobe. Late-arriving Angels kept rolling in, and rather than go off on their own, they elected to stick with whatever crowd was available. Now and then somebody would do a wheelstand across the parking lot. Others squatted on the ground, making last-minute carburettor adjustments, and those with nothing else to do stood quietly beside their bikes, smoking cigarettes or sipping from one of the beer cans that were being passed around. Bill, the Jokers' president, was deep in serious pondering over a road map with Dirty Ed, president of the Hayward Hell's Angels. Hutch, the Jokers' vice-president and chief spokesman, stood next to my car with two angels and listened to the newscast. 'Man, those mothers up there are double-shook,' said one of the Angels. 'I just hope they don't hide the broads.'

The certain knowledge than an emergency force of cops and dogs was waiting for them – a knowledge now reinforced by radio bulletins – had already made a difference in the make-up of the run. Many who would ordinarily take their 'old ladies' had left the girls behind in case of a serious clash with the law. Getting locked up in a country town is bad enough if you're by yourself, but to have your wife or girl friend locked up in the same jail – instead of back home to call lawyers and bondsmen – is a kind of double jeopardy that the Angels have learned to avoid.

When I found such perennial double packers as Sonny, Terry, Tiny, Tommy and Zorro without their women, I realized the outlaws were expecting real trouble. But instead of trying to avoid it, as they often have in the past, this time they were determined to meet it head on. 'It ain't that we're really so hot for Bass Lake,' said Barger, 'but with all this newspaper and radio stuff saying they're laying for us up there, we can't back out. This is one run we got to make or they'll never give us any peace again. We don't want trouble, but by God if it comes, there won't nobody be able to say we ducked out.'

This was the kind of talk that was making the rounds in the parking lot when the eight-thirty radio alert led into a rock-'n'-roll song called 'A World of Our Own'.

We'll build a world of our own –
that no one else can share.
All our sorrows we'll leave far behind us there . . .

The song made the whole scene jell. As I sat there in the car, sipping coffee from an Army surplus canteen on a mean cold morning when all of us should have been home in bed, I tried to fit the lyrics to the scene I was part of. At first it seemed like just another teen-age pipe dream with a good swinging beat:

And I know you will find
there'll be peace of mind –
when we live in a world of our own.

A World of Our Own . . . and then, sweet Jesus, it dawned on me that I was right in the middle of it, with a gaggle of righteous dudes that no man could deny . . . weird flotsam on the rising tide, Giant Boppers, Wild Ones, Motorcycle Outlaws.

I had a feeling that at any moment a director would appear, waving cards saying 'Cut' or 'Action'. The scene was too strange to be real. On a peaceful Saturday morning in Oakland, in front of a dumpy, Turkish-looking bar, this weird hellbroth of humanity had gathered . . . wearing labels saying 'Hell's Angels' and 'Gypsy Jokers', and now they were anxious to shove off on their annual Independence Day picnic . . . a Monster rally too rotten for Hollywood, crude parody of the crazy-cool melodramatic scene that Brando had already made famous.

Yet the action was certified by *Time*, *Newsweek* and *The New York Times*. It was at least that real. Grant Wood might have titled it *American Modern*. But there were no artists on hand – nor photographers, nor legmen for the New York Press establishment. Here was the radio chattering crazily about the impending destruction of a California resort by an army of five hundred motorcycle hoodlums, and not even a wire-service stringer was there to get a first-hand report. As it turned out, the Press was getting the story from the police, by telephone – which seemed odd in light of all the advance publicity they had whipped up.

Finally the Joker president gave the word and we thundered out of the parking lot. The lead bikes peeled off into the street, and the others followed, whooping and gunning their engines. But the noise died down instantly. By the time the formation turned on to the freeway, just a few blocks away, the riders were strung out two abreast in each lane, holding a steady sixty-five miles an hour. Everybody looked grim and purposeful; there was no talk at all between riders.

*

> Here's the man who doesn't have any identity. But *tonight* he has the Los Angeles Police Department and the Los Angeles Fire Department upset. He has the National Guard called out. Tonight he is somebody. Tonight he has an identity. – *Reverend G. Mansfield Collins, a Watts minister, speaking in the wake of the 1965 riots*

As the most reprehensible celebrities in years, it was inevitable that their trek to Bass Lake would draw large crowds of horrified burghers all along the route. In Tracy, a town of about eleven thousand on U.S. 50, people ran out of stores to get a better look. I was standing in an air-conditioned liquor store buying beer when the outlaws rolled through town. 'Good God Almighty!' said the clerk. He rushed to the door, throwing it open to let in a blast of noise and hot air from the street. He stood there for several minutes with his hand on the arm of a customer who moved up beside him. All of downtown Tracy was silent except for the roar of motorcycle engines. The outlaws passed slowly down the main street, as if in review, keeping a tight formation with no talk and strictly dead pan. Then, at the eastern city limit, they accelerated up to sixty-five and roared out of sight.

In Modesto, on U.S. 99 in the Central Valley, there were crowds on the sidewalks and photographers at downtown inter-sections. Some of the photos later appeared on the Associated Press wire . . . wonderful shots, Independence Day in California, with the natives taking to the hills done up in the latest West Coast styles.

While the main clusters of outlaws rolled in lawful splendour towards the destination, there were others, late-running stragglers and double-tough independents, who were hustling to catch up. Somewhere near the Manteca turnoff a quartet of Hangmen from El Cerrito came thundering past. They materialized out of traffic in my rear-view mirror. I saw them coming before I heard the noise . . . and suddenly they were right next to the car, filling the sunshine peace of the morning with a roar that drowned out the radio.

Traffic veered to the right as if to make room for a fire engine. In front of me was a station wagon with several children in the back. They pointed excitedly as the hoodlums came past, almost close enough to reach out and touch. The whole line of traffic slowed down; the bikes went by so fast that some people probably thought they'd been buzzed by a low-flying crop duster. But that wouldn't have bothered anyone for more than an instant. What made the sudden appearance of the outlaws unnerving was the element of intrusion. The Central Valley is healthy, rich-looking farmland. There are hand-painted signs along the road, advertising fresh corn, apples and tomatoes for sale at wooden stands; in the fields tractors moving slowly along the furrows, their drivers shielded from the sun by yellow umbrellas mounted above the seats. It is an atmosphere as congenial to crop-dusting airplanes as to horses and cattle. But not to outlaw motorcyclists: they seemed as out of place as a crowd of Black Muslims at the Georgia State Fair. The sight of these refugees from big-city saloon society running around loose in Norman Rockwell country was hard to accept. It was brazen, unnatural and uppity.

11

Were it not for the presence of the unwashed and the half-educated, the formless queer and incomplete, the unreasonable and absurd, the infinite shapes of the delightful human tadpole, the horizon would not wear so wide a grin. – *Frank Moore Colby*, Imaginary Obligations

*

THE Hell's Angels as a group are often wilfully stupid, but they are not without *savoir-faire*, and their predilection for travelling in packs is a long way from being all showbiz. Nor is it entirely due to warps and defects in their collective personality. No doubt these are factors, but the main reason is purely pragmatic. 'If you want the cops to leave you alone you have to shake 'em up,' explains Barger. 'If we make the scene with less than fifteen bikes they'll always bust us. But if we show up with a hundred or two hundred they'll give us a goddamn escort, they'll show a little respect. Cops are like anybody else: they don't want any more trouble than they think they can handle.'

This was obviously true at Bass Lake, which had already hosted one Hell's Angels rally, in 1963, an occasion which resulted in the defiling of a local church. Because of this previous hurt to the community – coupled with a fear of disrupted tourist trade – the law enforcement agencies of Madera County decided to fight the Hell's Angels with a new kind of stratagem. The district attorney, Everett L. Coffee, drew up a document – a 'legal restraining order' designed to keep the outlaws out of Madera County forever. Or at least that was the general idea.

Sometime around noon it became apparent from the multitude of radio alarms that several bands of Hell's Angels were indeed headed for Bass Lake. Yet there were other reports of communities in both northern and southern California still 'braced for invasion'. This was because various elements of the Press had managed to convince each other that there were actually five hundred to a thousand Hell's Angels – so when only two hundred showed up at Bass Lake both the news media and the police felt certain that the others would strike somewhere else. When a half-dozen of the Frisco Angels appeared in Marin County they were immediately surrounded and followed by sheriff's deputies who knew they were only the vanguard of a whole army just over the rise. (The sad truth was that Frenchy and a few of his Box Shop cohorts had cancelled out on the main run, wanting to avoid trouble, and had decided to go off on their own for a peaceful weekend. As it turned out, they were harassed more severely than they would have been at Bass Lake.)

If the Angels needed evidence to support their strength-in-numbers policy, they got it on Fourth July. The only outlaws who didn't get jerked around by the law were those who made the rally. The few splinter groups who went off by themselves were searched and ticketed from one end of the state to the other. Afterwards, a careful count of Hell's Angels sightings added up to less than three hundred, including all the rest of the clubs. Where the other seven hundred outlaws spent the holiday is any man's guess; if Mr Lynch knew, he wasn't talking.*

Somewhere near Modesto, about halfway between Oakland and Bass Lake, I heard on the radio that roadblocks were being set up to prevent the outlaws from entering the resort area. At the time I was running slightly ahead of the Joker–Angel convoy but behind the main Angel contingent that had left the El Adobe before I arrived. I wanted to be on hand when they got to Bass Lake, for the newscasts left no doubt that a major riot was inevitable.

There are two ways to get to Bass Lake from the freeway U.S. 99. I knew the Angels would go south to Madera and then take California 41, a wide, well-paved highway, all the way into Yosemite. The other access route is about fifty miles shorter, but it is a maze of switch-offs and half-paved backroads through the mountains. It took off at Merced and climbed up to Tuttle, Planada,

* Mr Lynch has consistently refused to talk about the Hell's Angels. The subject seems to embarrass him. As Attorney General of the nation's most populous state, he is living testimony to the theory that silence is wisdom. Governor Brown is his good friend and benefactor.

Mariposa and Bootjack. According to the map, the last twenty miles appeared to be a gravel goat track. My car had been wheezing and shimmying all the way from San Francisco, but I swung left at Merced and floored it for a long roller-coaster-run through the foothills. Only two of the outlaws, both strays, made the mistake of taking the same route. I passed one; he was kneeling over a road map in an ancient gas station near Mormon Bar. The other, with a girl on the back, came wailing past me on the climb to Mariposa. The temperature at noon was 105 degrees, and the brown California hills looked ready to burst into flame at any moment. The only green in the landscape was the fringe of scrub oaks looking down on the valley. People who claim to know say these knotty little trees exist in only two places – California and Jerusalem. In any case, they burn well, and if a fire gets started in the grass below, the main job of the stand-by fire crews is to keep it from reaching the oaks which squat there in the dry wind like an army of nervous virgins, a firestorm waiting for a spark.

I was labouring along behind a fire truck when the untracked outlaw came zooming past. He had apparently tired of the slow pace and whacked his hog down into second . . . winding it out until he got abreast of me and then crashing into third. The men in the fire crew stared as if a polar bear had just rushed across the road. The bike was gone in an instant, but the clang and blast of its gear changes hung on the wind like the sound of a jet passing over. And in that instant the firemen caught a glimpse of the hairy rider, the swastika on the gas tank, and the girl on the back – a sight so unutterably strange to their mountain eyes that they could only gape at it.

A few miles west of Mariposa, well into the mountains, I heard another radio bulletin: 'The Hell's Angels motorcycle club has arrived at Bass Lake, and members are reported trying to filter into the resort area. Authorities, armed with a court restraining order, are manning roadblocks in an effort to keep the motorcyclists out of the area during the long holiday weekend.'

If the roadblocks were strategically placed they could prevent a rendezvous by cutting off access to public campsites in the national forest and forcing the outlaws to congregate in places where they would be certain, by the very nature of their gathering, to violate some county or municipal ordinance. A blockade at Oakhurst, just short of the national-forest boundary, could have created a situation where the Angels could be arrested for either blocking the highway or moving off it and trespassing on private property. With a little imagination, the roadblocks might have been gerrymandered to force one group of outlaws off to the south and another to the north. There was no lack of methods the authorities might have used to prevent a Hell's Angels rally at Bass Lake. But it was the same old story: the police were expecting at least five hundred savages coming in for a rumble; roadblocks would detain them, but for how long? And what then? The idea that the Angels would ride two hundred miles for a party and then be turned back by a roadblock ten miles from their destination was obviously wishful thinking. There would surely be violence, a bloody clash on a major highway, with holiday traffic backed up for miles. The alternative was to let them pass, but that too was fraught with tragic possibilities. It was a certified conundrum, a rooty challenge to the legal and social machinery of Madera County.

At a gas station in Mariposa, I asked directions to Bass Lake. The attendant, a boy of about fifteen, advised me solemnly to go elsewhere. 'The Hell's Angels are gonna tear the place up,' he said. 'There's a story about them in *Life* magazine. Jesus, why would anybody want to go to Bass Lake? Those guys are terrible. They'll burn the place down.'

I told him I was a karate master and wanted to be in on the action. As I left he warned me to watch myself and not take chances. 'The Hell's Angels are worse than you think,' he said. 'They'll run right down a shotgun barrel.'

The next stretch of road was like something from a Lewis and Clark diary. The car suffered so badly that I figured I would have to abandon it before the weekend was out and catch a ride back to San Francisco in one of the swastika trucks. I amused myself between creek crossings by telling the tape recorder how weird it was to be seeking out a gang of big-city psychopaths in this kind of country. The road was not even numbered on the map. Now and then I would pass an abandoned log house or the remains of a gold-panning rig. Except for the radio I felt as remote from civilization as any lone poacher in the jagged Mission Range peaks of northern Montana.*

Somewhere around two in the afternoon I reached the smooth pavement of Highway 41, just south of Bass Lake. I was flipping the radio dial for bulletins when I passed a hot-dog stand and saw two outlaw bikes parked conspicuously beside the road. I made a U-turn, parked beside the bikes and found Gut and Buzzard brooding over the restraining order. Buzzard, formerly of Berdoo, is a Hell's Angel straight out of Central Casting. He is a weird combination of menace, obscenity, elegance and genuine distrust of everything that moves. He turns his back on photographers and thinks all journalists are agents of the Main Cop, who lives in a pent-house on the other side of some bottomless moat that no Hell's Angel will ever cross except as a prisoner – and then only to have his hands chopped off as a lesson to the others. There is a beautiful consistency about Buzzard; he is a porcupine among men, with his quills always flared. If he won a new car with a raffle ticket bought in his name by some momentary girl friend, he would recognize it at once as a trick to con him out of a licence fee. He would denounce the girl as a hired slut, beat up the raffle sponsor, and trade off the car for five hundred Seconals and a gold-handled cattle prod.

I enjoy Buzzard, but I have never met anyone outside the Angels who thought he deserved anything better than twelve hours of the bastinado. One morning when Murray was doing his research for the *Post* article I assured him it would be safe to go over to Barger's house in Oakland for an interview. Then I went back to sleep. Several hours later the phone rang, and it was Murray, yelling with rage. He'd been talking quietly with Barger, he said, when suddenly he was confronted by a wild-eyed psychotic who shook a knotty cane under his nose and shouted: 'Who the fuck are you?' The assailant's description didn't fit any Angel I'd ever met, so I called Sonny and asked what had happened. 'Aw hell, it was just Buzzard,' he said with a laugh. 'You know how he is.'

Indeed. Anyone who has ever met Buzzard knows how he is. It took Murray several hours to calm down after his introduction, but weeks later – after lengthy reflection and a distance of three

* Home turf of the largest grizzly-bear gang in the United States – about four hundred in all.

thousand miles – he was still sufficiently affected by the incident to describe it like this:

> We talked affably enough for half an hour or so and at one point Barger grinned and said, 'Well, nobody never wrote nothin' good about us, but then we ain't never done nothin' good to write about.' But the convivial atmosphere began to change noticeably when four or five other Angels, including Tiny, the chapter's huge sergeant at arms, stopped by and joined in. One, a surly blackbearded youth named Buzzard, was sporting a pork-pie hat and a cane he had picked up somewhere; he waved the cane about as he talked and jabbed it at me from time to time. I suddenly got the clear impression that he would have enjoyed using it on somebody. I was the only candidate in the room. I was certain Barger and the other Angels weren't about to pick on me, but I knew that if Buzzard began going to work with the cane I couldn't count on anyone stopping it before I got hurt. To resist would have been folly, because the Angel code would then have called for all of them to pitch in for old Buzzard and I would have been demolished. I sensed menace in the room, and as soon as I could manage it without giving the impression that I was bolting (which might have been a fatal mistake), I said good-bye to Sonny and strolled out of the house.

I quote Murray because he gives me a sense of balance. His perspective on the Angels was very different from mine. Buzzard was the only one who really gave him a jolt. The others only made his flesh crawl. The fact of their existence was an insult to everything he considered decent. He may have been right, and in a way I hope he was, for it would add to the satisfaction – the sense of culture and old-world solidity – that I got from agreeing with him now and then.

Actually, Buzzard is not that dangerous. He has a keen dramatic sense and a taste for weird props. The pork-pie hat Murray referred to is an expensive straw Panama with a madras band. They sell for about $18 at the best shops in San Juan and are worn by American businessmen all over the Caribbean. Buzzard's cane – which Murray saw as a cudgel of some kind – is an integral part of his uniform, his image. Next to Zorro, Buzzard is the Angels' fashion plate. Except for his colours and his neatly trimmed black beard, he looks almost collegiate. In his late twenties, he is tall, wiry and articulate. During the daylight hours he is easy enough to joke with, but at dusk he begins to eat Seconal, which affects him in the same general way that a full moon affects a werewolf. His eyes glaze over, he snarls at the juke box, pops his knuckles and wanders around the premises in a mean funk. By midnight he is a real hazard, a human lightning bolt looking for something to zap.

My first encounter with Buzzard was at the hot-dog stand just out of Bass Lake. He and Gut were sitting at a patio table, pondering the five-page legal document they'd been handed moments earlier. 'They have a roadblock down by Coarsegold,' said Gut. 'Everybody who comes through gets one of these – and they take your picture when they give it to you.'

'That dirty sonofabitch,' said Buzzard.

'Who?' I asked.

'Lynch, that bastard. This is his work. I'd like to get my hands on that cheap-ass punk.' He suddenly shoved the document across the table. 'Here, *you* read this. Can *you* tell me what it means? Hell no, you can't! Nobody could make sense of this shit!'

The thing was titled: ORDER TO SHOW CAUSE WHY PRELIMINARY INJUNCTION SHOULD NOT ISSUE AND TEMPORARY RESTRAINING ORDER MADE. It named as plaintiff 'The people of the State of California', and as defendants 'John Does 1 through 500, Jane Does 1 through 500, individually and as associated under the name and style of HELL'S ANGELS or ONE PERCENTERS, or COFFIN CHEATERS, or SATAN'S SLAVES, or IRON HORSEMEN, or BLACK AND BLUE, or PURPLE AND PINK, or RED AND YELLOW, unincorporated associations.'

The intent of the order was clear, but the specific language was as vague and archaic as the list of defendants, which must have been taken from some yellowed newspaper clipping dating from the late fifties. What it amounted to was a temporary injunction, applicable to anyone photographed in the act of receiving it from the police, against (1) violating any public law, statute or ordinance or committing any public nuisance ... (2) any conduct which is indecent or offensive to the senses ... or (3) carrying or possessing, for the purpose of using same as weapons, any blackjack, sling shot, billy, sandclub, sawed-off shotgun, metal knuckles, switchblade knives, tyre chains, and firearms of any type....

It cited, as reason for the order, the incident two years earlier at the Little Church in the Pines: 'Defendants were drunk ... and entered said Church without authority and without permission took possession of numerous choir robes, donned the same, and paraded on foot and by motorcycles in a lewd manner using vile and obscene language. At said time and place it was necessary for a Deputy Sheriff to threat [*sic*] said defendants in order to recover said robes.'

Page two of the document struck a plaintive note, saying it is 'well known in the State of California' that the members of these associations, 'by intimidations, assault, and other generally violent means, attempt to take over the area in which they congregate; that an outbreak of violence habitually attends such actions, with resulting injury and possible loss of life to members of the public; that the only reasonably certain way for any individual to avoid this violence is to remain at home or to depart from the area in which members of defendant associations are present'.

To Buzzard's vast amusement, I couldn't explain what the document meant. (Nor, several weeks later, could a San Francisco lawyer who tried to interpret it for me.) As it turned out, the Madera County police couldn't explain it either, but their roadside translation was relatively clear: at the first sign of trouble everybody on a motorcycle would be clapped in jail and denied bond.

Gut seemed more depressed than angry at this turn of events. 'Just because I have a beard,' he muttered, 'they want to put me in jail. What's this country coming to?' I was trying to think of an answer when a Highway Patrol car drove up to within ten feet of where we were sitting. I hastily wrapped the court order around the can of beer I was drinking. The two cops just sat there and stared at us, a shotgun mounted in front of them on the dashboard. A high-pitched dispatcher's voice crackled urgently from their radio, telling of various Hell's Angels movements: 'No arrests reported in Fresno . . . large groups on Highway Ninety-nine . . . group of twenty stopped at roadblock west of Bass Lake. . . .'

I made a point of talking to my tape recorder, hoping the sight of it would keep them from shooting all three of us if the radio suddenly ordered them to 'take appropriate action'. Gut slumped in his wooden chair, sipping an Orange Crush and staring off at the sky. Buzzard seemed to quiver with rage, but he kept himself under control. The surface resemblance between the two was striking: both tall, lean, dressed for the road, but neither looking particularly scraggy – beards trimmed, medium-long hair, and neither with any sign of weaponry or weird extras. Without the Hell's Angels' insignia they wouldn't have attracted any more attention than a couple of touring hipsters from L.A.

At that time, Gut was not technically a Hell's Angel. Several years earlier he had been one of the charter members of the Sacramento chapter – which, like the Frisco chapter, began with a distinctly bohemian flavour. Terry the Tramp was another charter member of the North Sac Angels. They had always got along well with Sacramento's beatnik element, and when the chapter moved to Oakland they brought some of this influence with them. It didn't go over too well at the El Adobe. The original Oakland Angels were hard-ass brawlers – a purer strain, as it were – and they had never made contact with the jazz, poetry and protest element of Berkeley and San Francisco. Because of this conflict in backgrounds the sudden consolidation in Oakland of Angel refugees from Sacramento and Berdoo had an unsettling effect on the whole scene.

A wanderer like most of the others, Gut had also been a member of the Berdoo chapter, but now – at twenty-seven – he was having second thoughts about making another plunge. Membership doesn't transfer automatically. The fellowship does, and the assumption is always that a transient Angel will eventually be absorbed into whatever chapter he chooses to ride with, but there is always a waiting period . . . just to make sure. In Gut's case the trial period was a very mutual thing. He wanted to go back to college in the fall, he said. He already had a year at a junior college down south; he wanted to be a commercial artist, and his sketchbook of motorcycle drawings showed a natural talent. 'I'm not so sure I want to join the Angels again,' he said one night. 'But I hate to lose friends. Sometimes I think I'd like to drop the club and settle down to something different, but it's hard to tell the Angels that.' A friend of Gut's, a non-Angel predicted: 'He'll join again. Hell, he doesn't know how not to.'*

The three of us were still sitting there, talking aimlessly, when the patrol car suddenly jumped backwards, made a tight circle in

* Gut eventually drifted away from the Angels and into the Berkeley–LSD scene.

the parking lot and zoomed off down the highway. I quickly finished my beer and was picking up the tape recorder when there was a tremendous sound all around us. Seconds later, a phalanx of motorcycles came roaring over the hill from the west. Both Gut and Buzzard rushed towards the highway, waving and shouting happily. The road was dense with bikes. The hot-dog stand was on the crest of a hill above Bass Lake; it was the last geographic barrier between the Angels and their destination. The police, in their wisdom, had managed to pile up at least a hundred bikes at the roadblock – where the restraining orders were ceremoniously handed out – and then release them all at once. So instead of arriving in quiet knots, the outlaws crested the hill in a great body . . . howling, hooting, waving bandannas and presenting the citizens with a really terrifying spectacle. The discipline of the highway had broken down entirely; now it was madness. The sight of Gut and Buzzard cheering beside the road caused Little Jesus to fling his hands in the air and utter triumphant screams. His bike veered off to the right and nearly collided with Charger Charley the Child Molester. An Angel I had never seen came by on an orange three-wheeler, kicking his feet straight out like a rodeo rider. Andy from Oakland, who has no driver's licence, came by with his wife sitting in front of him on the gas tank, ready to grab the handlebars at the first sight of the fuzz. The noise was like a landslide, or a wing of bombers passing over. Even knowing the Angels, I couldn't quite handle what I was seeing. It was like Genghis Khan, Morgan's Raiders, *The Wild One* and the Rape of Nanking all at once. Both Gut and Buzzard leaped on their bikes and roared off to join the pack.

As I was getting into my car another bike pulled into the lot. It was an outlaw B.S.A., a rare animal in this league, and on it was a stocky, tough-looking man in his late thirties with a $400 Nikon camera hanging on his neck . . . Don Mohr, then a photographer for *The Oakland Tribune*. Except for the Nikon and the lack of colours, Mohr looked as grimy and menacing as any Hell's Angel, and with good reason. He was a veteran motorcyclist, who had been riding longer than most of the Hell's Angels. Unlike many of his contemporaries, he had developed at least one of his talents and gained some leverage in the world of squares and money, but he had never given up bikes. In Oakland he wore a blue suit to work and drove a white Thunderbird, but when the Angels went out on a run he joined them on his old Beezer. He wore boots, greasy Levis and a sleeveless denim vest, showing tattoos on both arms. He looked like a middleweight Rocky Marciano and talked the same way.*

We speculated briefly on the nature of the weekend, but by that time the last of the bikes had gone over the hill and we both wanted to catch up. I followed him down the winding road to Bass Lake and we soon fell in with the tail of the caravan. The outlaws weren't exceeding the speed limit, but they were gearing down noisily and zooming four abreast through the curves, yelling and waving at people beside the road . . . doing everything possible to inject the maximum degree of civic trauma into their arrival. If I had been a citizen of Bass Lake at the time I would have gone home and loaded every gun I owned.

*Not long after the Bass Lake Run, Mohr was made an honorary Hell's Angel.

12

> Everyone knows our horsemen are invincible. They fight because they're hungry. Our empire is surrounded by enemies. Our history is written in blood, not wine. Wine is what we drink to toast our victories. – *Anthony Quinn as Attila in the film* Attila the Hun

*

BASS Lake is not really a town, but a resort area – a string of small settlements around a narrow, picture-postcard lake that is seven miles long and less than a mile wide at any point. The post office is on the north side of the lake in a cluster of stores and buildings all owned by a man named Williams. This was the Angels' rendezvous point . . . but the local sheriff, a giant of a man named Tiny Baxter, had decided to keep them out of this area by means of a second roadblock about a half-mile from the centre of downtown. It was Baxter's decision and he backed it with his three-man force and a half-dozen local forest rangers.

By the time I got there the outlaws were stopped along both sides of the highway, and Barger was striding forth to meet Baxter. The sheriff explained to the Angel chieftain and his Praetorian Guard that a spacious campsite had been carefully reserved for them up on the mountain above town, where they wouldn't 'be bothered'. Baxter is six-foot-six and built like a defensive end for the Baltimore Colts. Barger is barely six feet, but not one of his followers had the slightest doubt that he would swing at the sheriff if things suddenly came down to the hard nub. I don't think the sheriff doubted it either, and certainly I didn't. There is a steely, thoughtful quality about Barger, an instinctive restraint that leads outsiders to feel they can reason with him. But there is also a quiet menace, an egocentric fanaticism tempered by eight years at the helm of a legion of outcasts who, on that sweaty afternoon, were measuring the sheriff purely by his size, his weapon and the handful of young rangers who backed him up. There was no question about who would win the initial encounter, but it was up to Barger to decide just what that victory would be worth.

He decided to go up the mountain, and his legion followed without question or bitterness. The ranger who pointed out the route made it sound like a ten-minute drive up a nearby dirt road. I watched the outlaw horde boom off in that direction, then talked for a while with two of the rangers who stayed to man the roadblock. They seemed a little tense but smiled when I asked if they were afraid the Hell's Angels might take over the town. They had shotguns in the cab of their truck, but during the confrontation the guns had remained out of sight. Both were in their early twenties, and they seemed very cool, considering the much-publicized threat they had just met and sidetracked. I chalked it up later to the influence of Tiny Baxter, the only cop I've ever seen put Sonny Barger on the defensive.

It was about 3.30 P.M. when I started up the dirt road to the designated Angel campground. Thirty minutes later I was still following motorcycle tracks up a fresh bulldozer cut that looked like something hacked out of a Philippine jungle. The angle was low gear all the way, it zigzagged like a deer trail and the campsite itself was so high that when I finally arrived it seemed that only a heavy ground fog lay between us and a clear view of Manhattan Island, at the other end of the continent. There was no trace of water, and by this time the Angels had worked up a serious thirst. They had been shunted off to a parched meadow nine or ten thousand feet up in the Sierras, but it was obviously a bum trip. They hadn't minded the climb, but now they felt deceived and they wanted to retaliate. The prevailing ugly mood was shared by Barger, who felt the sheriff had duped him. The campsite was fit only for camels and mountain goats. The view was excellent, but a camp without water on a California Fourth of July is as useless as an empty beer can.

I listened to the war talk and shouting for a while, then hustled down the mountain to call a Washington newspaper I was writing for at the time, to say I was ready to send one of the great riot stories of the decade. On the way down the road I passed outlaw bikes coming the other way. They'd been stopped at the Bass Lake roadblock and pointed up to the campsite. The Frisco swastika truck came by in first gear, with two bikes in the back and a third trailing twenty feet behind at the end of a long rope in a cloud of dust. Its rider was hanging on grimly behind green goggles and a handkerchief tied over his nose and mouth. Following the truck was a red Plymouth that erupted with shouts and horn blasts as I passed. I stopped, not recognizing the car, and backed up. It was Larry, Pete and Puff, the new president of the Frisco chapter. I hadn't seen them since the night of the meeting at the DePau. Pete, the drag racer, was working as a messenger in the city, and Larry was carving totem poles out of tree stumps in other Angels' front yards. They had broken down on the freeway near Modesto and been picked up by three pretty young girls who stopped to offer help. This was the Plymouth, and now the girls were part of the act. One was sitting on Pete's lap in the back seat, half undressed and smiling distractedly, while I explained the problem of the campsite. They decided to push on, and I said I'd see them later in town . . . or somewhere, and at that point I thought it would probably be in jail. A very bad scene was building up. Soon the Angels would be coming down the mountain *en masse*, and in no mood for reasonable talk.

In the Carolinas they say 'hill people' are different from 'flatlands people', and as a native Kentuckian with more mountain than flatlands blood, I'm inclined to agree. This was one of the theories I'd been nursing all the way from San Francisco. Unlike Porterville or Hollister, Bass Lake was a mountain community . . . and if the old Appalachian pattern held, the people would be much slower to anger or panic, but absolutely without reason or mercy once the fat was in the fire. Like the Angels, they would tend to fall back in an emergency on their own native sense of justice – which bears only a primitive resemblance to anything written in law books. I thought the mountain types would be far more tolerant of the Angels' noisy showboating, but – compared to their flatlands cousins – much quicker to retaliate in kind at the first evidence of physical insult or abuse.

On the way down the mountain I heard another Monitor newscast, saying the Hell's Angels were heading for Bass Lake and big trouble. There was also mention of a Los Angeles detective who had shot one of the suspects rounded up for questioning about the rape of his daughter the day before. The sight of the suspect being led through the hall of the police station was too much for the detective, who suddenly lost control and began firing point blank. The victim was said to be a Hell's Angel, and newspapers on sale in Bass Lake that afternoon were headlined: HELL'S ANGEL SHOT IN RAPE CASE. (The suspect, who survived, was a twenty-one-year-old drifter. He was later absolved of any connection with either the Angels or the rape of the detective's daughter . . . who had been selling cookbooks, door to door, when she was lured into a house known to be frequented by dragsters and hot-rod types. The detective admitted losing his head and shooting the wrong man; he later pleaded temporary insanity and was acquitted of all charges by a Los Angeles grand jury.) It took several days, however, for the Press to separate the rape-shooting from the Hell's Angels, and in the meantime the headlines added fuel to the fire. On top of the Laconia stories, including the one in *Life*, the radio bulletins and all the frightening predictions in the daily press – now this, a Hell's Angels rape in Los Angeles, and just in time for the 3 July papers.

Given all these fiery ingredients, I didn't feel a trace of alarmist guilt when I finally got a Bass Lake–Washington connection and began outlining what was going to happen. I was standing in a glass phone booth in downtown Bass Lake – which consists of a small post office, a big grocery, a bar and cocktail lounge, and several other picturesque redwood establishments that look very combustible. While I was talking, Don Mohr pulled up on his bike – having breached the roadblock with his Press credentials – and indicated that he was in a hurry to call the *Tribune*. My editor in Washington was telling me how and when to file, but I was not to do so until the riot was running under its own power, with significant hurt to both flesh and property . . . and then I was to send no more than an arty variation of the standard wire-service news blurb: Who, What, When, Where and Why.

I was still on the phone when I saw a big burr-haired lad with a pistol in his belt walk over to Mohr and tell him to get out of town. I couldn't hear much of what was going on, but I saw Mohr produce a packet of credentials, stringing them out like a card shark with a funny pack. I could see that he needed the phone, so I agreed with my man in Washington that first things would always come first, and hung up. Mohr immediately occupied the booth, leaving me to deal with the crowd that had gathered.

Luckily, my garb was too bastard for definition. I was wearing Levis, Wellington boots from L. L. Bean in Maine, and a Montana sheepherder's jacket over a white tennis shirt. The burr-haired honcho asked me who I was. I gave him my card and asked why he had that big pistol on his belt. 'You know why,' he said. 'The first one of these sonsofbitches that gives me any lip I'm gonna shoot right in the belly. That's the only language they understand.' He nodded towards Mohr in the phone booth, and there was nothing in his tone to make me think I was exempted. I could see that his pistol was a short-barrelled Smith & Wesson ·357 Magnum – powerful enough to blow holes in Mohr's B.S.A. cylinder head, if necessary – but at arm's length it hardly mattered. The gun was a killer at any range up to a hundred yards, and far beyond that in the hands of a man who worked at it. He was wearing it in a police-type holster on the belt that held up his khaki pants, high on his right hip and in an awkward position for getting at it quickly. But he was very conscious of having the gun and I knew he was capable of raising bloody hell if he started waving it around.

I asked him if he was a deputy sheriff.

'No, I'm working for Mr Williams,' he said, still studying my card. Then he looked up. 'What are you doing with this motorcycle crowd?'

I explained that I was only a journalist trying to do an honest day's work. He nodded, still fondling my card. I said he could keep it, which seemed to please him. He dropped it in the pocket of his khaki shirt, then tucked his thumbs in his belt and asked me what I wanted to know. The tone of the question implied that I had about sixty seconds to get the story.

I shrugged. 'Oh, I don't know. I just thought I'd look around a bit, maybe write a few things.'

He chuckled knowingly. 'Yeah? Well, you can write that we're ready for 'em. We'll give 'em all they want.'

The dusty street was so crowded with tourists that I hadn't noticed the singular nature of the group that surrounded us. They weren't tourists at all; I was standing in the midst of about a hundred vigilantes. There were five or six others wearing khaki shirts and pistols. At a glance they looked like any bunch of country boys at any rustic hamlet in the Sierras. But as I looked around I saw that many carried wooden clubs and others had hunting knives on their belts. They didn't seem mean, but they were obviously keyed up and ready to bust some heads.

The merchant Williams had hired a few private gunmen to protect his lakefront investment; the rest were volunteer toughs who'd been waiting all day for a fight with a bunch of hairy city boys who wore chains for belts and stank of human grease. I remembered the mood of the Angels up on the mountain and I expected at any moment to hear the first of the bikes coming down the hill into town. The scene had all the makings of a king-hell brawl, and except for the pistols it looked pretty even.

Just then the door of the phone booth opened behind me, and Mohr stepped out. He looked curiously at the mob, then raised his camera and took a picture of them. He did it as casually as any Press photographer covering an American Legion picnic. Then he straddled his bike, kicked it to life and roared up the hill towards the roadblock.

Burr-head seemed confused and I took the opportunity to stroll off towards my car. Nobody said anything and I didn't look back, but at any instant I expected to be whacked on the kidneys with a big stick. Despite the Press credentials, both Mohr and I had been firmly identified with the outlaws. We were city boys, intruders, and under these circumstances the only neutrals were the tourists, who were easily identifiable. On my way out of town I wondered if anybody in Bass Lake might take one of my aspen-leaf cheques for a fluorescent Hawaiian beach suit and some stylish sandals.

The scene at the roadblock was surprisingly peaceful. The bikes were again parked along both sides of the highway, and Barger was talking to the sheriff. With them was the chief forest ranger for the area, who was explaining cheerfully that another campsite had been set aside for the Angels . . . Willow Cove, about two miles down the main road and right on the edge of the lake. It sounded too good to be true, but Barger signalled his people to follow the rangers' jeep and check it out. The strange procession moved slowly down the highway, then veered into the pines on a narrow jeep trail that led to the campsite.

There were no complaints this time. Willow Cove lacked only a free-beer machine to make it perfect. A dozen of the Angels leaped off their bikes and rushed into the lake fully clothed. I parked under a tree and got out to look around. We were on a small peninsula jutting into Bass Lake and cut off from the highway by a half-mile of pine forest. It was an idyllic kind of setting and a very unlikely place to be put aside for an orgy. But it was, and the outlaws set about occupying it like a victorious army. Sheriff Baxter and the head ranger explained to Barger that there were only two conditions on their use of the site: (1) that they would leave it as clean and unlittered as they found it and (2) that they would keep to themselves and not menace the campgrounds on the other side of the lake, which were full of tourists. Sonny agreed, and the weekend's first crisis was over. The outlaw clan, which now numbered about two hundred, was agreeably settled in a private kingdom, with nothing of substance to bitch about. Beyond that, the Maximum Angel was committed to the task of keeping his people under control. It was an unnatural situation for Barger to find himself in. Instead of spending the weekend rallying his boozy legion from one piece of unfriendly turf to another, beset at all times by a cruel authority wearing guns and badges, he now found his people in a pleasant cul-de-sac... a state of rare equality with the rest of humanity, which they could only disturb by committing some deliberate outrage – by violating an agreement that the Prez had honoured with his word.

The transaction had been carried out in Hollywood Indian style. There was a childlike simplicity in the dialogue between Barger and the lawmen:

'If you play straight with us, Sonny, we'll play straight with you. We don't want any trouble and we know you guys have as much right to camp on this lake as anybody else. But the minute you cause trouble for us or anyone else, we're gonna come down on you hard, it's gonna be powder valley for your whole gang.'

Barger nods, seeming to understand. 'We didn't come here for trouble, Sheriff. The way we heard it, you had trouble waitin' for us.'

'Well, what did you expect? We heard you were coming in for a rumble, to tear things up.' Baxter forces a smile. 'But there's no reason why you can't enjoy yourselves here like everybody else. You guys know what you're doing. There's nothing wrong with you. We know that.'

Then Barger smiles, very faintly, but he smiles so seldom that even a grimace means he thinks something is very funny. 'Come off it, Sheriff. You know we're all fuck-up or we wouldn't be here.'

The sheriff shrugged and walked back to his car, but one of the deputies picked up the conversation and soon found himself telling five or six grinning Angels what basically decent fellows they were. Barger went off to get a beer kitty going. He stood in the middle of the big clearing and called for donations. We had been there about half an hour and by this time I'd suffered a fatal run on my own stock. Puff had spotted the cooler in my car. I hadn't planned to roll into camp and instantly dispose of my beer supply for the weekend, but under the circumstances I had little choice. There was no hint of intimidation, but neither was there any question in anyone's mind that I'd brought the beer for any other purpose than to share it at this crucial bone-dry time. As it happened, I had barely enough money for gas back to San Francisco. Once my two cases were gone I couldn't buy a single can all weekend without cashing a cheque, and that was out of the question. Beyond that, I was – and might still be – the only journalist the Angels had ever seen who didn't have an expense account, so I was a little worried at their reaction when I'd be forced to plead poverty and start drinking out of the kitty. My own taste for the hops is very powerful, and I had no intention of spending a beerless weekend in the withering sun.

In retrospect this seems like a small point, but it didn't at the time. It was an ill-chosen moment to cast my bread on the waters . . . the suck-tide was running. Somewhere in the cacophony of foaming and hissing that followed the discovery of my cache, I recall saying, to nobody in particular: 'All right, goddamnit, this thing had better work both ways.' But there was no reason to believe it would. At that stage of their infamy the Angels equated all reporters with *Time* and *Newsweek*. Only a few of them knew me, and the others were not going to be happy when I began lurking around the beer supply, draining one can after another in a feverish effort to even the score.

Many hours later, after the beer crisis had passed, I felt a little foolish for having worried. The outlaws gave it no thought. To them it was just as natural for me to have their beer as for them to have mine. By the end of the weekend I'd consumed three or four times as much as I'd brought with me . . . and even now, looking back on nearly a year of drinking with the Angels, I think I came out ahead. But that isn't the way they balance the books. Despite their swastika fetish, the fiscal relationship between Angels is close to pure communism: 'from each according to his abilities and to each according to his needs'. The timing and the spirit of the exchange are just as important as the volume. Much as they claim to admire the free enterprise system, they can't afford it among themselves. Their working ethic is more on the order of 'He who has, shares'. There is nothing verbal or dogmatic about it; they just couldn't make it any other way.

But none of this was apparent that afternoon in Bass Lake as I watched my stock disappear while Barger called for funds. Although Sheriff Baxter had left, six deputies had attached themselves to the camp on what appeared to be a permanent basis. I was talking to one of them when Barger joined us with a handful of money. 'The sheriff said that place by the post office will sell us all the beer we want,' he said. 'How about using your car? There's likely to be trouble, if we take one of the trucks.'

I didn't mind and the deputy said it was a socko idea, so we counted out the money on the hood of the car. It came to $120 in bills and roughly $15 in change. Then, to my amazement, Sonny handed me the whole bundle and wished me well. 'Try to hustle,' he said. 'Everybody's pretty thirsty.'

I insisted that somebody come with me to help load the beer in the car . . . but my real reason for not wanting to go alone had nothing to do with loading problems. I knew all the outlaws lived in cities, where the price of a six-pack ranges from $.79 to $1.25. But we were nowhere near a city, and I also knew, from long experience, that small stores in remote areas sometimes get their pricing policy from *The Gouger's Handbook*.

Once, near the Utah–Nevada border, I had to pay $3 for a six-pack, and if that was going to be the case at Bass Lake, I wanted a reliable witness – like Barger himself. At normal city prices $135 would fetch about thirty cases of beer, but up in the Sierras it would only cover twenty, or maybe fifteen if the merchants were putting up a solid front. The Angels were in no position to do any comparison shopping, and if they were about to be taught a harsh lesson in socio-economics, I figured they'd be more receptive to the bad news if it came from one of their own people. There was also the fact that sending a penniless writer to get $135 worth of beer was – as Khrushchev said of Nixon – 'like sending a goat to tend the cabbage'.

I mentioned this on the way to town after Sonny and Pete had agreed to come with me. 'You'd of come back with it,' Sonny said. 'A person would have to be awful stupid to run off with our beer money.' Pete laughed. 'Hell, we even know where you live. And Frenchy says you got a boss-lookin' old lady, too.' He said it jokingly, but I noted that raping my wife was the first form of retaliation that came to his mind.

Barger, like the politician he is, hastened to change the subject. 'I read that article you wrote about us,' he said. 'It was okay.'

The article had appeared a month or so earlier, and I remembered a night in my apartment when one of the Frisco Angels had said, with a beery smile, that if they didn't like what I wrote they'd come over some night to kick down my door, throw gasoline into the hall and then put a match to it. We were all in good spirits at the time, and I recall pointing to the loaded double-barrelled shotgun on my wall and replying, with a smile, that I would croak at least two of them before they got away. But none of this violence had come to pass, so I assumed they either hadn't read the article or had managed to live with what it said. Nonetheless, I was leery of having it mentioned, and especially by Barger, whose opinions automatically become the Hell's Angels' official line. I had written the piece with the idea that I would never again have any contact with motorcycle outlaws, whom I'd referred to as 'losers', 'ignorant thugs' and 'mean hoodlums'. None of these were terms I looked forward to explaining while surrounded at a remote Sierra campsite by two hundred boozing outlaws.

'What are you doin' now?' Barger asked. 'Are you writin' somethin' else?'

'Yeah,' I said. 'A book.'

He shrugged. 'Well, we don't ask for nothin' but the truth.* Like I say, there's not much good you can write about us, but I don't see where that gives people the right to just make up stuff ... all this bullshit, hell, ain't the truth bad enough for 'em?'

We were almost to Williams's store, and I suddenly remembered my burr-haired inquisitor with his high-powered language barrier. We made the turn at the bottom of the hill and I parked the car as inconspicuously as possible about thirty yards from the store. According to the deputy at the campsite, the sale was already arranged. All we had to do was pay, load the beer and leave. Sonny had the cash, and as far as I was concerned, I was just the chauffeur.

It took about fifteen seconds to understand that something had queered the plan. As we stepped out of the car the vigilantes began moving towards us. It was very hot and quiet, and I could taste the dust that hung over the parking area. A Madera County paddy wagon was parked at the other end of the shopping centre, with two cops in the front seat. The mob stopped short of the car and formed a bristling human wall on the boardwalk outside the store. Apparently they hadn't been informed of the pending transaction. I opened the trunk of my car, thinking that Sonny and Pete would go in for the beer. If things got serious I could jump into the trunk and lock it behind me, then kick out the back seat and drive away when it was all over.

Neither Angel made a move towards the store. Traffic had stopped and the tourists were standing off at a safe distance, watching. The scene reeked of Hollywood: the showdown, *High Noon*, *Rio Bravo*. But without cameras or background music it didn't seem quite the same. After a long moment of silence the burr-haired fellow took a few steps forward and shouted: 'You better get your asses out of here. You don't have a chance.'

I walked over to talk with him, thinking to explain the beer agreement. I wasn't particularly opposed to the idea of a riot, but I didn't want it to happen right then, with my car in the middle and me as a participant. It would have been ugly: two Hell's Angels and a writer against a hundred country toughs on a dusty street in

* Several months later they decided that truth was not enough. There would have to be money too. This created tension, which blossomed into resentment and finally violence.

the Sierras. Burr-head listened to my reasoning, then shook his head. 'Mr Williams changed his mind,' he said. And then I heard Sonny's voice right behind me: 'Well, fuck that! We can change our minds too.' He and Pete had walked out to join the argument, and now the vigilantes moved forward to support Burr-head, who didn't look worried.

Well, I thought, here we go. The two cops in the paddy wagon hadn't moved; they were in no hurry to break the thing up. Getting beaten by a mob is a very frightening experience . . . like being caught in a bad surf: there is not much you can do except try to survive. It has happened to me twice, in New York and San Juan, and it came within seconds of happening again at Bass Lake. All that prevented it was the suspiciously timely arrival of Tiny Baxter. The crowd parted to make room for his big car with the flashing red light on top. 'I thought I told you to stay out of town,' he snapped.

'We came for the beer,' Sonny replied.

Baxter shook his head. 'No, Williams says he's running low. You gotta go over to the market on the other side of the lake. They have plenty.'

We left instantly. Like the first campsite, the first beer contact had all the signs of a calculated botch. Baxter may or may not have known what he was doing, but if he did he deserves credit for coming up with a subtle and ingenious strategy. He made a limited number of appearances during that weekend, but each one came at a critical moment and he always arrived with a solution. After the fixing of the beer crisis the Angels began to view him as a secret sympathizer, and by midnight of the first day Barger had been made to feel almost personally responsible for the welfare of everybody in Bass Lake. Each time Baxter fixed something he put the Angels more in his debt. The strange burden eventually ruined Barger's holiday. The vagaries of the restraining order and the numerous agreements he'd made with the sheriff caused him to worry constantly. One of his few pleasures was the knowledge that Baxter wasn't getting any sleep either.

On the way around the lake we speculated about what sort of mob might be waiting at the next store. 'Those bastards were gonna stomp us,' said Pete.

'Yeah, and that would have been it,' Sonny muttered. 'That sheriff don't know how close he was to havin' a war on his hands.'

I didn't take his remark very seriously, but by the time the weekend was over I knew he hadn't been kidding. If Barger had been stomped by a mob of locals, nothing short of a company of armed militia could have kept the main body of outlaws from swarming into town for vengeance. An attack on the Prez would have been bad enough, but under those circumstances – a police-planned beer run – it would have been evidence of the foulest treachery, a double cross, and the Angels would have done exactly what they all came to Bass Lake expecting to do. Most would have finished the weekend in jail or the hospital, but they were expecting that too. It would have been a good riot, but looking back, I no longer think the initial clash would have been evenly matched. Many of the vigilantes would have lost their taste for the fight the moment they realized that their opponents meant to inflict serious injury on anybody they could reach. Big Frank from Frisco,* for instance, is a black belt in karate who goes into any fight with the idea of jerking people's eyeballs out of their sockets. It is a traditional karate move and not difficult for anyone who knows what he's doing . . . although it is not taught in 'self-defence' classes for housewives, businessmen and hot-tempered clerks who can't tolerate bullies kicking sand in their faces. The intent is to demoralize your opponent, not blind him. 'You don't really jerk out the eyeball,' Big Frank explained. 'You just sorta *spring* it, so it pops outta the socket. It hurts so much that most guys just faint.'

Red-blooded American boys don't normally fight this way. Nor do they swing heavy chains on people whose backs are turned . . . and when they find themselves in a brawl where things like this are happening, they have good reason to feel at a disadvantage. It is one thing to get punched on the nose, and quite another to have your eyeball sprung or your teeth shattered with a wrench.

So if there had been a full-strength fight that afternoon, the locals would probably have been routed after the first clash. But it would have taken a while for the police to muster enough strength to prevail, and in the meantime the outlaws would have wreaked

* Or Frank Number Two – not legendary Frank, ex-outlaw and ex-president.

all manner of destruction on the merchant Williams's property – breaking windows, looting beer coolers and probably rifling some cash registers. A few would have been shot by Burr-head and his crew, but most would have tried to flee at the first sign of serious police action. This would have led to wild chases and skirmishing, but Bass Lake is a long way from Angel turf and not many of them could have made it all the way home without being captured at roadblocks.

Barger knew this and he didn't want it to happen. But he also knew that it was not a sense of hospitality or concern for social justice that had got them a campsite. Tiny Baxter had a bomb on his hands, and he had to tread carefully to keep it from going off. This was Barger's leverage – the certainty that his people would behave like wild beasts if they were pushed too far. But it would last only as long as things stayed quiet. John Foster Dulles might have called it a 'balance of terror', a volatile stand-off which neither side wanted to upset. Whether this was a just or desirable situation for a woodsy American community to find itself in is, again, pretty much beside the point. As weird and unreal as the Bass Lake confrontation might have sounded to radio listeners in New York or Chicago, nobody on the scene had any doubt about what they were seeing. Right or wrong, it was happening, and by the time the Angels were settled at Willow Cove, even the locally made restraining order was irrelevant. The outlaws simply had to be dealt with in terms of moment-to-moment reality.

I hadn't planned to get physically involved, but after the narrow escape at Williams's store I was so firmly identified with the Angels that I saw no point in trying to edge back to neutrality. Barger and Pete seemed to take me for granted. As we drove around the lake they tried earnestly to explain the importance of the colours. Pete seemed puzzled that the question had ever come up. 'Hell,' he said, 'that's what it's all about.'

The other market was in the centre of the main tourist area, and when we got there the crowd was so dense that the only place to park was between the gas pump and the side door. If trouble broke out we'd be hopelessly penned in. At a glance the scene looked even worse than the one we'd just been rescued from.

But this was a different crowd. They'd apparently been waiting for hours to see the Angels in action, and now, as the two stepped out of the car, a murmur of gratification went up. These were not locals, but tourists – city people, from the valley and the coast. The store was full of newspapers featuring the Hell's Angels rape in Los Angeles, but nobody looked frightened. A curious crowd gathered as the outlaws bargained with the owner, a short moon-faced man who kept saying: 'Sure thing, boys – I'll take care of you.' He was aggressively friendly, even to the point of putting his arm around Pete's grimy shoulders as they made their way to the beer vault.

I bought a paper and went to the bar and lunch counter at the far end of the store. While I was reading the rape story I heard a little girl behind me ask: 'Where are they, Mummy? You said we were going to see them.' I turned to look at the child, a bandy-legged pixie just getting her permanent teeth, and felt thankful once again that my only issue is male. I glanced at the mother and wondered what strange grooves her mind had been fitted to in these wonderfully prosperous times. She was a downbeat thirty-five, with short blonde hair and a sleeveless blouse only half tucked into her tight Bermuda shorts. It was a vivid tableau . . . on a hot California afternoon a sag-bellied woman wearing St Tropez sunglasses is hanging around a resort-area market, trailing her grade-school daughter and waiting in the midst of an eager crowd for the arrival of The Hoodlum Circus, as advertised in *Life*.

I remembered the previous spring, when I was driving one night from San Francisco to Big Sur and heard a radio bulletin about a tidal wave due to strike the California coast around midnight. Shortly before eleven I got to Hot Springs Lodge – which sits on a cliff just above the ocean – and rushed inside to sound the alarm. It was a slow night, and the only people still awake were a half-dozen locals sitting around a redwood table with some bottles of wine. They'd already heard the warnings and were waiting for the thing to hit. A tidal wave, by God – it was a sight worth waiting up for. That same night, according to anguished police reports, more than ten thousand people flocked to Ocean Beach in San Francisco, creating a night-long traffic jam on the Coast Highway. They too were curious, and if the wave had come up on schedule most of them would have been killed. Luckily it petered out somewhere between Honolulu and the West Coast . . .

A crowd of about fifty people gathered to watch us load the beer. Several teenagers got up the nerve to help. A man wearing madras shorts and black business socks kept asking Pete and Sonny to pose while he backed off for panoramic sequences with his home-movie camera. Another man, also wearing Bermudas, sidled up to me and asked quietly: 'Say, are you guys really Nazis?'

'Not me,' I said. 'I'm Kiwanis.'

He nodded wisely, as if he had known all along. 'Then what's all this stuff you read?' he asked. 'You know, this stuff about swastikas.'

I called to Sonny, who was showing our helpers how to stack the cases in the back seat. 'Hey, this man wants to know if you're a Nazi.' I expected him to laugh, but he didn't. He made the usual disclaimers regarding the swastikas and Iron Crosses ('That don't mean nothin', we buy that stuff in dime stores'), but just about the time the man seemed satisfied that it was all a rude put-on, Barger unloaded one of those jarring ad libs that have made him a favourite among Bay Area newsmen. 'But there's a lot about that country we admire,' he said, referring to pre-war Germany. 'They had discipline. There was nothin' chickenshit about 'em. They might not of had all the right ideas, but at least they respected their leaders and they could depend on each other.'

The audience seemed to want to mull this over, and in the meantime I suggested we get back to Willow Cove. At any moment I expected somebody to start yelling about Dachau and then to see some furious Jew lay Barger out with a campstool. But there was no sign of anything like that. The atmosphere was so congenial that we soon found ourselves back inside the store, eating hamburgers and sipping draught beer. I was beginning to feel almost relaxed when we heard motorcycles outside and saw the crowd surge towards the door. Seconds later, Skip from Richmond appeared, saying he'd waited as long as he could for the beer and had finally decided to seek it on his own. Several more Angels arrived, for the same reason, and the owner scurried around behind the bar, serving up the mugs with a nice enthusiasm: 'Drink up, boys, and take it easy – I bet you're thirsty as hell after that long ride, eh?'

The man's attitude was very odd. As we left he stood by the car and told us to come back real soon, 'with the other fellas'. Considering the circumstances, I listened closely for a telltale lilt of craziness in his voice. Maybe he's not even the owner, I thought. . . . Maybe the owner had fled with his family to Nevada, leaving the village loony to mind the store and deal with the savages in his own way. Whoever he was, the eager little person had just sold eighty-eight six-packs of beer at $1.50 each and guaranteed himself a booming trade for the rest of the weekend. . . . Without spending a penny, he'd landed the West Coast's top animal act, a surefire crowd-pleaser that would put the traditional lakeside fireworks display in deep shade. All he had to worry about was the good possibility that the act might go haywire at any moment, destroying both the profits and the customers in a brutal eruption which the next day's newspapers would describe as:

THE RAPE OF BASS LAKE: FIRE AND PANIC IN MOUNTAIN RESORT; COPS BATTLE HELL'S ANGELS AS RESIDENTS FLEE

The locals seemed resigned to it, and it was no surprise to find them armed and surly. Nor was it strange to find the police unusually tense. This was the first major rally since Monterey, and the vast publicity surrounding it was a factor that neither the outlaws nor the police had ever had to contend with. Things like roadblocks and restraining orders were new problems for both sides. The idea of a carefully reserved campsite had been tried before, but it had never been effective except late at night, when the outlaws were not likely to move around anyway. The real shocker, however, was the beer situation. The Angels have always prided themselves on the one contribution they inevitably make to any community they visit. In spite of the terror they inspire, they leave many dollars in local taverns. Because of this, they found it unthinkable that anyone would refuse to sell them beer – and especially without fair warning, which would have caused them to bring a whole truckload from the city.

But Bass Lake was a different scene. The locals had had nearly a week to work themselves into a swivet, and by Saturday morning they were braced for the worst. Among the safety measures they were counting on was the knowledge that the hoodlums would be much less dangerous if denied large quantities of drink. This was evident to everyone concerned – even the beer-sellers – and besides it was going to be a bad money weekend anyway, since the rotten publicity would cause large numbers of vacationers to go elsewhere. What manner of man would bring his family to camp on a battleground, a place almost certain to be invaded by an army of vicious rabble?

The question still pertains, but it doesn't alter the fact that people came from all over California that weekend to enjoy the rustic pleasures of Bass Lake. When they were turned away from motels or regular campsites they slept in roadside turn-outs and dirty ravines. By Monday morning the lakefront looked like the White House lawn after Andrew Jackson's inaugural ball. The crowd was abnormal even for a big summer holiday.

Californians are known to be enthusiastic outdoorsmen; in 1964, near Los Angeles, thousands of weekend campers had to be restrained by barriers from moving into an area that had just been gutted by a forest fire. When it was under control and the barriers were opened, the blackened campsite quickly filled to capacity. A reporter on the scene said the campers were 'pitching their tents among smoking stumps'. One man who had brought his family explained that there was 'no place else to go, and we only have two days'.

As a pathetic comment, it made a pathetic kind of sense. But nothing that simple and tangible could explain the capacity crowd at Bass Lake. Anybody who really wanted no part of the outlaws had plenty of time to find a safer vacation spot. Police reports of possible 'Hell's Angels strikes' had Bass Lake near the top of every list.

So it must have been a giddy revelation for the Bass Lake Chamber of Commerce to discover that the Hell's Angels' presence – far from being a plague – was in fact a great boon to the tourist trade. It is eerie to consider the meaning of it. If the Hell's Angels draw standing room only, any half-hip chamber-of-commerce entertainment chairman should see the logical follow-up:

next year, bring in two fighting gangs from Watts and pit them against each other on one of the main beaches . . . with fireworks overhead while the local high-school band plays *Bolero* and 'They Call the Wind Maria'.

13

That was the trouble with Porterville – they had four thousand people downtown watchin' two hundred of us. – *Terry the Tramp*

*

OUR final purchase at the beer market was a dozen cans of horse-meat for Pete's big redbone hound. The dog had been on other runs and seemed to know the spirit. It ate constantly, never seemed to sleep and went into long fits of howling for no apparent reason.

We drove back to camp very slowly. The car was so jammed with loose six-packs that I could barely move my arms to steer, and each bump in the road caused the springs to drag on the rear axle. When we got to the Willow Cove turnoff the car wouldn't climb the dirt hill that led into the pines . . . so I backed off and made a fast run at it, driving the junker straight into the hill like a cannon ball. Our momentum took us over the hump, but the crash pushed the right fender back on the tyre. The car lurched far enough down the trail to block it completely and stopped just short of crashing into a dozen bikes *en route* to the store. It took some rough work with a bumper jack to get it moving again, and just as we freed the front wheel a purple truck came grinding over the crest and rammed into my rear bumper. The rhythm of the week-end was picking up . . . a huge beer delivery, the rending of metal, greedy laughter and a rumble of excitement when Sonny told what had happened at Williams's store.

We had been away about two hours, but the interim peace had been preserved by the arrival of several carloads of girls and beer. By six the whole clearing was ringed with cars and bikes. My car was in the middle, serving as a communal cooler.

During Barger's absence, the other chapter presidents had seen to the gathering of wood for a bonfire. The task fell to the newest member in each chapter, a tradition that nobody questioned. After all, as Tiny has said, the Hell's Angels are like any other fraternity, and like the others, they have a fine sense of ritual, hierarchy and organization. At the same time, they take pride in a certain uniqueness, a distinctive sort of life orientation that sets them apart from the Elks and the Phi Delts. Inevitably members of other fraternities have questioned the Angels' traditions – calling them eccentric, or criminal. Among the most controversial are Rape, Assault and Body Odour. Another, not so repellent to the public, is the outlaws' powerful disdain for either home telephones or mailing addresses. With rare exceptions, they have assigned this aspect of reality to various wives, 'mamas', girl friends and friendly hustlers whose pads are always open, day or night, to anyone wearing the colours.

The outlaws are very comfortable with their inaccessibility. It saves them a lot of trouble with bill collectors, revenge seekers and routine police harassment. They are as insulated from society as they want to be, but they have no trouble locating each other. When Sonny flies down to Los Angeles, Otto meets him at the airport. When Terry goes to Fresno, he quickly locates the chapter president, Ray – who exists in some kind of mysterious limbo and can only be found by means of a secret phone number, which changes constantly. The Oakland Angels find it convenient to use Barger's number, checking now and then for messages. Some use various saloons where they are well known. An Angel who wants to be reached will make an appointment either to meet somewhere or to be at a certain phone at a designated time.

One night I tried to arrange a contact with a young Angel named Rodger, a one-time disc jockey. It proved to be impossible. He had no idea where he might be from one day to the next. 'They don't call me Rodger the Lodger for nothing,' he said. 'I just make it wherever I can. It's all the same. Once you start worrying about it, you get hung up – and that's the end, man, you're finished.' He didn't use cards, not wanting even a cardboard illusion of worldly permanence. If he'd been killed that night he'd have left no footprints in life, no evidence and no personal effects but his bike – which the others would have quickly raffled off. Hell's Angels don't find it necessary to leave wills, and their deaths don't require much paperwork. . . . A driver's licence expires, a police record goes into the dead file, a motorcycle changes hands and usually a few 'personal cards' will be taken out of wallets and dropped into wastebaskets.

Because of their gypsy style of life, their network has to be functional. A lost message can lead to serious trouble: an Angel who might have fled will be arrested; a freshly stolen bike will never reach the buyer; a pound of marijuana might miss a crucial connection; or at the very least a whole chapter will never get word of a run or a big party.

The destination of a run is kept secret as long as possible – hopefully, to keep the cops guessing. The chapter presidents will figure it out by long-distance telephone, then each will tell his people the night before the run, either at a meeting or by putting the word with a handful of bartenders, waitresses and plugged-in chicks who are known contacts. The system is highly efficient, but it has never been leakproof, and by 1966 the Angels had decided that the only hope was to keep the destination a secret until the run was actually underway. Barger tried it once, but the police were able to track the outlaws by radioing ahead from one point to another. Radio tracking is only a device to give the cops an edge, a sense of confidence and control. Which it does, as long as no lapses occur . . . but it is safe to predict that on one of these crowded holidays a convoy of Angels is going to disappear like a blip shooting off the edge of a radar screen. All it will take is one of those rare gigs the outlaws are forever seeking: a ranch or a big farm with a friendly owner, a piece of rural turf beyond the reach of the fuzz, where they can all get drunk and naked and fall on each other like goats in the rut, until they all pass out from exhaustion.

It would be worth buying a police radio, just to hear the panic:

*

'Group of eighty just passed through Sacramento, going north on U.S. Fifty, no violence, thought to be headed for Lake Tahoe area. . . .' Fifty miles north, in Placerville, the police chief gives his men a pep talk and deploys them with shotguns on both sides of the highway, south of the city limits. Two hours later they are still waiting and the dispatcher in Sacramento relays an impatient demand for a report on Placerville's handling of the crisis. The chief nervously reports no contact and asks if his restless troops can go home and enjoy the holiday.

The dispatcher, sitting in the radio room at Highway Patrol headquarters in Sacramento, says to sit tight while he checks around . . . and moments later his voice squawks out of the speaker: 'Schwein! You lie! Vere are dey?'

'Don't call me no swine,' says the Placerville chief. 'They never got here.'

The dispatcher checks all over northern California, with no result. Police cars scream up and down the highways, checking every bar. Nothing. Eighty of the state's most vicious hoodlums are roaming around drunk somewhere between Sacramento and Reno, hungry for rape and pillage. It will be another embarrassment for California law enforcement . . . to simply lose the buggers, a whole convoy, right out on a main highway . . . heads will surely roll.

By now, the outlaws are far up a private road, having left the highway at a sign saying: OWL FARM, NO VISITORS. *They are beyond the reach of the law unless the owner complains. Meanwhile, another group of fifty disappears in the same vicinity. Police search parties stalk the highway, checking for traces of spittle, grime and blood. The dispatcher still rages over his mike; the duty officer's voice cracks as he answers urgent queries from radio newsmen in San Francisco and Los Angeles: 'I'm sorry, that's all I can say. They seem to have . . . ah . . . our information is that they . . . they disappeared, yes, they're gone.'*

*

The only reason it hasn't happened is that the Hell's Angels have no access to private property in the boondocks. One or two claim to have relatives with farms, but there are no stories of the others being invited out for a picnic. The Angels don't have much contact with people who own land. They are city boys, economically and emotionally as well as physically. For at least one generation and sometimes two they come from people who never owned anything at all, not even a car.

The Hell's Angels are very definitely a lower-class phenomenon, but their backgrounds are not necessarily poverty-stricken. Despite some grim moments, their parents seem to have had credit. Most of the outlaws are the sons of people who came to California either just before or during the Second World War. Many have lost contact with their families, and I have never met an Angel who claimed to have a home town in any sense that people who use that term might understand it. Terry the Tramp, for instance, is 'from' Detroit, Norfolk, Long Island, Los Angeles, Fresno and Sacramento. As a child, he lived all over the country, not in povery but in total mobility. Like most of the others, he has no roots. He relates entirely to the present, the moment, the action.

His longest bout with stability was a three-year hitch in the Coast Guard after finishing high school. Since then he has worked half-heartedly as a tree-trimmer, mechanic, bit actor, labourer and hustler of various commodities. He tried college for a few months but quit to get married. After two years, two children and numerous quarrels, the marriage ended in divorce. He had another child, by his second wife, but that union didn't last long either. Now, after two hugely publicized rape arrests, he refers to himself as an 'eligible bachelor'.

Despite his spectacular rap sheet, he estimates his total jail time at about six months – ninety days for trespassing and the rest for traffic offences. Terry is one of the most arrest-prone of all the Angels; cops are offended by the very sight of him. In one stretch, covering 1964 and 1965, he paid roughly $2,500 to bail bondsmen, lawyers and traffic courts. Like most of the other Angels he blames 'the cops' for making him a full-time outlaw.

At least half the Hell's Angels are war babies, but that is a very broad term. There are also war babies in the Peace Corps, in corporate training programmes, and fighting in Vietnam. The Second World War had a lot to do with the Hell's Angels origins, but you have to stretch the war theory pretty thin to cover both Dirty Ed, in his early forties, and Clean Cut from Oakland, who is twenty years younger. Dirty Ed is old enough to be Clean Cut's father – which is not likely, though he's planted more seeds than he cares to remember.

It is easy enough to trace the Hell's Angels' mystique – and even their name and their emblems – back to the Second World War and Hollywood. But their genes and real history go back a lot farther. The Second World War was not the original California boom, but a rebirth of a thing that began in the thirties and was already tapering off when the war economy made California a new Valhalla. In 1937 Woody Guthrie wrote a song called 'Do-Re-Mi'. The chorus goes like this:

California is a garden of Eden
A Paradise for you and for me,

But believe it or not,
You won't think it's so hot,
If you ain't got the Do-Re-Mi.

The song expressed the frustrated sentiments of more than a million Okies, Arkies and hillbillies who made a long trek to the Golden State and found it was just another hard dollar. By the time these gentlemen arrived, the Westward Movement was already beginning to solidify. The 'California way of life' was the same old game of musical chairs – but it took awhile for this news to filter back East, and meanwhile the Gold Rush continued. Once here, the newcomers hung on for a few years, breeding prolifically – until the war started. Then they either joined up or had their pick of jobs on a booming labour market. Either way, they were Californians when the war ended. The old way of life was scattered back along Route 66, and their children grew up in a new world. The Linkhorns had finally found a home.

Nelson Algren wrote about them in *A Walk on the Wild Side*, but that story was told before they crossed the Rockies. Dove Linkhorn son of Crazy Fitz, went to hustle for his fortune in New Orleans. Ten years later he would have gone to Los Angeles.

Algren's book opens with one of the best historical descriptions of American white trash ever written.* He traces the Linkhorn ancestry back to the first wave of bonded servants to arrive on these shores. These were the dregs of society from all over the British Isles – bums, misfits, criminals, debtors, social bankrupts of every type and description – all of them willing to sign oppressive work contracts with future employers in exchange for ocean passage to the New World. Once here, they endured a form of slavery for a year or two – during which they were fed and sheltered by the boss – and when their time of bondage ended, they were turned loose to make their own way.

In theory and in the context of history the set-up was mutually advantageous. Any man desperate enough to sell himself into bondage in the first place had pretty well shot his wad in the old country, so a chance for a foothold on a new continent was not to

* A story called *Barn Burning*, by William Faulkner, is another white-trash classic. It provides the dimension of humanity that Algren's description lacks.

be taken lightly. After a period of hard labour and wretchedness he would then be free to seize whatever he might in a land of seemingly infinite natural wealth. Thousands of bonded servants came over, but by the time they earned their freedom, the coastal strip was already settled. The unclaimed land was west, across the Alleghenies. So they drifted into the new states – Kentucky and Tennessee; their sons drifted on to Missouri, Arkansas and Oklahoma.

Drifting became a habit; with dead roots in the Old World and none in the New, the Linkhorns were not of a mind to dig in and cultivate things. Bondage too became a habit, but it was only the temporary kind. They were not pioneers, but sleazy rearguard camp followers of the original westward movement. By the time the Linkhorns arrived anywhere the land was already taken – so they worked for a while and moved on. Their world was a violent, boozing limbo between the pits of despair and the Big Rock Candy Mountain. They kept drifting west, chasing jobs, rumours, homestead grabs or the luck of some front-running kin. They lived off the surface of the land, like armyworms, stripping it of whatever they could before moving on. It was a day-to-day existence, and there was always more land to the west.

Some stayed behind and their lineal descendants are still there – in the Carolinas, Kentucky, West Virginia, and Tennessee. There were dropouts all along the way: hillbillies, Okies, Arkies – they're all the same people. Texas is a living monument to the breed. So is southern California.

Algren called them 'fierce craving boys' with 'a feeling of having been cheated'. Freebooters, armed and drunk – a legion of gamblers, brawlers and whorehoppers. Blowing into town in a junk Model-A with bald tyres, no muffler and one headlight . . . looking for quick work, with no questions asked and preferably no tax deductions. Just get the cash, fill up at a cut-rate gas station and hit the road, with a pint on the seat and Eddy Arnold on the radio moaning good back-country tunes about home sweet home, that Bluegrass sweetheart still waitin', and roses on Mama's grave.

Algren left the Linkhorns in Texas, but anyone who drives the Western Highways knows they didn't stay there either. They kept moving until one day in the late 1930s they stood on the spine of a scrub-oak California hill and looked down on the Pacific Ocean – the end of the road. Things were tough for a while but no tougher than they were in a hundred other places. And then came the war – fat city, big money even for Linkhorns.

When the war ended, California was full of veterans looking for ways to spend their separation bonuses. Many decided to stay on the Coast, and while their new radios played hillbilly music they went out and bought big motorcycles – not knowing exactly why, but in the booming, rootless atmosphere of those times, it seemed like the thing to do. They were not all Linkhorns, but the forced democracy of four war years had erased so many old distinctions that even Linkhorns were confused. Their pattern of intermarriage was shattered, their children mixed freely and without violence. By 1950 many Linkhorns were participating in the money economy; they owned decent cars, and even houses.

Others, however, broke down under the strain of respectability and answered the call of the genes. There is a story about a Linkhorn who became a wealthy car dealer in Los Angeles. He married a beautiful Spanish actress and bought a mansion in Beverly Hills. But after a decade of opulence he suffered from soaking sweats and was unable to sleep at night. He began to sneak out of the house through the servants' entrance and run a few blocks to a gas station where he kept a hopped-up 1937 Ford with no fenders . . . and spend the rest of the night hanging around honky-tonk bars and truck stops, dressed in dirty overalls and a crusty green T-shirt with a Bardhal emblem on the back. He enjoyed cadging beers and belting whores around when they spurned his crude propositions. One night, after long haggling, he bought several Mason Jars full of home whiskey, which he drank while driving at high speed through the Beverly Hills area. When the old Ford finally threw a rod he abandoned it and called a taxi, which took him to his own automobile agency. He kicked down a side door, hot-wired a convertible waiting for tune-up and drove out to Highway 101, where he got in a drag race with some hoodlums from Pasadena. He lost, and it so enraged him that he followed the other car until it stopped for a traffic light – where he rammed it from the rear at seventy miles an hour.

The publicity ruined him, but influential friends kept him out of jail by paying a psychiatrist to call him insane. He spent a year in a rest home; and now, according to the stories, he has a motorcycle dealership near San Diego. People who know him say he's happy – although his driver's licence has been revoked for numerous violations, his business is verging on bankruptcy, and his new wife, a jaded ex-beauty queen from West Virginia, is a half-mad alcoholic.

It would not be fair to say that all motorcycle outlaws carry Linkhorn genes, but nobody who has ever spent time among the inbred Anglo-Saxon tribes of Appalachia would need more than a few hours with the Hell's Angels to work up a very strong sense of *déjà vu*. There is the same sulking hostility towards 'outsiders', the same extremes of temper and action, and even the same names, sharp faces and long-boned bodies that never look quite natural unless they are leaning on something.

Most of the Angels are obvious Anglo-Saxons, but the Linkhorn attitude is contagious. The few outlaws with Mexican or Italian names not only act like the others but somehow look like them. Even Chinese Mel from Frisco and Charley, a young Negro from Oakland, have the Linkhorn gait and mannerisms.

14

Basically they're just like Negroes. By themselves they're no more trouble than anybody else – but the minute they get in a group they go all to pieces, they really do. – *San Francisco policeman*

*

JUST before dusk on the first afternoon a sudden scrambling tension swept over the camp. People had been coming and going for several hours, but with no sense of urgency. The odd welcome at the beer market had undermined the sheriff's edict about keeping away from the tourists, and many of the outlaws rode over to sample the hostility. The atmosphere at Willow Cove was festive. New arrivals were greeted with shouts, kisses, flying tackles and sprays of beer. The deputies were taking pictures. At first I thought it was for evidence, but after watching them urge the Angels to strike colourful poses and dive into the lake with their clothes on, I realized that the cops were as fascinated as any first-time visitor at the Bronx Zoo. One told me later: 'Hell, I wish I had a movie camera, this is the damnedest thing I ever saw. People wouldn't believe it unless they saw pictures. Wait'll I show these to my kids!'

Just before lunch, for no obvious reason, the tempo changed abruptly. Barger and several others went into a huddle with two deputies, then jumped on their bikes and disappeared down the trail. About ten of the outlaws left camp in a group, all looking grim. Moments later two police cars left. Most of the outlaws seemed content to let Barger handle whatever was happening, but about twenty gathered around Tiny, in the middle of camp, and muttered darkly at the news, on the police radio, of 'an attack on a motorcyclist'. They didn't know who it was, or even if it was one of their own. (A motorcycle hill-climb-and-scrambles event was scheduled the next day near Yosemite, and there were many respectable bikes in the area. Somebody said a group wearing

Seventh Sons colours had been seen near Mariposa, but none of the Angels had ever heard of that outfit, or knew if they were outlaws.)

When a gathering of Angels and their allies gets word that 'a motorcyclist' has been attacked, it comes as an ominous signal that some enemy is on the move. Barger and his escort were gone for almost an hour, and many of the others would have gone out to look for them if Tiny hadn't insisted on waiting for further word. I recall somebody cursing the untenable position: 'Jesus, look where we are! The bastards got us trapped out here! There's no way out except that one path!'

Willow Cove was a natural Dunkirk. I watched the two remaining deputies; the moment they left, I was leaving too . . . their departure could only mean that things had gotten out of hand somewhere else and that the Angel campsite would be next. I didn't want to be there when the vigilantes came whooping through the trees.

But the deputies didn't leave, and just before dark Barger's patrol came back in good spirits. Dirty Ed, it seemed had been riding peacefully beside the lake when five friendly looking youths, on foot, had flagged him down. Always conscious of public relations, he had stopped to chat. What followed, according to one version was an unconscionable bushwhacking:

'Are you going to compete in the scrambles tomorrow?' one of them asked.

Just as Ed was about to answer no, the sixth man snuck up behind him.

'He knocked me clean off my bike,' cringed Ed. 'Hit me with an eight-foot length of two-inch pipe. My head exploded. I thought I'd been hit by a locomotive!

'The six young men had been drinking. The only reason I can figure for them doing it was to make a name for themselves,' complains Ed. 'They were "joe citizens", and had been drinking for about five days. The other "citizens" in the campground were afraid we would come back and stomp them. Some of them were so scared they started folding their tents and moving out. "Rather Switch Than Fight", they said.'

This absurd and fraudulent account appeared in what is known in the trade as a 'newstand quickie', titled 'The Real Story Behind the Hell's Angels and Other "Outlaw" Motorcycle Groups'. It was whipped up by the photographer who was arrested later that weekend for 'obstructing justice', and although it contained some excellent photos, the text was apparently put together by somebody like Whittaker Chambers.

Yet Dirty Ed now insists – for public consumption – that the 'Real Story' version is pretty close to the truth, although he chuckles indulgently at lines like 'The six young men had been drinking . . . Rather Switch Than Fight' . . . and the lunatic assertion that he somehow sensed, without ever seeing it, the exact length and width of the pipe that laid his scalp open. Twenty years on the outlaw circuit have not done much to mellow his view of the Press and the world of devious squares he thinks it represents. He would no more trust a reporter than he would a cop or a judge. To him they are all the same – the running dogs of whatever fiendish conspiracy has plagued him all these years. He knows that somewhere behind that moat, the Main Cop has scrawled his name on a blackboard in the Big Briefing Room – with a notation beside it: 'Get this boy, give him no peace, he's incorrigible, like an egg-sucking dog.'

Dirty Ed has been a motorcycle outlaw for all of his adult life. He works as a bike or auto mechanic around the East Bay cities, but he is not professionally ambitious. At six foot one and weighing 225, he looks like a beer-bellied wrestler. His hair is balding on top and grey at the temples. If he shaved off his stringy oriental beard he would look almost distinguished. As it is, he just looks mean.

Later that night, standing by the bonfire with a beer, he talked briefly about the encounter. The eight stiches in his head had cost a dollar each, and he'd had to pay cash. That was the worst part of it – having to pay. Hell, eight dollars was a case of beer and gas back to Oakland. Unlike the younger Angels, Ed has to underplay his action and keep his image at least double tough. He has been around longer than almost anybody, which is plenty long enough to know he won't get any sympathy when he starts showing signs of old age. Few of the younger Angels would have made a screeching U-turn on the road and roared back to confront five punks who'd yelled an insult. But Dirty Ed did. He would ride his bike into a river to fight a bull moose if he thought the beast had it in for him. Probably it was lucky for everybody that the kids pole-axed him off his bike before he hurt one of them. They told the police they'd panicked when he swung around and came at them, for what they considered no reason at all. The fact that they just happened to have a lead pipe on hand didn't seem to surprise anybody.

The teenage assailants were arrested – 'to make sure we didn't kill 'em', Barger explained – and then driven to their homes, where they were released with a warning to avoid any contact with the outlaws for the rest of the weekend. The fact of their arrest gave Barger the excuse he needed to let the incident pass. Had the bushwhackers not been taken into custody, the Angels would have insisted on revenge – perhaps not instantly, but the threat would have changed the whole tone of the weekend. As it turned out, the formality of arrest satisfied everybody. Barger wasn't pleased, but after weighing the alternatives and talking with Baxter, he decided to give the jury-rigged truce another chance. His legionnaires agreed, which they would have in any case – even if he'd called for a frontal assault on the sheriff's home. But when he opted for prudence, peace and more beer the others seemed genuinely relieved. They had saved face without having to fight, and they still had two days to party.

The outlaws don't mind a fight, even if it means a good chance of getting hurt, but getting arrested can be a very expensive proposition. Once jailed, they have to post bond to get out, and unlike the solid citizen, who is a jobholder or property owner or at least has friends who can sign for the amount, the Angels have no recourse but their friendly bondsmen. Each chapter has one, who is always on call. If necessary he will drive two hundred miles in the dead of night to get an Angel out of jail. His fee for this service is ten per cent of whatever he signs for; and in rural situations where tensions are running high, a Hell's Angel who winds up in jail will invariably be socked with a maximum bond, which can run as high as $5,000 for drunkenness and assault, or $2,500 for indecent exposure . . . netting the bondsman $500 and $250 respectively. These fees are not refundable; they are interest on a short-term loan. But the Angels are such good customers that some bondsmen will give them a group rate, scaling down the fees to fit the circumstances. The outlaws appreciate their bondsmen and rarely welsh, although many are so far in debt that they have to pay off in instalments, $10 or $15 a week.

The Frisco chapter's bondsman once had a windfall of forty-six arrests in one night, at $100 to $242 each.* The clubhouse was raided, and those captured – including eighteen girls – were charged across the board with 'suspicion of (1) robbery, (2) assault with deadly weapons, (3) possession of marijuana, (4) harboring fugitives, (5) conspiracy to harbor fugitives and (6) contributing to the delinquency of minors'.

It was a spectacular bust, causing huge headlines in the Press, but all charges were dropped when the Angels mounted a countersuit for false arrest. Not one of the forty-six was ever tried, much less convicted . . . yet all those caught in the raid had to sign for ten per cent of his bond to get out of jail. There was no alternative. They have no friends either willing or wealthy enough to put up $2,500 in cash or property in the middle of the night, or the next day either. A cheque won't make it, and no court has ever released a Hell's Angel on his own recognizance. The only way out of the slammer is to pay the bondsman, and he only answers the call for those with good credit. An outlaw who has welshed in the past will sit in jail indefinitely.

The Oakland chapter's 'bondsman' is a handsome middle-aged woman with platinum-blonde hair named Dorothy Connors. She has a pine-panelled office, drives a white Cadillac and treats the Angels gently, like wayward children. 'These boys are the backbone of the bail-bond business,' she says. 'Ordinary customers come and go, but just like clockwork, the Angels come down to my office each week to make their payments. They really pay the overhead.'

At Bass Lake the situation was further complicated by the restraining order, which, according to the police, ruled out any possibility of bail, even at ten per cent. Despite this, the sunset mood at Willow Cove was loose and happy. There was a feeling

* Not all of this was paid, and the Frisco Angels were forced to change bondsman. The new man charges them a firm ten per cent.

that the crises were all past and that now the serious drinking could begin.

In accordance with their ethic of excess in all things, the Angels booze with a zeal that seems hardly human. As drinkers, they are binge-oriented. Around home they seldom get drunk, but at parties they go completely out of their heads – screaming gibberish and running headlong at each other like crazed bats in a cave. The bonfire is always a hazard. On one run Terry fell into the fire and was burned so badly that he had to be rushed to a hospital. Those who avoid the fire and refrain from shoving their fists through car windshields might, at any moment, go roaring off on their bikes to seek out some populated area where they can put on a show.

In 1957 several hundred outlaws made a disastrous run to Angels Camp, where the American Motorcycle Association was staging a big race in conjunction with the annual frog-jumping contest. Many of the top riders in the country were on hand, along with some three thousand cyclists of every description. The Angels were not invited, but they went anyway – knowing that their presence would cause violence.

The A.M.A. includes all kinds of motorcyclists – from those on 50-cubic-centimetre Hondas to devotees of full-dress Harley 74s – but it centres on competition riders, either professional or amateur, who take their bikes very seriously, spend a lot of money on them and ride all year round. Their idea of a good party is an argument about gear ratios or the merits of overhead cams. Unlike the outlaws, they frequently take long trips either alone or in groups of two or three . . . and often into areas where anybody on a motorcycle is automatically treated like a Hell's Angel, a raping brute unfit to eat or drink among civilized people. This has made them bitter, and most can't even discuss the Angels without getting angry. The relationship of the two groups is not quite as venomous as that of owls and crows – who will attack each other on sight – but the basic attitudes are not much different. Unlike the general public, many competition riders have had painful experience with the outlaws, for they move in the same small world. Their paths cross at bike-repair shops, races or late-night hamburger stands. According to respectable cyclists, the Angels are responsible for the motorcycle's sinister image. They blame the outlaws for many of the unpleasant realities of being a bike-owner – from police harassment to public opprobrium to high insurance rates.

The 'respectability' of A.M.A. people is entirely relative. Many are as mean and dishonest as any Hell's Angel, and there is a hard core – mainly race riders and mechanics – who will go out of their way to tangle with outlaws. A.M.A. officials deny this, for obvious reasons, but in almost the same breath they denounce the Angels as criminal scum. I've heard cops call motorcycle outlaws 'the lowest of the low' and 'the scum of the earth', but they do it with a certain amount of self-control. Most cops were bitterly amused at the Hell's Angels' publicity boom. By contrast, the A.M.A. people were outraged; it was like a bunch of owls reacting to the news that a crow warlord had won the Nobel Peace Prize.

In Sacramento in the fall of 1965 a handful of Hell's Angels attended a national championship race and afterwards got in a brief scuffle, in the parking lot, with two men who said something to offend them. Nobody was hurt, and the Angels, five of them, drove off in a car towards San Francisco. They had not gone far when they were forced off the road by two cars full of respectable riders and mechanics . . . who jerked the outlaws out of their car, and as one said later: 'We beat the bastards bloody; they couldn't stand up; they were crying.'

On the disastrous run to Angels Camp in 1957 the outlaws were outnumbered about ten to one, but the opposition couldn't have mustered enough strong-arms to meet them head on. The Angels arrived early and bought up the entire beer supply of four bars, which they drank in a pasture several miles from the site of the races. By nightfall most of the outlaws were raving drunk, and when somebody suggested they go over and check out the A.M.A. camp the reaction was automatic. Their howling frightened the townspeople and sent the sheriff running for his car. The outlaw pack filled both lanes of the narrow road . . . gunning their engines and sending the beams of their headlights into trees and bedroom windows as they weaved and jockeyed for running room. They were only going for a party, they said later, but the party never got started. The lead bikes took the crest of a hill at over a hundred miles an hour and crashed blindly into a group of cyclists beside the road. Two outlaws died in the bloody pile-up, which immediately drew a large crowd. There were not enough police to keep the scene under control, and fights broke out as cyclists shoved and shouted among the wreckage. Flashing lights and sirens added to the confusion, which grew worse as the fighting spread. It continued all night and most of the next day – not a full-scale riot, but a series of clashes that kept local police racing from one spot to another.

The casualty list showed two dead, a dozen serious injuries and the final demise of the old notion that rural communities are geographically insulated from 'city trouble'. Angels Camp was a major goad to the development of the mutual assistance concept, a police version of mobile warfare, which meant that any town or hamlet in California, no matter how isolated, could summon help from nearby police jurisdictions in case of emergency. There is no official list of these emergencies, but if there were, any rumour of a Hell's Angels visitation would be right at the top.

15

> The fact that people are poor or discriminated against doesn't necessarily endow them with any special qualities of justice, nobility, charity or compassion. – *Saul Alinsky*

*

TO squelch any possibility of the Angels roaring drunkenly out of camp during the night, Baxter and the Highway Patrol announced a 10-P.M. curfew. At that time, anyone in camp would have to stay, and nobody else could come in. This was made official just after dark. The deputies were still trying to be friendly and they assured the Angels that the curfew was as much for their protection as anything else. They kept talking about 'bunches of townspeople, coming through the woods with deer rifles'. To forestall this, the police set up a command post at the point where the Willow Cove trail joined the highway.

Meanwhile, a mountain of six-packs was piling up in the middle of the camp. This was in addition to the original twenty-two cases in my car. By the time it got dark the car was half empty, so I put the rest of the beer in the back seat and locked my own gear in the trunk. I decided that any symbolic alienation I might incur by securing my valuables was worth the risk of having them all lost – which they probably would have been, for it was not long before the camp became like an animal pen. A reporter from *The Los Angeles Times* showed up the next day and said it 'looked like Dante's Inferno'. But he arrived about noon, when most of the outlaws were calm and stupefied from the ravages of the previous night. If the midday lull seemed that awful the bonfire scenes might have permanently damaged his mind.

Or perhaps not, for the ten-o'clock curfew had a drastic effect on the action. By driving all the fringe elements out of camp it forced the Angels to fall back on their own entertainment resources. Most of those who left were girls: they had seemed to be enjoying things until the deputies announced that they would either leave by the deadline or stay all night. The implications were not pleasant – at ten the law was going to pull out, seal off the area and let the orgy begin.

All afternoon the scene had been brightened by six or ten carloads of young girls from places like Fresno and Modesto and Merced who had somehow got wind of the gathering and apparently wanted to make a real party of it. It never occurred to the Angels that they would not stay the night – or the whole weekend, for that matter – so it came as a bad shock when they left. The three nurses who'd picked up Larry, Pete and Puff earlier in the day made a brave decision to stay – but then, at the last moment, they fled. 'Man, I can't stand it,' said one Angel as he watched the last of the cars lurch off down the trail. 'All that fine pussy, just wasted. That wiggy little thing with the red shoes was all *mine*! We were groovin'! How *could* she just split?'

It was a rotten show by almost any standards. Here were all these high-bottomed wenches in stretch pants and sleeveless blouses, half unbuttoned . . . beehive hairdos and blue-lidded eyes . . . ripe, ignorant little bodies talking horny all afternoon ('Oh Beth, don't these bikes just drive you kinda wild?'). Yeah, baby, wild for the open road . . . and off they went, like nuns hearing the whistle, while the grief-stricken Angels just stood there and watched. Many of them had left their own women behind, fearing trouble, but now that the trouble was dissipated, there was not going to be any strange ginch either.

Among the hardest hit was Terry the Tramp, who immediately loaded up on LSD and spent the next twelve hours locked in the back of a panel truck, shrieking and crying under the gaze of some god he had almost forgotten, but who came down that night to the level of the treetops 'and just stared – man, he just looked at me, and I tell you I was scared like a little kid'.

Other Angels rushed off to the beer market when the curfew was first announced, but their hopes for a party with the tourists were dashed when the place closed right on the dot of ten. There was nothing to do but go back to camp and get wasted. The police were lenient with late arrivals, but once in, there was no getting out.

The hours between ten and twelve were given over to massive

consumption. Around eleven I ducked into the car and worked for a while on the tape, but my monologue was constantly interrupted by people reaching through the back windows and trying to wrench the trunk open. For hours there had been so much beer in camp that nobody worried about seeing the end of it, but suddenly it all disappeared. Instead of one beer at a time, everybody who reached into the car took a six-pack. The stash had begun. It was like a run on a bank. Within minutes the back seat was empty. There were still twenty or thirty six-packs piled up near the bonfire, but these weren't for stashing. The cans were clipped off one at a time. Nobody wanted to start a run on the public-beer stock. It would have been very bad form . . . and if the hoarding became too obvious, those who planned to drink all night might get violent.

By this time various drug reactions were getting mixed up with the booze and there was no telling what any one person might do. Wild shouts and explosions burst through the darkness. Now and then would come the sound of a body plunging into the lake . . . a splash, then yelling and kicking in the water. The only light was the bonfire, a heap of logs and branches about ten feet wide and five feet tall. It lit up the whole clearing and gleamed on the headlights and handlebars of the big Harleys parked on the edge of the darkness. In the wavering orange light it was hard to see faces except those right next to you. Bodies became silhouettes; only the voices were the same.

There were about fifty girls in camp, but nearly all were 'old ladies' – not to be confused, except at serious risk, with 'mamas' or 'strange chicks'. An old lady can be a steady girl friend, a wife or even some bawdy hustler that one of the outlaws has taken a liking to. Whatever the connection, she is presumed to be spoken for, and unless she makes obvious signs to the contrary, she will usually be left alone. The Angels are very solemn about this, insisting that no member would think of violating the sanctity of another's liaison. This is true, but only up to a point. Unlike wolves, old ladies don't mate for life, and sometimes not even for a month. Many are legally married, with several children, and exist entirely apart from the general promiscuity. Others are borderline cases who simply change their minds now and then. . . . They switch loyalties without losing rank, establishing just as firm a relationship with one Angel as they previously had with another.

These can be very shifting sands. Like beauty and honesty, promiscuity is in the eyes of the beholder – at least among the Angels. An old lady who changes her mind once too often, or perhaps only once, will find herself reclassified as a mama, which means she is common property.

There are mamas at any Angel gathering, large or small. They travel as part of the troupe, like oxpeckers,* fully understanding what's expected: they are available at any time, in any way, to any Angel, friend or favoured guest – individually or otherwise. They also understand that the minute they don't like the arrangement they can leave. Most hang around for a few months, then drift on to something else. A few have been around for years, but this kind of dedication requires an almost preterhuman tolerance for abuse and humiliation.

The term 'mama' is all that remains of the original expression 'Let's go make somebody a mama', which was later shortened to 'Let's go make a mama'. Other fraternities have different ways of saying it, but the meaning is the same – a girl who's always available. A widely quoted section of the Lynch report says these girls are called 'sheep', but I have never heard an Angel use that word. It sounds like the creation of some police inspector with intensely rural memories.

The mamas aren't pretty, although some of the newer and younger ones have a sort of demented beauty that erodes so fast that you have to see it happen, over a period of months, to feel any sense of tragedy. Once the girls have developed the proper perspective, it's easy to take them for granted. One night in Sacramento the Angels ran out of beer money and decided to auction off Mama Lorraine in a bar. The top bid was twelve cents, and the girl laughed along with the others. On another occasion, Magoo was packing Mama Beverly on a run to Bakersfield when he ran out of gas. 'Do you know,' he recalls, 'I couldn't find a single gas-station attendant who would give me a free gallon of gas for a

* Webster defines oxpeckers as small, dull-coloured birds that feed on ticks which they pick from the backs of infested cattle and wild animals.

go at her.' The public prints are full of testimony by men who take pride in having 'sold their talents dearly', but people who understand that their only talent is not worth fifteen cents or a gallon of gas are not often quoted. Nor do they usually leave diaries. It would be interesting to hear, sometime, just exactly what it feels like to go up on the auction block, willing to serve any purpose, and get knocked down for twelve cents.

Most mamas don't think about it, much less talk. Their conversation ranges from gossip and raw innuendo, to fending off jibes and haggling over small amounts of money. But every now and then one of them will rap off something eloquent. Donna, a stocky, good-natured brunette who came north with the exodus from Berdoo, once put the whole thing in a nut. 'Everybody believes in something,' she said. 'Some people believe in God. I believe in the Angels.'

Each chapter has a few mamas, but only Oakland maintains as many as five or six at a time. Among other outlaw clubs the situation varies. The Gypsy Jokers are not as mama-oriented as the Angels, but the Satan's Slaves are so keen on the practice that they take their communal women down to the tattoo parlour and have 'Property of Satan's Slaves' etched permanently on the left rump-cheek. The Slaves feel that branding gives the girls a sense of security and belonging. It erases any doubt about peer-group acceptance. The branded individual is said to experience powerful and instantaneous sensations of commitment, of oneness with the organization, and those few who have taken the step form a special elite. The Angels are not given to branding their women, but the practice will probably catch on because some of them think it 'shows real class'.*

'But it takes the right girl,' said one. 'She has to really mean it. Some girls won't go for it. You know, like who wants to go to the baby doctor with a big tattoo sayin' your ass belongs to the Satan's Slaves? Or what if a girl wants to cop out sometime and get

*** In early February 1966, Terry and a Frisco Angel named George Zahn were arrested for 'contributing to the delinquency' of a fifteen-year-old girl who had 'Property of Hell's Angels' tattooed across her back at the shoulder-blade level. She also had the clap, which worries the Angels about as much as bad breath.**

married? Man, imagine the wedding night. She drops her nightie and there it is. Wow!'

There were about twenty Slaves at Bass Lake, but they didn't do much mixing. They staked out a small corner of the clearing, parked their bikes around it and spent most of the weekend lying around with their women and drinking their own wine. The Gypsy Jokers were less inhibited, but their behaviour was oddly subdued in the presence of so many Hell's Angels. Unlike the Slaves, few of the Jokers had brought girls, so they were spared the constant worry that some pill-crazed Angel might try to move in and provoke a fight that the Angels would have to win. In theory the Hell's Angels confederation is friendly with all other outlaws, but in practice the half-dozen Angel chapters clash frequently with various clubs around their own turf. In San Francisco the Jokers and the Angels nurse a long-standing enmity, but the Jokers get along famously with other Angel chapters. A similar situation prevailed for years in the Los Angeles area, where the Berdoo Angels had sporadic rumbles with the Slaves, Commancheros and Coffin Cheaters. Yet these three clubs continued to speak well of every Hell's Angel in the state except those dirty bastards from Berdoo, who kept muscling in on other people's turf. All this was changed, however, by the Monterey rape, which resulted in such overwhelming heat that the Berdoo Angels were forced into desperate coexistence with the Slaves and other L.A. clubs, who were not much better off.

The Satan's Slaves are still a power in outlaw circles, but they have lost their slashing style of the early 1960s.* Other outlaws say the Slaves have never recovered from the loss of Smackey

* The Slaves returned to prominence with a vengeance in the summer of 1966, when thirty of them ransacked an apartment house in Van Nuys, a suburb of Los Angeles. On the morning of Saturday, 6 August, three Slaves were served with eviction notices and forced to leave an apartment they had occupied for only a week. On Saturday night the three evictees returned to the building with a noisy raiding party and wreaked havoc for several hours. The terrified occupants locked their doors while the outlaws smashed sixteen windows and threw thirty pieces of furniture into the swimming pool. The Slaves threatened their ex-neighbours with further attacks if anyone called the police – which somebody finally did, but not until the motorcyclists had roared off into the night, seeking new nadirs, etc.

Jack, their legendary president, who had so much class that even the Angels held him slightly in awe. Smackey Jack stories still circulate whenever the clan gets together. I first heard about him from an easygoing Sacramento Angel named Delbert:

'Man, that Jack was outta sight. Sometimes he'd run wild for three or four days on pills and wine. He carried a pair of rusty pliers around with him and we'd sic him on strange broads. Man, he'd jerk 'em down on the ground and start pullin' their teeth out with those goddamn pliers. I was with him in a place one time when the waitress wouldn't give us any coffee. Jack climbed right over the counter and took out three of her front teeth with his pliers. Some of the things he did would turn your stomach. Once he pulled out one of his own teeth in a bar. People couldn't believe it. A lot of 'em ran out when they saw he was serious. When he finally got the thing out, he laid it down on the bar and asked if he could trade it for a drink. He was spittin' blood on the floor, but the bartender was too shook up to say anything.'

Smackey Jack's turbulent three-year reign came to an end in 1964. Few of the outlaws seem to know what happened to him. 'I heard he took a real bad fall,' said one. 'He pushed his luck about as hard as a guy could.' Motorcycle outlaws are reluctant to talk seriously about former buddies who came to a bad end; the implications are too depressing. Smackey Jack, with his penchant for free-lance dentistry, was not the type to retire peacefully. Whatever happened – whether he was jailed, killed or forced to flee anonymously – he exists in outlaw legend as a rollicking, unpredictable monster who always prevailed. His loss was a demoralizing blow to the Satan's Slaves, whose spirit was already faltering under continued police pressure. By the end of 1964 the club was on the verge of disbanding.

The Slaves, along with several of the Hell's Angels chapters, were saved from extinction by the Lynch report and the nationwide infamy that followed. It gave the outlaws something to live up to, but they could never make it big unless they stopped fighting among themselves. Barger was among the first to realize this, and the other clubs were not far behind. Their long struggle for equality was suddenly rendered futile. The publicity breakthrough gave the Angels such prestige that the other clubs had no choice but to get on the bandwagon or perish. The process of consolidation took most of 1965, and it was only in the first stages at the time of the Bass Lake Run. Of the dozen or so functioning outlaw clubs in the state, only the Jokers and the Slaves felt confident enough to show up at Bass Lake in significant strength. Individual Angel chapters might have lost their supremacy, but when all of them got together, there was no question about who had the action. All things considered, it was a nervous time for the Slaves to show up with their women, who tend towards a wispy, blondish prettiness – a tempting sight for any Hell's Angel brooding drunkenly on the whys and wherefores of an unjust sex ratio.

By eleven it was plain that every girl in camp was not only spoken for, but taken. Off in the bushes there were sounds of giggling and groaning and twigs snapping, but the hundred or so outlaws who remained around the bonfire were discreetly oblivious. Many had worked off excess energy in the traditional war games. On some earlier run they had formed two secret battle societies: The Lodge and U-Boat 13. At any moment, at the sound of a prearranged signal, the U-Boat mob would rush on some hapless Lodge partisan, crushing him under a pile of bodies. Other Lodgers would then come to the rescue, adding to the pile-up. It looked like a scramble for a loose ball in a game between the Chicago Bears and the Green Bay Packers, except at Bass Lake the human heaps involved fifty or sixty people. I remember seeing Puff, who weighs about 225, sprint for about twenty yards and dive head first into the pile with a beer in each hand. For some reason there were no injuries. The outlaws are not athletic in the sense that any are ex-lettermen, but nearly all of them stay in good shape. They don't work at it, but the way most of them live they don't have to. What work they get paid for is usually physical anyway, and when they're not working they exist on hamburgers, doughnuts and whatever else they can hustle. Many swell up with beer, but the swelling bears little resemblance to the stylish pot of the desk-bound world. Even the few fat Angels are built more like beer barrels than water balloons.

There are those who claim the outlaws don't need food because they get all their energy from pep pills. But this is a bit far-fetched. The substitution doesn't work, as anyone who ever tried it can tell you. There are drugs to stimulate latent energy, but they are worthless and enervating unless the energy is there in the first place. Taken in excess on an empty stomach, pep pills induce a kind of nervous stupor characterized by fatigue, depression, chills and soaking sweats. The Angels deal freely on the black market, and if any pill really worked as a substitute for food they would use it in large quantities, for it would vastly simplify their lives. As it is, they take their nourishment wherever they can. Girls cook for them, waitresses give them 'credit' at greasy diners, and there are always the married men, whose wives rarely balk at feeding five or six of the brethren at any hour of the day or night. According to the code, there is no such thing as one Angel imposing on another. A hungry outlaw will always be fed by one of the others who has food . . . and if times are lean all around, a foraging party will hit a supermarket and steal everything they can carry. Few clerks will try to stop a dangerous hoodlum rushing out the door with two hams and three quarts of milk. The outlaws are not apologetic about stealing food, even though it goes against their pride. They prefer to think they don't have to – but whenever they do, they aren't sneaky. While one is gathering hams or steaks another will create a disturbance to draw the clerks. A third will fill a rucksack full of cans and vegetables on the other side of the store . . . and then they will all flee at the same time through different exits. There is nothing difficult about it. All it takes is gall, a threatening appearance and a surly disregard for whatever the neighbours might think. As for the police, by the time they reach the scene of the crime the food is already being cooked, twenty blocks away.

The outlaws are not articulate when it comes to the strengths and weaknesses of the world they function in, but their instincts are finely honed. They have learned from experience that some crimes are likely to be punished, and some aren't. A Hell's Angel who wants to make a long-distance call, for instance, will usually go to a pay phone. He will deposit enough money for the first three minutes, acknowledge the operator's signal at the end of that time and talk for as long as he wants. When he finally hangs up, the operator will tell him how many coins he should put in the black box . . . but instead of paying, he laughs, spits obscenities into the phone and finishes. Unlike the normal, middle-class, hard-working

American, a motorcycle outlaw has no vested interest in the system that is represented by the voice of a telephone operator. The values of that system are completely irrelevant to him. He doesn't give a damn, and besides, he knows the phone company can't catch him. So he completes his call, abuses the operator and goes off to get happily wasted.

16

> The psychopath, like the child, cannot delay the pleasures of gratification; and this trait is one of his underlying, universal characteristics. He cannot wait upon erotic gratification which convention demands should be preceded by the chase before the kill: he must rape. He cannot wait upon the development of prestige in society: his egotistic ambitions lead him to leap into headlines by daring performances. Like a red thread the predominance of this mechanism for immediate satisfaction runs through the history of every psychopath. It explains not only his behaviour but also the violent nature of his acts. – *Robert Lindner*, Rebel Without a Cause

*

ON a run everybody gets wasted. As midnight approached, the Willow Cove campsite took on an air of bedlam. People with glazed eyes wandered into the lake and sat down. Others fell against bikes or shouted meaningless abuse at friends they couldn't recognize. Rather than mix in the deranged traffic around the bonfire, I drifted back to my car, on the edge of darkness, and joined a group of Gypsy Jokers. They were still holding back, letting the Angels put on the show.

Hutch, the spokesman, seemed to have a philosophic bent and he wanted to talk. Just what was the meaning of this whole goddamn thing about motorcycle gangs? He didn't claim to know, but he wanted to explore it. 'We aren't really bad,' he said. 'But we aren't good either. Hell, I don't know. Sometimes I like this scene, and sometimes I don't. But the thing that really pisses me off is the newspapers. I don't mind them calling us punks and that kind of stuff, but you know? Even when we pull off some really bad shit, they *still* get it wrong. When I read those things I don't even recognize myself. Hell, we should probably kick your ass just for being a reporter.'

The others chuckled, but it occurred to me that the same remark might spark a different reaction later on, when the drink began to take hold. Yet it seemed that if the outlaws really wanted no part of the Press, they would have bounced me out of camp much earlier. Just before dark Tiny had driven off two cameramen who claimed to be from C.B.S., and shortly after that he'd warned me about using the tape recorder, saying he'd throw it in the fire if he saw it. Except in posed or prearranged situations most Angels are leery about being photographed or recorded and even of talking to a man with a notebook. Tapes and film are regarded as especially dangerous because they can't be denied. This is true even in peaceful situations, where a casual photograph can place a man at the scene of a crime not yet committed. An Angel who gets arrested on suspicion of manslaughter in Oakland can always find witnesses to swear he was in San Francisco that night – but he is done for if any newspaper has a photo of him talking to the victim ten minutes prior to the fatal fight. Tape recordings can also be incriminating, particularly if one of the outlaws gets strung out on booze or pills and begins bragging about what Senator Murphy calls 'their wild acts and defiance of decency'. This has happened. In one instance Barger took three hours of tape from a reporter and went over it carefully, erasing anything that seemed incriminating. Since then he has passed the word that nobody gives interviews without checking with him first.

The Jokers don't answer to Barger, however, and at that point they were eager to get the ear of any journalist who might give them a boost up the status ladder. Hutch is a bright fellow, about six-two, with thick blond hair and a face that any Arthur Murray studio would hire on sight. He works as a labourer now and then, but only to stay eligible for unemployment insurance, known in outlaw circles as the 52-26 Club. At twenty-seven he exists on the fringe of the labour market, working only in emergencies. When I saw him several weeks later at his parents' apartment in a prosperous residential district of San Francisco, he talked about motorcycle outlaws with a lazy objectivity that was hard to mesh with his concern for more and better Press notices. I was only dimly aware of it then, but after a while I realized that if the outlaws were ever forced to choose between consistently bad and biased publicity or no publicity at all, they wouldn't hesitate to choose the former.

While Hutch and I were talking, another Joker joined the conversation. He introduced himself as Bruno, or Harpo, or something along those lines, and handed me one of his cards. Many outlaws carry business cards, some of them very elaborate. Frenchy from Frisco hands out shiny black ones with silver lettering. The idea of cards was born when the Frisco Angels, lamenting their rotten image, decided to win the public over to their side by aiding every stranded motorist they could find and then leaving a card saying, on one side. 'You Have Been Assisted by a Member of the Hell's Angels, Frisco', and on the other, 'When we do right no one remembers. When we do wrong no one forgets'. It was not quite as classy as leaving a silver bullet or a chromed headbolt, but they felt it was better than nothing. For several years the Frisco Angels made a point of offering their mechanical talents to any motorist with problems, but that was before all the publicity. It would be very risky now.

Consider the reaction of a middle-aged roofing-and-siding salesman, cruising along with his wife and two children in the family Mustang on a remote stretch of Highway 101. Something in the engine begins to clank, so he pulls on to the shoulder and gets out to look. Suddenly he hears a rumble of motorcycles. A dozen Hell's Angels pull over, get off their bikes and walk towards him. Thinking quickly, he jerks the oil dipstick out of his engine and begins lashing at the thugs. His wife, terror-stricken, leaps out of the car and runs into a nearby cornfield, weaving through the stalks like a lizard. The children cower, the man is punched, and moments later a Highway Patrol car arrives. The outlaws are jailed on $3,000 bond for aggravated assault and attempted rape. A week later, when things are explained and all charges are dropped, the man apologizes . . . but each Angel is $300 poorer, and the 'courtesy cards' are left at home next time. The outlaws still carry cards, but not the highway variety. Most show only the club emblems, the member's name and the ever-present one-percenter sign. None give printed addresses or phone numbers. These are sometimes written on the back of the cards, but they change so frequently that it's impossible to keep them current. Most of the cards I have contain three or four phone numbers, nearly all disconnected for nonpayment.

For some reason I no longer have Bruno's (or Harpo's) card, but I remember him because he stole a full beer from me. I couldn't quite believe it, for he had gone to great lengths to make sure I didn't have any wrong impressions about the Gypsy Jokers. From time to time we would put our beers down on the trunk of the car we were leaning against. Just before he left I opened a fresh can, put it down and saw Bruno–Harpo exchange it deftly for his own, which was empty. When I mentioned this to Hutch, he shrugged and said: 'It was probably just a habit, one of those tricks you pick up from drinking in bars when you're broke.'

Habits like these are widespread in outlaw society. The outlaws can be very friendly with outsiders, but not all of them equate friendship with mutual trust. Some will steal senselessly, out of sheer habit or compulsion, while others will take pains to protect a naïve outsider against the more light-fingered of the brethren – who are not to be pitied or censured, but only watched.*

There is a story about an Angel who went to use the bathroom in the home of a stranger he was visiting. While there, he rummaged through the medicine cabinet and found a bottle of orange pills that looked like Dexedrine – which he promptly ate. Later, when he felt sick, he told the host about the pills and sheepishly asked if he might have made a mistake. It developed that he had taken a massive overdose of cortizone, a drug well known for its anti-arthritic properties, unpredictable reactions and weird side effects. The man whose pills had been eaten was not happy and told the Angel he would probably break out in a rash of boils and running sores that would keep him in agony for weeks. On hearing this, the outlaw nervously retired to whatever bed he was using at the time. The boils never came, but he said he felt sick and weak and 'queer all over' for about ten days. When he recovered, he said the incident had taught him a valuable lesson: he no longer had to worry about what kind of pills he ate, because his body could handle anything he put into it.

The theft of my beer sent me back across the clearing for

* In twelve months of relatively careless dealing with the Angels, I had only two things stolen: the Lynch report was the first; the second was a heavy classic-looking Italian switch-blade knife, which I kept on my mantelpiece and used as a letter opener.

another. By this time it was obvious to everyone standing around the campfire that the beer mountain was almost gone. Within an hour or so, those with nothing stashed were going to be thirsty. This would cause tension, and the hoarders were among the most insistent that another beer run should be made. Otherwise, they would have to share their stash or fight. Some people were too stoned and wasted to care about beer, but a hard core of about fifty drinkers who intended to stay on their feet all night began the laborious process of getting up a collection. By now the camp was badly disorganized. Barger had disappeared somewhere in the trees, and those remaining around the fire were the least likely to have money.

The fact that all the Bass Lake stores were closed was immaterial. Tiny said he had a 'friend' who ran a market out on the highway. He would open the store at any hour of the night if somebody came around the back and rapped on the window of his bedroom. I listened carefully because I knew who would have to go get the stuff. The police were not going to let any Angels out of camp, and the only non-Angels still around were me and a young boy who had wandered in earlier and was now worried about getting home. Until he announced this, everybody thought he was somebody else's friend, but in fact he was a stowaway. Nobody was particularly anxious to help him get out of camp, but he insisted that he had to meet some friends who were cruising up and down the highway, looking for him. For a moment he was standing next to Tiny by the fire, and the contrast was mind-bending. A clean-cut lad about sixteen, wearing a white T-shirt and chinos, taking the mountain air with a huge hairy outcast given over to all forms of depravity and wearing a patch on his jacket saying, 'I'm bound to go to heaven because I've already served my time in hell'. Together they looked like figures in some ominous painting, a doomsday portrait of the human animal confronting itself . . . as if a double-yolked egg had hatched both a chicken and a wildebeest.

Tiny would make a good reporter or an actor's agent. He has a fine sense of 'contacts', of being in touch with what's happening, inside dope, the latest. He is an inveterate phone-user. Long distance means nothing to him. In Oakland he has several pay phones on which he takes collect calls from Boston, Providence, New York,

Philadelphia and God knows where else. He operates like a master criminal, always checking the action, the chances, the possibilities. When he sits down in a bar he faces the door. While other Angels drink and talk aimlessly Tiny broods about unreachable contacts, unreported action and all the loose ends that might come unravelled at any moment.

He is six foot five, and his weight varies between 250 and 270, depending on his frame of mind – which gyrates so wildly that he is probably the most dangerous of the Angels and also one of the best-humoured. Others are quicker to fight, but they don't cause half as much damage. Tiny hurts people. When he loses his temper he goes completely out of control and his huge body becomes a lethal weapon. It is difficult to see what role he might play in the Great Society.

While the beer collection was being taken up, the headlights of a car came poking through the trees. A few bikes had come in since ten, but this was the first car, and the sight of it caused a stir. It turned out to be Filthy Phil, an ex-president of the Frisco chapter, who explained that he'd hidden a fifteen-year-old girl on the highway and needed some help to get her past the roadblock.

This jelled things. It was decided to do everything at once. Phil and I would go for the beer, try to get the boy past the roadblock on the way out, and take Pete and Puff to a point in the woods where they could locate the girl. Phil was looking anything but filthy. He was wearing dress slacks, a white shirt and a blue cashmere sweater. He'd had a hard time getting into camp, he said, because the cops wouldn't believe he was an Angel. He looked more like an off-duty cop, or maybe a brawny bouncer from some club on the Sunset Strip. His car, a new white Chevrolet Impala, was as out of place as his clothes.

About fifty yards short of the highway he pointed out where the girl was hiding, and the two Angels went off through the woods to get her. We continued along the trail to the roadblock. There were three cars and at least ten cops, with a white-haired Highway Patrol captain in charge. Our stowaway was sitting in the back seat, and just as the captain began asking us what we were up to, another car came by and the boy shouted: 'That's them! That's them!' I reached over and blew the horn, the other car stopped, the boy leaped out, and seconds later he was gone. The police thought something had been put over on them. 'You mean, that kid was in there all this time?' one asked. 'Was he hurt? What's going on in there?'

'Nothing,' I said. 'It's dull. Go in and see for yourself. You'll be surprised.'

The captain, who'd been mulling over the bogus Press credentials I'd given him, then told us we couldn't leave. A long argument ensued, having to do with freedom of the Press, a citizen's right to buy beer at any legal hour, and the possibility that the Angels might go looking for beer on their own hook if we were turned back.

'Where would you buy it?' the captain asked. 'All the places are closed.'

'We'll go as far as we have to,' I said. 'There's plenty of time.'

They had a quick huddle and then said we could go – thinking, no doubt, that we'd have to drive sixty miles to Madera, to find an open bar. As we left, one of the cops smiled and said, 'Have a good trip'.

Ten minutes later we parked beside what appeared to be Tiny's friend's market, but it was hard to be sure. It was farther away than he'd said, and much bigger than his description. Because of this I was a little hesitant to go around back and start rapping on dark windows. If we had the wrong market it could be a serious mistake. But it seemed worth a try, so I rapped, keeping ready to sprint around the corner at the first sound of a gun being cocked. Nobody answered, so I rapped again. At any instant I expected to hear a woman shrieking: 'Henry! They're here! Oh God, they've come for us! Shoot, Henry! Shoot!' And even if Henry didn't blow my head off, he'd be sure to call the police and we'd be busted for attempted burglary, trying to crash a beer market in the dead of night.

Finally I heard movement inside, and somebody yelled: 'Who is it?'

'A friend of Tiny's,' I said quickly. 'We need beer.'

A light came on and a friendly face appeared. The man came out in his bathrobe and opened the store. He didn't seem at all upset. 'Yeah, good old Tiny,' he said. 'He's a real gas, ain't he?' I agreed, and gave him the $35 the Angels had collected around the fire. Phil added $5 more, and we left with eight cases. The man held Tiny in such high esteem that he charged only $1.25 a six-pack instead of the $1.50 we'd paid at the other place. When we got back to the roadblock, the captain flashed his light in the car and seemed shocked to see the beer. We'd been gone less than a half-hour. 'Where'd you get it?' he asked.

'Down the road,' I said.

He shook his head glumly and waved us into camp. Obviously, some dirty work was afoot. I felt a little sorry for him. Here he was, standing out on the highway all night, sworn to protect the citizens of Bass Lake, and the very people most likely to suffer looting if the Hell's Angels ran wild were helping to get the hoodlums drunk.

We were received in camp with cheers and shouting. Our eight cases made the nut. The hoarders wisely fell back on their own stash, and sometime around four a big contingent from the south rolled in with several more cases. The rest of the night was more a question of endurance than enjoyment. Magoo, a twenty-six-year-old teamster from Oakland, stayed by the fire and kept stoking. When somebody warned him not to burn everything up on the first night he replied: 'What the hell? There's a whole forest. We got plenty of firewood.' Magoo is one of the most interesting of the Angels because his mind seems wholly immune to the notions and tenets of twentieth-century American life. Like most of the others, he is a high-school dropout, but his gig with the teamsters gives him a decent income and he doesn't have much to worry about. He drives a truck whenever he gets the call – sometimes six days a week and sometimes only one – and he says he enjoys the work especially after a long layoff. One night in Oakland he showed up wearing a white shirt under his colours and seeming very pleased with himself: 'I did some righteous work today for the first time in a long time,' he said. 'I unloaded thirty-five thousand pounds of frozen chickens, even stole one. It made me feel good to do some work for a change.'

Magoo is a pill freak, and when he gets wired up, he does a lot of talking. Despite his Cro-Magnon appearance, he has a peculiar dignity that can only be dealt with on its own terms. He is easily insulted, but unlike some of the others, he distinguishes between accidental insults and those which are obviously intentional. Instead of bashing people he doesn't like – in the style of Fat Freddy, a heavy-set Mexican, the Oakland chapter's punchout artist – Magoo will simply turn his back on them. His opinions are flavoured with a morality that seems more instinctive than learned. He is very earnest, and although much of his talk is weird and rambling, it is shot through with riffs of something like primitive Christianity and a strong dose of Darwin. Magoo started the Porterville riot in 1963. He was the one who, according to the news magazines, 'mercilessly beat' the old man in the tavern. Here is Magoo's version:

'I was sitting there at the end of a horseshoe bar, just drinking beer and minding my own business when this old bastard came up, picked up my beer and threw it in my face. "What the hell!" I yelled, and I stood up quick. "Uh-oh," says the guy, "I made a mistake." So I clipped him with a right and he stumbled. Then another and he was going down, then I finished him off with another punch and left him there on the floor. That's all. Hell, what would you do if some sonofabitch threw a beer in your face?'

One night in Oakland, Magoo and I got into a long conversation about guns. I expected the usual crap about 'dum-dums' and 'shoot-outs' and 'cooling guys with a rod', but Magoo talked more like a candidate for the Olympic pistol team. When I casually mentioned man-size targets, he snapped: 'Don't tell me about shooting at *people*. I'm talking about match sticks.' And he was. He shoots a Luger ·22 revolver, an expensive, long-barrelled, precision-made gun that no hood would even consider. And on days when he isn't working, he goes out to the dump and tries to shoot the heads off match sticks. 'It's hard as hell,' he said. 'But now and then I'll do it just right, and light one.'

Magoo is more self-contained than most of the Angels. He is one of the few who doesn't mind telling you his real name. He is married to a quiet, ripe-looking girl named Lynn, but he seldom takes her to any Angel party that might get wild. Usually he comes alone and he doesn't say much unless he decides to drop some pills, which cause him to rave like Lord Buckley.

At Bass Lake he tended the fire with the single-minded zeal of a man who's been eating bennies like popcorn. The flames lit up his glasses and his Nazi helmet. Earlier in the day he had chopped his Levis at knee level with a hunting knife, exposing his thick white legs for about ten inches before they disappeared again into black motorcycle boots. The effect was an obscene mockery of Bermuda shorts.

Sometime before dawn I was standing by the fire and listening to Magoo make one of his classy propositions. He was talking to two other Angels and a girl, trying to convince them: 'Let's the four of us go off in the bushes,' he said. 'We'll smoke up some weed, get all fucked up, feel no fuckin' pain – and if she wants to lay some body on us, why not?' He waited a moment, but there was no reply, so he continued: 'You're an Angel, aren't you? I never manhandled you, did I? Never given you a hard time. So what's wrong? Let's go over to the bushes and smoke up some weed. She's an Angel woman. Hell, she should swing.'

At that moment, without waiting for a reply, Magoo turned slightly at the hip, not moving his feet, and urinated into the fire. There was a loud hiss as some of the embers went black. The stench caused people to move away. Perhaps he meant it as a mating signal, a carnal gesture designed to strip away all pretence, but all it did was queer his act. The Angel whose woman was being hustled had not been happy with the situation, and Magoo's mindless indulgence of his bladder gave the others a good excuse to drift off, seeking an upwind position.

Sometime later, on the other side of the fire, I heard two Angels several feet behind me. They were sitting on the ground, leaning against one of the bikes and talking very seriously while they passed a joint back and forth. I listened for a moment, keeping my back to them, but all I heard was one emphatic sentence: 'Man I'd give all the weed in the world to clear up the mess in my head.' I quickly moved away, hoping I hadn't been recognized.

At my car I found several people rummaging through the back seat, looking for beer. They had been out in the woods for a while and didn't realize that another delivery had come in. One of these was the inscrutable Ray, president of the Fresno chapter. Not even the Angels understand Ray. He is too friendly with outsiders, he introduces himself formally and always shakes hands. There is nothing threatening about him except perhaps his size – about six foot three, and two hundred pounds. His blond hair is short by Angel standards, and his face is as wholesome as the cover on a Boy Scout handbook. Some of the outlaws call him a socialite, implying that his connection with the Angels is more dilettantish than desperate. Which is probably true. Ray gives the impression of having options, so the others assume he'll eventually cop out for something with more of a future. Something like stoop labour, or a steady job in a grease pit. Ray is twenty-five and enjoys being an Angel, but he is not entirely committed – and because of this, he is a bone in the throat of those outlaws who don't have even the illusion of an option. If Ray moved to Oakland he would have to show some really fiendish class before he could get into Barger's chapter. He would have to beat up a cop in public, or rape a waitress on the counter of her own hash house. Only then, after burning his bridges back to the square world, would he be welcome in the legion of the damned.

But Ray is content to stay in Fresno, where he stages wild parties and does a booming trade in motorcycles. He is such a bike zealot that Angels in both L.A. and the Bay Area use him as a sort of clearing house. He travels constantly, and always on his hog. One weekend he will be at the Blue Blazes Bar in Fontana, checking on the Berdoo action, and on the next he'll turn up at the Luau or the Sinners Club in Oakland . . . cheerfully giving advice, shaking hands and trying to organize a party. At the height of the civil rights upheaval in Alabama, Ray rode his bike all the way to Selma – not to march, but just to see what was happening. 'I thought maybe them niggers was getting out of hand,' he explained with a smile. 'So I just went down to check on 'em.'

When Ray met Bill Murray in Fontana and learned he was doing an article for *The Saturday Evening Post*, he invited him up to Fresno and gave him specific instructions on how to make the connection. 'When you get to town,' he said, 'go out Blackstone Avenue until you find Ratcliff Stadium. Ask for me in the filling station across the street. I'm sometimes hard to find, but they'll know where I am.'

But something went wrong, and Murray spent half a day futilely checking leads – which were all false, because Ray's human antennae took Murray for a cop. He did, however, locate a house where the Fresno Angels had recently staged a party. It made such an impression on him that he quickly left town. Here is the way he described it:

The house was set back 100 or 200 yards from Blackstone Avenue, which is the main road north to Yosemite, and it was just one of many similar ones in the neighborhood – a one-storey, white-frame, three-room bungalow with a tiny front yard and a general air of dilapidation. Nonetheless, it was hard to miss. Part of the fence had been flattened, all of the windows had been smashed, one of the fenceposts had been rammed through a door, and the branches of two small trees in the front yard had been torn away from the trunks and dragged grotesquely on the ground; between them, an armchair sprawled face down, gutted, its arms smashed. On the back of the chair, written in red ink, were the words:

Hells Angels
13 卐 69er
Dee – Berdoo

I went into the house and stood in the center of what must have once been the living room. It was hard to tell, because I had never seen such utter chaos: every piece of furniture had been smashed; debris littered the floors – broken glass, torn clothing, empty cans, wine and beer bottles, crockery, boxes. Every door had been ripped off its hinges, and a large hole gaped where an air conditioner had been torn away and carted off. The word 'cops' had been scrawled in large red letters over a caved-in bed and used as a target for bottles and anything else that had come to hand. Under it was written, 'Yea, Fresno', over another swastika. All the walls had been defaced. . . .

The immediate neighbors were respectable people whose houses were not more than a few yards away; they said that the house had been rented to a single girl who had seemed all right. The next morning the motorcyclists had started to arrive; there must have been twenty or twenty-five of them, including their girls, and their party had lasted nearly two weeks, until the police had finally come without being summoned. No one had protested or called for help. The man who lived directly in back of the house, and who hadn't had a night's sleep in all that time, explained why. 'You're not going to buck an army,' he said. 'They wouldn't have stood for it. They're like a bunch of animals.'

17

rapere: to seize, enjoy hastily . . . – *Latin dictionary*

*

THE Fresno Angels don't make news very often, but when they do, it is usually for something outlandish, some genuinely wretched affront to everything the squares hold dear. One of these was a brutal 'rape' in a little town called Clovis, near Fresno, in the Central Valley. When the story hit the papers, the citizens were outraged for miles around.

A thirty-six-year-old widow and mother of five claimed she'd been yanked out of a bar where she was having a quiet beer with another woman, then carried to an abandoned shack behind the bar and raped repeatedly for two and a half hours by fifteen or twenty Hell's Angels and finally robbed of $150. That's how the story appeared in the San Francisco newspapers the next day, and it was kept alive for a few more days by the woman's claims that she was getting phone calls threatening her life if she testified against her assailants.

Then, four days after the crime, the victim was arrested on charges of 'sexual perversion'. The true story emerged, said the Clovis chief of police, when the woman was 'confronted by witnesses. Our investigation shows she was not raped,' said the chief. 'She participated in lewd acts in the tavern with at least three Hell's Angels before the owners ordered them out. She encouraged their advances in the tavern, then led them to an abandoned house in the rear. . . . She was not robbed, but according to a woman who'd accompanied her, had left her house early in the evening with five dollars to go bar-hopping.'

This incident did not appear in the Attorney General's report, but it is as valid as any that did and it is one of the classic Hell's Angels stories. The O. Henry gimp in the plotline gives it real style. Somebody should have done a public opinion survey in Fresno, getting one set of reactions after the first version of the 'rape' appeared, and another when the worm did a full turn. Like the Monterey rape, the Clovis outrage was one of those cases where the prosecuting attorneys would have fared better if their witness *had* been intimidated into silence.

The Clovis story is amusing not because of what happened, but because of the thundering disparity between accusation and reality. Here was the *rape mania*, the old bugaboo, one of the big keys to the whole Hell's Angels phenomenon.

Nobody is objective about rape. It is a horror and a titillation and a mystery all at once. Women are terrified of being raped, but somewhere in the back of every womb there is one rebellious nerve end that tingles with curiosity whenever the word is mentioned. This is even more terrifying, for it hints at basic depravity and secret lusts too dangerous to even think about. Men speak of rapists with loathing, and talk about their victims as if they carried some tragic brand. They are sympathetic, but always aware. Raped women have been divorced by their husbands – who couldn't bear to live with the awful knowledge, the visions, the possibility that it *wasn't really rape*. There is the bone of it, the unspeakable mystery. Everybody has heard the joke about the lawyer who used a quill and an ink bottle to get his client acquitted on a rape charge. He told the jury there was no such thing as rape, and proved it by having a witness try to put the quill in the bottle – which he manipulated so deftly that the witness finally gave up.

That sounds like one of Cotton Mather's jokes, or the wisdom of somebody very much like him – somebody who never had his arm bent up between his shoulder blades. Any lawyer who says there's no such thing as rape should be hauled out to a public place by three large perverts and buggered at high noon, with all his clients watching.

California averages more than 3,000 reported cases of forcible rape every year – or almost three a day. This would be a menacing statistic if it were not meaningless. In 1963, an average year, 3,058 forcible rapes were reported. But only 231 of these cases were brought to trial, and only 157 rapists were actually convicted. There is no way of knowing how many rapes were actually committed. Many went unreported or were hushed up by victims who feared the publicity and possible humiliation of a public trial.

Rape victims concerned for their reputations often refuse to press charges, and few prosecutors will compel them to testify. A rapist who confines his lust to middle- and upper-class ladies is on pretty safe ground. But he is taking his life in his hands when he preys on women to whom the rape stigma has little meaning. Given a victim willing to testify in open court, an articulate prosecutor can re-create the 'attack' in such vivid, carnal detail that even the meekest defendant will appear to the jury as a depraved Hun. The small percentage of rape cases that come to trial would indicate that the state only tries those it feels sure of. Despite this, only seven out of ten California rape trials end in conviction, while the figure for all other felony trials is eight out of ten.

The rape mania is such a complex phenomenon that it will eventually have to be dealt with by Presidential fiat. A blue ribbon commission will have to probe it, along with logrolling and the fatback syndrome. Meanwhile, the Hell's Angels will continue to be arrested for rape with monotonous regularity. It has come to be known as one of their specialities – particularly gang rape, the most painful and degrading kind of sex assault. Yet although most of the membership has been arrested for rape at one time or another, in fifteen years less than half a dozen have been convicted. The outlaws insist they don't rape, but police say they do it continually. Convictions are hard to get, the cops say, because most women are reluctant to testify, and those few who are willing usually change their minds after the Angels – or some of the mamas – threaten to cut them up or 'turn them out' for the whole club.

In July 1966 four Angels went on trial in Sonoma County for the forcible rape – at an Angel Party – of a nineteen-year-old San Francisco model. Nineteen Angels were charged, but the county attorney narrowed it down to four – Terry, Tiny, Mouldy Marvin and Magoo Two* – and went into court with no doubt in his mind that he would get four convictions. Two weeks later, after three Angel defence attorneys had cross-examined the victim, a jury of eleven women and one man voted for acquittal. They needed less than two hours to reach a unanimous verdict.

There is a certain amount of truth in the intimidation charges,

* Another Magoo – different from Oakland Magoo.

but not nearly enough to explain why the Angels are so often charged and seldom convicted. The biggest part of the truth lies in the problem of defining an act of rape in terms of what actually happened. Obviously, if a woman is jerked off the street and forced to commit fornication against her will, that is rape. Yet the Angels say this never happens.

'Why take a chance on a fifty-year rape rap?' said one. 'Hell, rape's no fun anyway – not if it's real – and we get all the action we can handle just by standing around. Christ, I've had women proposition me at stoplights, I've had 'em open my fly in bars without even saying hello, and if nothing happens by accident I just call around and find out who's horny.'

'Sure, we'll take whatever we can get,' said another. 'But I've never yet heard a girl yell rape until it was all over and she got to thinking about it. Let's face it, a lot of women can't make it with just one guy at a time, they can't get their jollies. But the trouble is that sometimes a girl wants to stop before we do, or maybe while she's taking on fifteen guys in the back of a pickup truck somebody heists a few bucks from her purse – so she flips her lid and brings the heat down on us. Or maybe we get rousted and there she is all naked in the middle of a bunch of Hell's Angels, so suddenly she's been raped. What can we say? It's an automatic bust. But all we have to do is get a lawyer in her ear, tell her all the stuff that'll come out in court, and she decides to drop charges. Most of our rape raps never even get to court.'

There are stories even in police records of girls who freely admitted to making it with two or three Angels and then trying to call a halt. What does a jury make of testimony to the effect that the first hump was for love, the next two for kicks and all the others were rape? An alleged rape victim in Oakland came to a bar one evening with an Angel she had met the night before and proceeded to do him on a pool table in a back room. One of the others looked in, saw what was happening, and naturally stood by for seconds. The girl protested, but when her true lover threatened to punch her she saw the light. After the third go she realized what she was in for and became hysterical, causing the bartender to summon the law.

Another girl rode a motorcycle up from Los Angeles and insisted on joining the club. The Angels told her she could, but only after she showed some class. 'Man, what a nutty broad,' said one. 'She came to the party the next night with a big St Bernard dog, and what an *act* she put on! I tell you it damn near blew my mind.' He smiled wistfully. 'After that, she took on everybody. Christ, what a bitch she was. She went right out of her gourd when she realized we weren't going to let her join the club. She called us all kinds of shit, then she went out to a phone booth and rang for the cops. We all got busted for rape, but we never heard nothin' more about it, because the broad split the next day. Nobody's seen her since.'

Whenever the word 'rape' comes up, Terry the Tramp tells the story about the 'off-the-wall broad who rolled up to the El Adobe one night in a taxi-cab – a really fine-lookin' chick. She paid the cabbie and just stood there for a minute, lookin' at us . . . and then, man, she walked across the parking lot like she owned the place and asked us what the hell we were starin' at. Then she started laughin'. "All right!" she yelled. "I fuck, I suck and I smoke a lot of dope, so let's get started!" Wow! We couldn't believe it. But by God, she wasn't lyin'. We put her in the back of that old panel truck we had then, and damn if she wasn't still yellin' for more when the bar closed. We had to take her out to the country.'

The Angels are full of stories about girls who seek them out. They tend to embellish both the action and the girls, but few of the stories are made up out of thin air. After dozens of long nights with the outlaws, I don't recall many when there wasn't at least one girl going down for the crowd, or whoever felt the sap rising. Usually they were mamas, but now and then what the Angels call 'a strange broad' or 'new pussy' would show up. Most of these seemed to be under the impression that they were 'with' one of the Angels, and sometimes it worked out that way. The new pussy would dance a bit, drink a few beers, then roar off into the night with her Shane. Other girls, however, were taken into the panel truck and not seen again for many hours. With a few rare exceptions, the fact of some gang action in a nearby truck or back seat does not cause much of a stir. Of the thirty or so outlaws at the El Adobe on a weekend night, less than half would take the trouble to walk across the parking lot for a go at whatever ginch is available. A girl might be kept humping for hours, but only because a group of ten or so will take several turns each. Any outlaw whose old lady is around will gallantly ignore the sex action. The wives and steady girl friends won't stand for it. They don't actively resent the mamas, but they observe a rigid social barrier. One of the Oakland old ladies, a pretty, dark-haired girl named Jean, thinks mamas are pretty sad people, born losers. 'I just feel sorry for girls like Mama Beverly,' she says. 'They think they have to put out and do anything at all just so they can be around guys like the Angels. But there are a lot of girls like that. One time at a party in Richmond a girl nobody had ever seen came in and started showing around a nude picture of herself. Then she went in the back room with half-dozen of the guys. Man, you ought to see the girls who flock around when the Angels are on a run, and just because they're Angels. If any girls claim she was raped by the Angels, it was most likely because she came up and asked for it.'

That sounds a bit harsh. Invariably, the girls who pursue the Hell's Angels are in the grip of some carnal urgency, and some are deranged sluts, but few really look forward to being gang-raped. It is a very ugly experience – a fact the Angels tacitly admit by classifying it as a form of punishment. A girl who squeals on one of the outlaws, or who deserts him for somebody wrong, can expect to be 'turned out', as they say, to 'pull the Angel train'. Some of the boys will pick her up one night and take her to a house where the others are sitting around with not much else to do. It is a definite ceremony, like the purging of a witch; the girl is stripped, held down on the floor and mounted by whoever has seniority. The punishment is administered in a place where everyone can watch, including the mamas and old ladies, although most of the Angel women are careful to avoid these shows. Not all the outlaws go for them either. The purging is usually done by the wronged Angel and a handful of others with a taste for this kind of discipline. Every chapter has a few gang-bang aficionados; they are usually the meanest of the lot . . . not the toughest, but the ones who are unpredictably hostile, day and night, in all kinds of situations.

At a party many months after I first met the Angels when they were taking my presence for granted, I came on a scene that still hovers, in my mind, somewhere between a friendly sex orgy and an all-out gang rape. It was not an Angel party, but they had been invited, and twenty or so showed up for what turned into a two-day bash. Almost immediately several of the outlaws located a girl, the ex-wife of another guest, who agreed to make the beast with two backs in a small building set apart from the main house. Which she did, and happily so, with the chosen trio. But word quickly spread of the 'new mama', and soon she was surrounded by a large group of onlookers . . . drinking, laughing and taking a quick turn whenever some vacancy occurred.

I keep a crumpled yellow note from that night; not all of the writing is decipherable, but some of it reads like this: 'Pretty girl about twenty-five lying on wooden floor, two or three on her all the time, one kneeling between her legs, one sitting on her face and somebody else holding her feet . . . teeth and tongues and pubic hair, dim light in a wooden shack, sweat and semen gleaming on her thighs and stomach, red and white dress pushed up around her chest . . . people standing around yelling, wearing no pants, waiting first second or third turns . . . girl jerking and moaning, not fighting, clinging, seems drunk, incoherent, not knowing, drowning . . .'

It was not a particularly sexual scene. The impression I had at the time was one of vengeance. The atmosphere in the room was harsh and brittle, almost hysterical. Most people took a single turn, then either watched or wandered back to the party. But a hard core of eight or ten kept at her for several hours. In all, she was penetrated in various ways no less than fifty times, and probably more. At one point, when the action slowed down, some of the Angels went out and got the girl's ex-husband, who was stumbling drunk. They led him into the shack and insisted he take his own turn. The room got nervous, for only a few of the outlaws were anxious to carry things that far. But the sight of her former old man brought the girl out of her daze just enough to break the silent tension. She leaned forward, resting on her elbows, and asked him to kiss her. He did, and then groggily took his turn while the others cheered.

Afterwards the girl rested for a while and then wandered around the party in a blank sort of way and danced with several people. Later she was taken back for another session. When she finally reappeared I saw her trying to dance with her ex-husband, but all she could do was hang on his neck and sway back and forth. She didn't seem to hear the music – a rock-'n'-roll band with a very swinging beat.

What would a jury make of that one – presuming they could know all the facts, circumstances and ramifications? If the girl was raped why didn't she protest or ask somebody for help? The Angels were vastly outnumbered, and it was not the sort of party they would have wanted to break up for the sake of a would-be mama. There was plenty of action around, and if anybody had protested the gang-bang the outlaws would have called it off. But nobody seemed bothered, and one or two of the non-Angel guests finally joined in. The girl had several chances to leave the party and call the police, but that would have been out of the question. Girls who get turned out at Hell's Angels parties don't think of police in terms of protection.

But sex is only one aspect of rape's broader definition. The word derives from the Latin *rapere*, 'to take by force'; and according to Webster, the contemporary translation ranges from (1) 'the crime of having sexual intercourse with a woman or girl forcibly and without her consent' to (2) 'the act of seizing and carrying away by force' or (3) 'to plunder or destroy, as in warfare'. So the Hell's Angels, by several definitions, including their own, are working rapists . . . and in this downhill half of our twentieth century they are not so different from the rest of us as they sometimes seem. They are only more obvious.

18

Now Bonnie and Clyde are the Barrow gang
I'm sure you all have read
How they rob and steal,
And how those who squeal
Are usually found dying or dead.
There are lots of untruths to their write-ups,
They are not so merciless as that;
They hate all the laws,
The stool pigeons, spotters and rats.
They class them as cold-blooded killers,
They say they are heartless and mean.
But I say this with pride,
That I once knew Clyde
When he was honest and upright and clean.

– Bonnie Parker who had nine notches on her pistol when Texas police finally did her in

Day & Night –
Whoever crashed; he painted & burnt
But!!!!
One day he crashed and –
was burnt –
and was also painted
But!!!!!!
Now he's off and running –
Strong –
He doesn't hold a grudge
But PLEASE *don't get him wrong*
Because if you CRASH
It will certainly be your ass!

– Poem found on a wall at a Hell's Angel party

*

NOBODY was raped at Willow Cove. The dearth of strange broads drove most of the outlaws to drunken despair, and by the time I decided to sleep that night there wasn't a sober human being in the camp. More than half of the fifty or so outlaws still standing around the bonfire had lost all contact with reality. Some just stood like zombies and stared vacantly at the flames. Others would brood for a while, then suddenly begin shouting gibberish, which echoed across the lake like the screaming of many loons. Now and then a cherry bomb would go off in the fire, blasting sparks and embers in all directions.

Before I went under, I made sure to lock the car doors and roll the windows up far enough so that nobody could reach in. The Angels are hell on people who pass out at parties, and one of their proudest traditions is the sleepless first night of any run. Several times when I was looking for somebody I was told 'He's hiding to crash'. For a while I thought the term had something to do with an overdose of brain-ticklers – the maddened victim having slunk off in the woods like a sick animal, to ride out his delirium without disturbing the others. But crashing means nothing more sinister than going on the nod, either from booze or simple fatigue. When this happens – if the unfortunate has not found a safe hiding-place – the others will immediately begin tormenting him. The most common penalty for crashing is the urine shower; those still on their feet gather quietly around the sleeper and soak him from head to foot. Other penalties are more sophisticated. Mouldy Marvin is widely admired for his work on crashers. He once wired Terry the Tramp to an electrical outlet, then soaked his Levis with beer and plugged him in. Jimmy from Oakland, one of the quieter Angels, recalls crashing on a run to Sacramento and being set on fire. 'The bastards painted my glasses black, wrote all over me with lipstick and then burned me,' he says with a grin. Magoo once woke up at a party to find himself handcuffed, clamped in leg irons, and two burning matchbooks in his lap. 'I begged somebody to piss on me,' he said. 'Man, I was on fire!'

As dawn approached there were less than twenty moving bodies in the camp. One of the Jokers I'd been talking to earlier had become fascinated with the word 'shunt'. It caught his ear when I referred to them having been 'shunted off' to a bad campsite. He repeated the word with a grin, then went off to play with it for a while. Several hours later I heard him urge another Joker: 'Say, man, let's go into town and shunt somebody.' By four in the morning the word had grown like a tumour in his consciousness and he wandered around the fire, buttonholing people and asking: 'What would you do if I said I was gonna shunt you?' Or: 'Say, man, can you lend me some shunt until morning? I'm hurtin'.' Then he would laugh distractedly and stagger off towards the remains of the beer mountain, which by that time was built almost entirely of empties. Now and then one of the outlaws, unable to find a full can, would fly into a rage and start kicking the empties in all directions until somebody came to help him. And behind all the other sounds, as always, was the revving and booming of motorcycle engines. Some of the Angels would sit on their bikes for a while, letting them idle, then kill the engine and move out again to socialize. It seemed to give them new energy, like a battery charge. The last sound I heard that night was the peaceful idling of a hog right next to the car.

The next morning I woke up to the same noise, but this time it was deafening. Apparently some enemy had crept in during the night and screwed every one of the carburettor adjustments, causing them all to need retuning. There was a big crowd by the still-smoking bonfire, and in the middle of it I could see Barger talking to a bald little man who seemed to have St Vitus's dance. He was a reporter from *The Los Angeles Times* and he was very much on edge, even though there were several deputies in camp. He was writhing and sweating like a man who'd burst into a cannibal fort to ask for the chief's daughter. He introduced himself as Jerry Cohen. Just as he started to explain what he wanted, Tiny rushed up to Barger, threw his arms around him and planted a sloppy wet kiss on his mouth. This is a guaranteed square-jolter, and the Angels are gleefully aware of the reaction it gets. 'They can't stand it,' says Terry. 'It blows their minds every time – especially the tongue bit.' The sight of a photographer invariably whips the Angels into a kissing frenzy, but I have never seen them do it among themselves, when there was nobody around to shock. There is an element of something besides showbiz to it and in serious moments now and then one of the Angels will explain it as 'just one of the ways we let the world know we're brothers'.

It is an unnerving way to be greeted. One night after I'd known the Angels for many months I walked into the Hyde Inn in San Francisco and joined a cluster at the bar. While I was reaching in my pocket for some beer money I was nearly knocked off my feet by a flying body that wrapped itself around me before I could see who it was. Everything went black, and my first thought was that they'd finally turned on me and it was all over: then I felt the hairy kiss and heard the laughter. Ronnie, the Oakland secretary, seemed offended that I hadn't caught him in mid-air, as he'd expected, and returned the kiss heartily. It was a serious social error and further proof to the outlaws that I was only about half bright. They considered me a slow learner, a borderline case with only splinters of real potential. My first plunge into folly was getting a limey bike, an insult that I only partially redeemed by destroying it in a high-speed crash and laying my head open. The wreck gave me a kind of minimum status that lasted until I blew the kissing act. After that they treated me with a gentle sort of detachment, as if I were somebody's little brother with an incurable disease – 'Let the poor fool have his way; God knows, it's the least we can do for him.'*

They treated *The Los Angeles Times* man the same way, but he never seemed to get over the feeling that somebody was going to sneak up behind him and scramble his brains with a tyre iron. It was a very funny scene. I was hoping Cohen would utter something like: 'President Barger, I presume?' But he was too nervous. He'd been talking to the cops, and his mind was full of atrocity stories; probably he was even then composing the article somebody else would write on his demise: '... the reporter struggled, but to no avail. The drug-crazed cyclists quickly hacked him into quarters, which they put on a spit. Their orgiastic cries floated across the water ... he is survived by ...'

The odd truth is that Cohen left Bass Lake with one of the longest and straightest interviews Barger has ever given anybody. The boss Angel was in rare spirits that morning. The sun was warm, his people were secure, and whatever he'd got hold of the night before had obviously been good for him. Cohen's demeanour was anything but hostile. Most reporters either patronized the outlaws or ask such pointed, opinionated questions that they

* I was eventually given to understand that not all of them felt this way.

would do just as well to get their answers from the Lynch report. One night in Oakland I watched a man from one of the East Bay papers make both mistakes at once. He came into the El Adobe and immediately asked to buy some marijuana. Then, before they could decide whether he was a poison toad or a narco agent, he pulled out some grass of his own and offered it around. This didn't work either, although it might have broken the ice if he'd rolled a joint for himself. Then he offered to buy a round of beers, talking constantly in bop jargon. The Angels tolerated him for a while, but after several beers he began asking questions about Hitler and gang rapes and sodomy. Finally Sonny told him he had thirty seconds to get his ass out of sight and if he showed up again they would work on his head with a chain.

Another journalist was eighty-sixed for being too sympathetic. 'There's somethin' creepy about that guy,' Barger told me. 'He's either a cop or he's crazy – and if it's neither one of those then he's usin' us for somethin' we don't know nothin' about.' Which proved to be true. His relationship with the Angels went from uneasy to critical, and the last time I talked to him, he said that they were after him for real. He was so worried that he'd bought a ·357 Magnum revolver. 'You're damn right I'm scared,' he said. 'If they come round here I'll shoot to kill.' This seemed to satisfy the Angels. 'The nutty sonofabitch was lookin' for a scare,' said one. 'Maybe it'll straighten him out.'

Cohen made none of these mistakes. He asked very short general questions and then stood quietly, sweating and shuffling, while his tape recorder gathered up the answers. I could almost hear the song when Barger led off with: 'We Angels live in our own world. We just want to be left alone to be individualists.'

Here are some of the other jewels that Cohen collected that morning, nearly all from Barger:

> Actually we're conformists. To be an Angel, you have to conform to the rules of our society, and the Angels' rules are the toughest anywhere. . . . Our bikes are first with us. We can do things with bikes that nobody else can. They can try but they can't. An Angel can tear a [hog] down and put it back together in two hours. Who else can? . . . This stuff [the Nazi insignia and headgear] – that's just to shock people, to let em know we're individualists, to let em know we're Angels. . . . There'd

be no trouble if we was left alone. The only violence is when people go after us. Couple of Angels will go into a bar and a few guys gettin' drunked up will start a fight, but we get blamed for it. Our two guys will put em down. Any two Angels can take on any other five guys. . . . You got to want to be an Angel. We don't just take anybody in. We watch em. We got to know they'll stick to our rules. . . .

Barger talked steadily for nearly an hour, fully aware that he was being taped and photographed. In that respect it was the end of an era, for soon afterwards he realized that the wisdom he dispensed and the poses he struck for the cameras were worth money, and by the time the article appeared, his expansive mood had turned to gall.

The rest of the stay at Bass Lake was relatively peaceful. Many of the Angels spent Sunday afternoon at the beer market, performing for an overflow crowd of tourists. They poured beer on each other, exchanged lewd chatter with the citizens and had a fine time keeping everybody on edge. Old men bought beer for them, middle-aged women called out insulting questions and the cash register clanged merrily.

Back at camp there were moments of tension when the Willow Cove inlet was invaded by three big hydroplanes full of muscle beach types and bikini girls. They weren't necessarily looking for a fight, but 'they came on strong', as one of the Angels put it, and for a while it looked as if something bad was building up. The police had made no provisions for staving off an attack by water, and when the hydroplanes arrived, there were no deputies in camp. The men on the boats were all in their twenties, wearing bright form-fit trunks with deep tans and shorted waxed hair that stayed combed even in the water. There were about twenty male specimens, and five or six girls who looked like something off the French Riviera. They tied up the boats to some trees across the inlet from the outlaw camp and began to play around lazily – diving, tossing the girls around, passing beers back and forth, but ignoring the outlaws completely.

A hundred feet away, on the other side of the inlet, the Hell's Angels lounged in all their grubby splendour. There were no sun tans, bikinis or waterproof watches on that side. The outlaws stood on the rocky beach in jockey shorts, wet Levis and matted beards that made their skins seem pale and mouldy. Several were splashing around with their clothes on. Some of the girls wore bras and panties, others rolled up their toreador pants as high as they would go, and a few were swimming in men's T-shirts. It looked like the annual picnic for the graveyard shift at the Never Sweat copper mine in Butte, Montana.

The Angels didn't do much swimming. It doesn't fit their style, and only a few know how. 'Shit, I'd sink like a stone if I went out in that water,' said one. 'I guess I could learn to swim if I wanted to, but what the hell? I wouldn't do it more'n once a year anyhow.'

Finally, after some roosterish banter, some of the muscle beach people swam gracefully across the inlet to answer questions the Angels had been yelling about the boats. They wanted to know about the engines, which looked so big that the outlaws couldn't understand why they didn't sink the hulls they were mounted in. One was a 400-horsepower Oldsmobile V-8 with a supercharger. This was the only common language the two groups had, but it served. After a half-hour of shop talk and a few shared beers, one of the boat boys offered to take some of the Angels for a spin. They came back laughing excitedly. 'Man, that thing did a big wheelie all across the lake,' said one. 'I couldn't believe it. That thing is outta sight!'

The only other incident of the run occurred on Sunday night, just before the beer market closed at ten. The Angels who'd been there all day were totally drunk when it came time to go, but they insisted on doing it up right. Whenever they exit in a group, drunk or sober, they boom off like a flight of jet fighters leaving a runway – one at a time, in rapid succession, and with overwhelming noise. The basic idea is that individual launches keep them from running into each other, but the Angels have developed the ritual to the realm of high drama. The order of departure doesn't matter, but the style and rhythm are crucial. They carefully prime their carburettors so the bikes will start on the first kick. An outlaw whose hog won't leap off like a thunderbolt feels a real stigma. It has the same effect as a gun jamming in combat or an actor blowing a key line: 'To be or not to be . . . quoth the raven.'

This is about the way it went at the beer market. A big crowd gathered in the driveway to watch the finale. A photographer rushed around frantically, flashing his strobe light every few seconds. But the Angels were too drunk to carry it off. Some of them flooded their carburettors, then raged and cursed as they jumped repeatedly on the kick starters. Others went careering off simultaneously or veered into the crowd with wild yells. Many were carrying six-packs, which made control even more difficult. Those who'd flooded on the first launch tried to atone for it by screeching off on one wheel, gunning their engines mercilessly to get up a head of steam before springing the clutch. Buck, a massive Joker, crashed into a police car before he got out of first gear and was taken straight to jail, where he spent the next thirty days. Frip from Oakland went flying off the road and hit a tree, breaking his ankle and blocking traffic on the narrow lakeside road.

A large crowd gathered, all wanting to help. The only cop on the scene was a Madera County Sheriff's deputy in a paddy wagon, but he claimed to have no authority and refused to call a private ambulance until somebody signed an agreement to pay the bill. This drew jeers and protests from the crowd. The photographer lost his head and began to curse the deputy. One of the four or five Angels on the scene went roaring off towards Willow Cove. Finally the photographer said he'd pay the ambulance bill and the deputy made the call.

Moments later two helmeted deputies rushed on to the scene, each with a German sheepdog on a leash. There was a flurry of yelling and pushing as people tried to get away from the dogs. A siren wailed somewhere down the road, but the police cars couldn't get through the traffic jam. Some cops left their cars and ran towards whatever was happening, waving their clubs and shouting: 'Stand back! Stand back!'

Barger's scout party arrived seconds behind the police, but they weren't stopped by the traffic. As they weaved between cars their headlights jerked around crazily, adding a new element of menace to the scene. I caught a glimpse of Barger shoving through the crowd towards the injured Angel. One of the helmeted cops reached out to stop him and was knocked about six feet up the road by Dirty Ed. I saw Ed coming, but I couldn't believe my eyes. The cop must have had the same feeling. Dirty Ed hit him on the run and grabbed the front of his jacket at the same time. The cop looked startled as he reeled backwards, trying to swing his club. One of the deputies jumped Ed, and the two had a brief wrestling match before the photographer tried to pull them apart.

Then, for reasons we can only speculate on, the cops seized the photographer instead of the Angel. Two handlers from the Kern County Canine Patrol got him in a double armlock, ignoring his piteous screams, and slammed him repeatedly against a dirt cliff until he lost his voice. He was then put in the paddy wagon. In the meantime Sheriff Baxter had arrived and was trying to calm things down. He found Barger and assured him that an ambulance was coming for his boy. This appeared to solve things, although Sonny and a dozen other Angels stayed until Frip was packed off to a hospital. Dirty Ed lurked quietly in the background, looking dangerous but not making any violent moves. The police ignored him, but Tiny Baxter went over to the paddy wagon and began screaming like a cheetah at the luckless photographer inside accusing him of trying to set off a riot. 'You crazy sonofabitch, I ought to come in there and break your goddamn head!' he yelled, and for a moment I thought he would. All the tension of the weekend was pounding in his voice as he berated the only enemy he could find who didn't have any allies. Grabbing Dirty Ed would have been like lighting a fuse, but the photographer was as harmless as a punching bag. He had no army to back him up, to avenge him if anything happened; and to make matters worse, he admitted being a free-lancer – a term most police interpret to mean a bum who can't even get a job. If they'd grabbed me that night I'd have admitted to being an Enforcer for the Opium Tong before saying I was a free-lance writer. Police are always more careful with people who're employed, even by the Tong. The only thing better is a wallet full of high-toned credentials . . . membership cards, all kinds of them, covered with filigreed wording and strange codes alluding to firm connections with various Power Combines and seats of influence that no smart cop should cross.

Unfortunately, the photographer had none of these, so he was kept in jail for three days, fined $167 for obstructing justice and released with a warning to keep out of Madera County for the rest of his natural life. Before being taken away, he gave me the keys to his new Sunbeam roadster and said he had $2,000 worth of camera equipment in the trunk. He didn't know me at all, and certainly there was nothing in my scraggy appearance to indicate that I would do anything but sell both the car and the equipment at the first opportunity. But he was not in a solid position; his only alternative was to let the car sit on the road for three days. Luckily, he had picked up two hitch-hikers earlier in the day, who said they'd hopped a freight from Los Angeles up to Fresno and then set out by thumb to see what was happening with the Hell's Angels. They agreed to drive the Sunbeam down to Madera, where the photographer was taken for booking. For some reason they followed me right to the jail. They could have fled down any side road. Nobody knew their names or where they might go, and the owner of the car was not in any position to start filing complaints.

At the jail we were told that nobody could speak to the prisoner until his bail had been posted. It was $275 and the only bondsman available refused to touch the case. He said there were too many bums running around loose that weekend. They parked the Sunbeam on the street, and while one went inside to give the keys to the desk sergeant a cop who'd been at the accident drove up and said I was going to be arrested for vagrancy the next time he laid eyes on me.

It didn't seem worth arguing about, so I dropped the hitch-hikers on 101 and drove north for about an hour, until I was sure the Madera county line was somewhere behind me. Then I found a back road next to an airport and went to sleep. The next morning I thought about going back to Bass Lake, but I didn't feel like spending the day scrounging beers and listening to the same dull noise.

I ate breakfast with a bunch of farmers in a diner on 101, then drove on to San Francisco. The holiday traffic was slow, but the only real bottleneck was in Tracy, where a large crowd had turned out for a hot-rod show. Somewhere west of Oakland I picked up two boys who said they were running away from a Job Corps camp. They didn't know exactly where they wanted to go, but one of them said he had a cousin up the coast in Ukiah, and they thought they'd go there for a while. I gave them a pack of cigarettes and let them off at a stoplight in Oakland.

Monday morning's newspapers were full of riot stories. *The Los Angeles Times* ran a king-size, eight-column headline:

HOLIDAY RIOTING – TEAR GAS, TROOPS QUELL YOUTHS – FOUR RESORTS IN MIDWEST DISRUPTED BY BATTLES OF CROWDS AND POLICE.

A front-page story in *The New York Times* said:

YOUTH RIOTS ERUPT IN THREE STATES; 25 HURT 325 HELD – OVERNIGHT OUTBREAKS ENGULF FOUR RESORTS, 200 SEIZED IN LAKE GEORGE TURMOIL.

It seemed like the only people who hadn't erupted on the Fourth of July were the Hell's Angels. Both San Francisco papers took note of this. A *Chronicle* headline said: HELL'S ANGELS FRONT ALL QUIET. But the *Examiner* gave the screw an extra turn: COPS CLIP WINGS OF ANGELS, MEEK CYCLISTS QUIT MADERA.

The only motorcycle story was a United Press dispatch from Sioux City, Iowa. It was very brief:

> A 30-member motorcycle gang called the 'Outlaw Club of the Midwest' left this city of 90,500 today after harassing its citizens over the holiday weekend. They blocked traffic, rode on sidewalks and played 'hide-and-seek' with squad cars. A spokesman for the gang said they came to Sioux City to 'give it a little class'.

The *Chronicle* story on the Angels said police in Madera County were still undecided on what to do about the restraining order. Apparently something had gone haywire, for the order called for the Angels to appear in Madera County Superior Court on 16 July or be permanently barred from the county. 'Police feared there might be trouble,' said the article, 'because the gang threatened to remain in Bass Lake until 16 July or return on that date with reinforcements.' County officials were faced with a choice between dismissing the order entirely or hosting another run – and Barger said they had every intention of going back to argue their case. Needless to say, the order was done away with. It had been a bummer from the start, and not even the cops charged with enforcing it knew what it meant. The final press comment on the Bass Lake Saga appeared in the *Examiner*, under a small headline: A VICTORY FOR HELL'S ANGELS. It said the order had been dismissed at the request of the district attorney, the same man who'd hatched it two weeks earlier.

In restrospect, there was unanimous agreement that both the Press and the police had done a spectacular job. There was massive publicity, a massive police presence and massive beer-drinking to justify all their concern. In a galaxy of nationwide riots and civic upheaval, Bass Lake was a star of peace. There were various explanations, some with ominous overtones. One of these came from a police official who attributed the lack of violence to the fact that 'there were almost as many officers as cyclists'. He estimated the Bass Lake task force at more than a hundred, all working overtime.*

The Angels had their own explanation. They belittled the idea that the cops had simply outmuscled them. Not at all. By the fact of sheer numbers they had forced both the cops and the citizens to leave them alone. Both sides claimed their own show of force had averted a crisis, and to a certain extent they were both right. But I think the real explanation was more complex.

It was the strange ambivalence of the public sentiment that kept Bass Lake confrontation so precariously balanced all week-end. It confused the Angels almost as badly as it did the police; they arrived to face a solid front of civic outrage . . . and then, for no reason they could hope to understand, they became the weekend's featured act, the main show, wild and randy proof that Bass Lake still knew how to put on a real Fourth of July pageant. The threat of violence was converted to dramatic tension. It put a definite zang in the air. The mood of the crowd was euphoric, even erotic. There were incidents, but not many . . . and when it was all over, the most serious offence of the weekend was laid to a photographer from Los Angeles.

If nothing else, the weekend was a monument to free enterprise. It is hard to say what might have happened if the outlaws hadn't

* Another interesting commentary on the Bass Lake spectacle came about a month after it was all over. In mid-August the Watts area of Los Angeles burst into massive rioting that lasted for four days. Thirty-four people were killed, hundreds wounded, and property damaged amounted to more than $1,000,000. Yet Watts erupted without an inch of pre-riot Press coverage, and the Los Angeles police were so unprepared that the National Guard had to be mobilized to bring things under control.

been able to buy beer, but the moon-faced man at the tourist market was the visionary who turned the tide. After the first purchase, the Angels were welcome or at least tolerated everywhere except at Williams's store – which even the vigilantes abandoned when it became apparent that the action was across the lake. Poor Williams was left holding the civic bag; he had taken a gutty stand, his image was all moxie . . . and on Monday night, when the Angels were finally gone, he had earned the leisure that enabled him to go out to the lakefront and gaze off in a proud, wistful way, like Gatsby, at the green neon lights of the taverns across the water, where the others were counting their money.

THE DOPE CABALA
AND
A WALL OF FIRE

19

> They get to drinking and smoking pot and popping them pills in their mouths . . . hell, absolutely anything can happen. They get into a kind of frenzy, like animals, and they'll tear you to bits, with chains, knives, beer-can openers, anything they can get their hands on. – *Fontana detective*

*

MOTORCYCLE outlaws have been accused of maintaining a dope network, a sinister web of sales and deliveries from one coast to the other. Federal narcotics agents say the Hell's Angels shipped more than $1,000,000 worth of marijuana from southern California to New York City between 1962 and 1965, sending it by air freight in boxes labelled 'motorcycle parts'. That is a lot of grass, even at street-corner retail prices. The 'network' was exposed in late 1965 when, according to *The Los Angeles Times*, 'eight persons who identified themselves as members [of the Hell's Angels] pleaded guilty in a San Diego court to charges of smuggling 150 pounds of marijuana from Mexico into the United States at San Ysidro'.

The convicted smugglers had little if anything to do with the Angels, despite their alleged claims to membership. Three of the eight were from New York, and of the five from Los Angeles two were girls. That left only three who could possibly have been Angels, but the outlaws I talked to said they'd never heard of them. Perhaps they lied, but I doubt it; normally they are proud to be connected with anything that makes headlines. Which is beside the point, really, because 150 pounds of pot is only a fraction of what crosses the Mexican border every week despite the sharp-eyed zeal of U.S. customs officials. These gentlemen hate dope like they hate sin; and when they're after it they know whom to grab; beatnik perverts and hairy sandal freaks. People with beards are shaken down thoroughly. I have crossed the border at Tijuana more than a dozen times, but the only time I was stopped and searched was after a week of skin-diving off the Baja California coast when three of us tried to get back into the States with a week's growth of hair on our faces. At the border we were asked the standard questions, gave the standard replies and were instantly seized. The customs agents took our truck, full of camping and Scuba gear, into a special shed and picked over it for an hour and a half. They found several bottles of liquor but no dope. They couldn't seem to believe it. They kept feeling the sleeping-bags and groping under the chassis. Finally they let us go with a warning to 'be more careful' in the future.

Meanwhile, out on the highway, the big-volume dope runners were being waved through with a smile. They were wearing neckties and business suits, driving late model rent-a-cars with electric-razor attachments. I didn't notice any outlaw motorcyclists roaring up to the border, but if any had appeared they'd have been jerked into the shed for a thorough shake-down. People who make a living smuggling narcotics into the States operate on the same principle as bad-cheque artists, who do not as a rule wear beards, earrings and swastikas.

Because of the headwaiter mentality that prevails among customs officials, no commercial shipper of marijuana or anything else illegal would make the mistake of using Hell's Angels for runners. It would be like sending a car up to the border with 'Opium Express' painted in red letters on both sides. If the God of the righteous could swoop down one night and char every Hell's Angel to ashes, marijuana traffic on the Mexican border would hardly be fazed. In February 1966 three men in a stolen truck passed through customs with almost a half-ton of marijuana – 1,050 pounds in one load. They got it all the way to Los Angeles, where they were arrested several days later on an anonymous tip – which netted the tipster close to $100,000 in reward money.

The Angels are too obvious for serious drug traffic. They don't even have enough capital to function as middlemen, so they end up buying most of their stuff in small lots at high prices. Three or four of them will nurse a joint until it is so short they have to hold it with alligator clips – which many outlaws carry for exactly this purpose. People with real access to marijuana can afford to smoke it in big pipes and hookahs . . . and if they have a serious commercial interest in the stuff they rarely smoke it at all except behind locked doors. A taste for pot is not part of the formula for success in a profit-oriented society. If Horatio Alger had been born near a field of locoweed his story might have been a lot different. He would have gone on unemployment and spent most of his time just standing around smiling at things, brushing off the protests of his friends and benefactors, saying: 'Don't bug me, baby – you'll never know.'*

The Angels insist there are no dope addicts in the club, and by legal or medical definitions this is true. Addicts are focused; the physical need for whatever they're hooked on forces them to be selective. But the Angels have no focus at all. They gobble drugs like vicitims of famine turned loose on a rare *smörgåsbord*. They use anything available, and if the result is a screaming delirium then so be it.

They smoke marijuana so openly that it's hard to understand why they're not all in jail for it. California's marijuana laws are among the most primitive manifestations of American politics. Two convictions for possession of a single joint – or even a tenth of one – will send a person to prison for a minimum of two years. A third conviction for possession means a minimum five years. The sentences are fixed by law, regardless of any circumstances a judge might find to be mitigating.

Except for the risk, the marijuana situation in California is a lot like the booze situation in the 1920s. Pot is everywhere; thousands of people smoke it as often as they take aspirins. But the fact of illegality has bred a cultishness, a pot underground whose partisans are forced to skulk around like spies, convening in dark rooms to pass their criminal pleasure from hand to nervous hand. Many get high from the sheer risk. Few people can 'turn on' without making a very spooky ordeal of it, but among those who do are the Hell's Angels – who have done it for so long and so often that they no longer confuse the mystique with the real effects. Marijuana seems

* The younger Angels – especially those who joined after the great publicity rash – are far more involved with the drug underground than the veterans. They are less cautious about the risks in selling and handling. The Angels have always been consumers, but in 1966 they were drifting towards a more businesslike involvement – such as selling junk in large quantities.

to relax them, but not much else. They refer to it as 'weed' or 'dope', shunning such hipster terminilogy as 'grass' and 'pot'. Most just take it for granted, as they do beer and wine. If the stuff is available they'll smoke it, but they rarely spend money for it. When they have to pay for kicks, they prefer something with more zang.

At Bass Lake it was pills. Soon after dark on Saturday I was standing with a group of Angels by the bonfire, talking about the Laconia riot, when somebody appeared with a big plastic bag and began passing out handfuls of whatever it contained. When my turn came I held out my hand and received about thirty small white pills. For a moment the talk ceased, while the outlaws gulped down their rations, chasing the pills with beer. I asked what they were and somebody beside me said: 'Cartwheels, man. Bennies. Eat some, they'll keep you going.' I asked him what they were in milligrams, but he didn't know. 'Just take about ten,' he advised. 'And if that don't work, take more.'

I nodded and ate two. They looked to be about five milligrams each, which is enough Benzedrine to keep most people awake and jabbering for several hours. Ten pills, or fifty milligrams, will send anybody but a pill freak to a hospital with symptoms of acute delirium tremens. Later several Angels assured me that their bennies were indeed 'fives' – at least that's what they were paying for. They never quoted their wholesale price, but they once offered to give me a break on as many as I wanted at the rate of $35 a thousand, or about twice what the same pills would cost me in a drugstore, with a prescription. It turned out that they were not even 'fives', but more like 'ones'. When I realised that the first two were having no effect, I took several more, and then more. By dawn I had eaten twelve – which, if they'd been honest, would have caused me to gnaw down trees like a beaver. As it was, they only helped me to stay on my feet about four hours longer than I would have otherwise. The next day I told the outlaws they were being cheated, but they shrugged it off. 'We got no choice,' said one. 'If you buy stuff on the black market you gotta take whatever you get. Who gives a damn anyway? If they're weak all you gotta do is take more. We're not gonna run out.'

Bennies ('cartwheels' or 'whites') are basic to the outlaw diet –

like weed, beer and wine. But when they talk about 'getting wasted', the action moves on to another level. The next step up the scale is Seconal ('reds' or 'red devils'), a barbiturate normally used as a sedative, or tranquillizer. They also take Amytal ('blue heaven'), Nembutal ('yellow jackets') and Tuinal. But they prefer the reds – which they take along with beer and bennies 'to keep from getting sleepy'. The combination brews up some hellish effects. Barbiturates and alcohol can be a fatal mixture, but the outlaws combine enough stimulants with their depressants to at least stay alive, if not rational.

A righteous Angel loading up on a run will consume almost anything, and in any quantity combination or sequence. I recall a two-day party, many months after Bass Lake, at which Terry began the first day with beer, had a stick of the grass at noon, then more beer, and another stick before dinner, then to red wine and a handful of bennies to keep awake . . . more grass in the middle of the evening, along with a red for some odd feeling, then all through the night more beer, wine, bennies and another red to get some rest . . . before taking off again for another twenty hours, on the same diet, but this time with a pint of bourbon and five hundred micrograms of LSD to ward off any possibility of boredom setting in. This is a pretty extreme diet, and not all of the Angels can handle the whole spectrum of stimulation, depression, hallucinations, drunkenness and wiped-out fatigue for forty-eight hours at a time. Most try to stick with limited combinations – such as beer, pot and Seconal; or gin, beer and bennies; or wine and LSD. But a few will go the whole route and on top of everything else shoot some methydrine or DMT and turn into total zombies for hours at a time.

20

The only way we can stop this is to arrest, arrest, arrest.
– *Los Angeles police chief, William Parker (since deceased), on the subject of Negro riots*

*

THE possibility of a Hell's Angels' dope network brings up, once again, the old bugaboo of expansion. Are the Angels spreading East? According to the New York *Daily News*, the dirty buggers have already made the leap. One night when the mist was on the river they boomed through the toll gate on the George Washington Bridge, chain-whipping a gatekeeper who noticed that their saddle-bags were full of dope and sex instruments. The *News* broke the story with a screaming headline: TERROR ON WHEELS.

THEY'RE A MOTORCYCLE MOB CALLED HELL'S ANGELS, AND THEY GET THEIR KICKS FROM SEX AND VIOLENCE.

Above the headline was a picture of Tiny, laughing in the grip of three Berkeley policemen. The caption beneath it said that bearded Tiny, 'blood streaming from his wrist, was clubbed down during brawl that erupted last week when free-swinging Angels took on Vietnam protest marchers. Towering Tiny and two others were jailed, and a cop suffered a broken leg in melee.' The caption must have got scrambled with one from a 'Beauty Slashes Self, Dies' story on another page. There is no other explanation for the strange line about 'blood streaming from wrist . . .'. Whose wrist? The picture shows three wrists, but none bleeding. And why is Tiny laughing? Is he hysterical after slashing his wrists at a Vietnam protest? If so, why was it necessary to club him? Which cop has the broken leg? And why are the others smiling?*

* Tiny was arrested for assaulting the officer whose leg got broken. A cop at the scene said he saw Tiny do it with a Coke bottle. Nine months later, after lengthy proceedings, the charge was reduced to 'disorderly conduct' and Tiny paid a $150 fine. The felony charge was dropped because films

The photo was very unsettling, but the one below it was even more so – especially to the Angels. It showed four neatly dressed suspects being booked in Greenwich Village for stabbing an AWOL Marine. They look no different from anyone else who might be arrested in the Village for stabbing a Marine, except that all four are wearing jackets with 'Hell's Angels' lettered on the back. There is no emblem, no death's-head, no class at all . . . and yet they claimed to be Hell's Angels. The account of their arrest was a model of police-blotter journalism. Several hours after the crime the four had been arrested – 'quite by coincidence', said the *News* – at the same hospital where the victim Marine was being treated. They just wandered in, 'jacketed, booted and wearing telltale gold earrings . . . to see about having a cyst removed from the neck of one of them'.

This immediately established a motive and a prime suspect – the man with the cyst. It was pressing on the tail of his medulla, causing great pain. After enduring it as long as possible he lost control of himself and stabbed a passing Marine. Then the whole pack ran aimlessly through the Village for several hours, like a family of hyenas, until they found themselves in front of a hospital, which they decided to enter and have done with the fiendish cyst that had caused all the trouble in the first place.

'Police quickly took them into custody,' said the *News*, 'and found knives, they [the police] said, on all four. Two were identified as being involved in the stabbing, and all were held on weapons charges.' (None of the four had motorcycles, and except for the lettering on their backs they looked like a bowling team from the Bronx.)

Then came the shocker: 'Brazenly the four announced they had come to town to "shake up New York", and that 15 to 24 other Angels were also roaming around the city.'

No doubt the others went underground, for they were never mentioned again in the 'Terror on Wheels' story or anywhere else. After placing The Terror in Manhattan, the *News* gave a dull summation of *Time* and *Newsweek* rumours, selections from the

---

showed Tiny falling on the officer's leg after being clubbed on the head by another cop.

Lynch report and old newspaper clippings. The article made it clear, however, that fifteen to twenty-four Hell's Angels were loose somewhere in Manhattan. And maybe they were. With a little luck they might have located one of the half-dozen opium dens that specialize in cyst reduction. If the *News* had put two and two together they would have known who caused the great power blackout that autumn. It was a Hell's Angels plot to take over the subway system and triple the fares. After weeks of intricate sabotage and recircuiting the power rails, the outlaws were attempting a final tie off under the Yale Club when one of their number, afflicted with bad hives, was overcome by abulia and wired the main subway voltage to the root of the Empire State Building's lightning rod. The resulting explosion killed them all, but their bones were carried off by water rats and there was no other evidence. As usual, the Angels beat the rap. And the *News* missed a hell of a story.

*

HELL'S ANGELS FACE PRISON FOR N. H. CYCLE RAMPAGE – New York Post (*June 1965*)

*

The New York power failure was not the first time the Hell's Angels have confounded the forces of decency and got off scot free. They are incredibly devious. Law enforcement officials have compared their guile to that of the snipe, a wily beast that many have seen but few have ever trapped. This is because the snipe has the ability to transform himself, when facing capture, into something entirely different. The only other animals capable of this are the werewolf and the Hell's Angel, which have many traits in common. The physical resemblance is obvious, but far more important is the *transmogrification factor*, the strange ability to alter their own physical structure, and hence 'disappear'. The Hell's Angels are very close-mouthed about this, but it is a well-known fact among public officials.

One of the best examples of how it can work showed up in the Laconia, New Hampshire, 'motorcycle riot' in June of 1965, which got more publicity than any other single event in the history of motorcycling. It was front page from coast to coast. *The New York Times* headline said: CYCLISTS' RIOT QUELLED, NEW HAMPSHIRE TOWN CLEANS UP. In San Francisco the *Examiner* put a little more zip to it: HELL'S ANGELS TERROR AT N. H. CYCLE RACES – COPS GUARD SLUG RIOTERS. The number of terrorists ranged from five thousand in *The New York Post* to twenty-five thousand in *The National Observer*, but twenty thousand more or less didn't seem to make much difference. Everybody agreed it was a wild and woolly bash. The mayor of the stricken hamlet, a thirty-five-year-old patriot named Peter Lessard, blamed the whole thing on the Hell's Angels. He said they had 'planned it in advance' and 'trained in Mexico for the riot'. On Monday, two days after the mêlée, Laconia's leading citizens gathered in the Tavern Hotel to hear their mayor explain what had happened. According to Lessard and Safety Commissioner Robert Rhodes, the Hell's Angels threw a ring around the whole area. 'They wouldn't let anybody get away. The thing blew up in our faces in minutes. There was some marijuana around too. Are the Communists behind it?'

Reporters picked up the quote with thinly veiled amusement, but it was at least a month before the initial, wild-eyed accounts of the Laconia riot were deflated by first-hand testimony from those without instant access to print. Even the *Life* article, on careful reading, indicated that many of the 'rioters' acted in self-defence when police and National Guardsmen launched an all-out, indiscriminate attack with tear gas, bayonets, nightsticks, and shotguns firing rock salt and Number 6 birdshot. Many of those arrested in the mop-up didn't own or ride motorcycles, and a fellow named Samuel Sadowski was sentenced to a year in jail after being arrested in a parking lot where there was no sign of rioting. According to an eye-witness, Sadowski's only offence was a hasty retreat from the line of fire.* The police used full-bore riot tactics, which they'd been practising for more than two months. The local police chief, Harold Knowlton, had called up two hundred National Guardsmen, sixty State Troopers and ten Civil Defence volunteers, in addition to his own force of twenty-eight regulars. 'We practised for ten weeks in crowd control and riot tactics,

* *Cycle World* magazine.

said the chief. 'But we did it under cover. We didn't want to challenge them.'

Shore nuff he didn't. The small army he trained was only for symbolic purposes. Just like the Hell's Angels – they don't want to challenge people either, but they manage to get provoked pretty often. One report of the riot quoted a local as saying: 'Luckily, there happened to be some National Guardsmen training nearby. If it hadn't been for them, this town would have been a gutted ruin – and there's no way of telling how many of our women would have been gang-raped, how many of our citizens might have been killed by those rotten bums on motorcycles. Thank God for the troops!'

The Lord was taking good care of Laconia that night; his troops came in and shot hell out of the place. One of the most critically injured was a photographer named Robert St Louis, who was shot in the face while trying to take pictures. Of the seventy reported injuries, sixty-nine were on the 'enemy' side.* *Life* quoted a seventeen-year-old boy as saying: 'They yanked me out of a car and knocked me bow-legged . . . then one cop stood on my head while another put handcuffs on.' Even the featured victim of the riot, a barber named Armand Baron, whose car was burned by rioters, attributed his injuries to the forces of the Almighty. While trying to flee he was hit in the mouth by a police billy and slammed on the hip by a Guardsman's rifle butt.

The Laconia riot was one of the most predictable outbursts in the history of civil chaos. The main event of that weekend was either the forty-fourth Annual New England Tour and Rally (as reported in *Life*) or the twenty-sixth running of the New England Motorcycle Races (according to *The National Observer*). Other promoters had different names for it: the A.M.A. called it a '100-Mile National Championship Road Race'. But by any name it was a huge, traditional motorcycle gathering. Non-racing cyclists know it as the New England 'Gypsy Tour', and it is one of those scenes they all like to make. The idea is about the same as any Hell's Angels run, but on a much bigger scale. Laconia, with a population of fifteen thousand in the winter and forty-five thousand in the

* The same casualty pattern prevailed in the Watts riot in August. Of the thirty-four killed, thirty-one were Negroes.

summer, attracts anywhere from fifteen to thirty thousand motorcyclists for the race weekend.

They have been an annual event since 1939 after the Belknap Gunstock Recreation Area was built outside Laconia as a winter ski run and summer campground. William Sheitinger, from nearby Concord, is a founder of both the American Motorcycle Association and the Laconia races. The races were not held in 1964, because of a riot the previous year.

'Anybody who knew anything about the event could predict to the hour that a riot would take place [again],' said Warren Warner, manager of the county-owned Belknap area. 'They rioted here before, but nobody saw it because it was away from town. We had seventy local and state police here, but they took a look at the mob and decided not to do anything at all. The cyclists threw cherry bombs, swung knives and chains, and threw beer cans at the police. We had fires started, buildings burned, the chair lift started in the middle of the night and wrecked, and picnic tables chopped up for kindling. The people in town who wanted these races weren't around and didn't want to be around. I tried to discuss the riots with them, but there was always the rebuttal that "nobody saw 'em, so what's the difference . . . ".'

In 1964 a new race track was built outside Laconia's jurisdiction, and the event was on again for 1965. The Laeonia Chamber of Commerce was enthusiastic enough to contribute $5,000 to the promotional fund . . . which was, after all, a pretty good investment, since the Chamber of Commerce estimates that motorcyclists spend between $250,000 and $500,000 in the area during the weekend of the races. This sounds like a lot, but considering the number of cyclists, it is only $25 to $50 each – most of which goes to motels, souvenir shops, beer joints and hamburger stands.

Mayor Lessard says the event 'has always been a good start to the tourist season', and that the economy 'suffered' in 1964, when the races were suspended. Former Mayor Gerald Morin, a beer distributor in Laconia, estimates that some fifteen thousand cases of beer were sold to cyclists during the 1965 weekend. 'Obviously, the races are good for our economy,' he said in the wake of the riot. 'We shouldn't be making any decisions now that emotions are high. We should wait until they cool down.' At the same time,

Mayor Lessard put it more bluntly: 'Even the people who want [the races] may have had some doubts until they deposited their cash in the banks.'

Fritzi Baer, a publicist for the New England Motorcycle Dealers Association – which sponsors the races – threw the weight of his prestige on the side of the mayor and the beer distributor: 'I believe when we get through this year the bad element won't come back. I know in my heart the bad elements won't come back to the state of New Hampshire after they've seen how we deal with them.'

Mr Baer did not define the 'bad element', but presumably it did not include anyone likely to purchase motorcycles in New England. In any case, some of them were dealt with rather harshly, under the provisions of a new riot law that United Press International reported was 'rushed through the state legislature' only a week before the Laconia races. It provides for fines up to $1,000 and imprisonment up to three years for persons who lead a disturbance or cause personal property damage during a riot. Under the old law, the maximum fine was $25. Contrary to rumours at the time of its enactment, the new law contained no provisions for punishment by dunking stool.

Even as the law was being passed, telephone poles on highways near Laconia were festooned with signs saying: COME TO THE RIOT – SEE WEIRS BEACH BURN SATURDAY NIGHT. Weirs Beach is a lakeside strip outside the town, with water on one side, and taverns, penny arcades and bowling alleys on the other. By nine o'clock Saturday night Lakeside Avenue, the main street, was thronged with some four thousand beer-drinking tourists, about half riding motorcycles. Crowds began appearing on rooftops above the arcade area, and police heard the shout go up: 'Let's have a riot!'

It was about this time that Mr Baron drove his car – for some excellent reason, no doubt – right down Lakeside and into the middle of the mob. He'd gone 'out for a ride', he explained later, taking his wife, his son, his son's wife and the two grandchildren: Duane, two, and Brenda, eight months old. By the time Mr Baron began creeping down the crowded street, the action was getting out of hand. People were throwing beer cans down from the rooftops. Police claimed somebody had chained the fire-call boxes and cut the phone lines to police headquarters, although this would hardly have seemed necessary. The police did not need telephones to hear five thousand people chanting, '*Sieg Heil!*' while somebody climbed up to hang a swastika on a beachfront flagpole. Then the mob began rocking cars back and forth – including Mr Baron's car, which was right in their midst. Baron got his family out, none of them injured, and watched his car roll over and begin burning when one of the rioters threw a match in the spilled gasoline.

The flames lit up the street just about the time the National Guard arrived on the scene with fixed bayonets and rifle butts swinging. With them came local gendarmes, firing shotguns. The mob scattered, many of them blinded by tear gas bombs. The police were pelted with firecrackers, rocks and beer cans, but they were wearing helmets, and their ten weeks of training served them well. According to Chief Knowlton, the riot area was cleared in fifteen minutes, 'but it took another hour to get the side-streets cleaned out'. This secondary action involved the rounding up of suspects. There are photos of people being clubbed off motorcycles, prodded out of sleeping-bags with bayonets, and according to the Associated Press, 'police rousted people registered in hotels . . .'.

Anyone reading the next day's headlines would have thought the whole Laconia area was a smoking ruin, with ragged survivors shooting at each other from behind the charred remains of automobiles. But this was not exactly the case. The state of martial law that had been declared on Saturday night was ended in time for Sunday's final racing events, which proceeded without incident. Liquor and beer sales, which had been halted during the riot, were also renewed. On Sunday morning there were reports of a naked man picketing on Lakeside Avenue with a large sign saying: HONI SOIT QUI MAL Y PENSE.

Mayor Lessard spent most of Sunday investigating the riot, and by Monday he was able to report it had been Communist-inspired and of Mexican origin, with the Hell's Angels doing the legwork. The mayor, the police chief and the local safety commissioner agreed that the Hell's Angels had 'caused all the trouble'. They had been plotting it for months.

'But they won't come back,' vowed the safety commissioner. 'And if they do, we'll just have to be ready for them like we were this time.' After all, nobody was killed or maimed, and property damage amounted to only a few thousand dollars at most.

Other merchants agreed. 'I think [the cyclists] will be invited back,' said the owner of the Winnipesaukee Gardens dance hall at Weirs Beach. The president of the Laconia National Bank said the riot had been caused by a 'small minority' that had been taught a good lesson and wouldn't try it again. One of the few dissenting voices in town was that of Warren Warner, who supervised the races for more than fifteen years, when they were at the old track in Belknap. 'The apologists will wait about six months or so,' he predicted. 'Then they'll start planting the idea that the riots were caused by police brutality or the Hell's Angels gang from California and that they can be controlled. But listen, in that crowd of twenty thousand cyclists there are two thousand who are no better than animals. There would have been a riot whether or not any one club decided to come or not.'

A local journalist not allied with the beer and hamburger industries put it more dramatically: 'The cyclists could have burned down the Weirs if they'd really wanted to. Maybe next time they will. Laconia is like a town playing Russian roulette. Five times out of six it pulls the trigger and nothing much happens. The sixth time it blows its brains out.'*

This did not jibe with the mayor's theory of foul winds from faraway places. Everyone seemed to agree that something Russian had been in the air that night, but I was curious about the Mexican influence and the role of the Hell's Angels. Actually, I couldn't believe the mayor had said the things he was quoted as saying when he analysed the riot. They were too absurd. So I decided to call him and check – not only his words, but random facts such as the number of arrests. For some reason it was impossible for the Press to divine how many alleged rioters had been arrested. This is usually a factor in crime stories, and in most cases it is an easy thing to find out. There is nothing interpretative about it, no hues or shadings. It is simply a number that anybody can get from the desk sergeant – if not immediately, then at least within twenty-four

* The Laconia racing weekend was held on schedule in 1966. There was massive police pressure and no rioting, perhaps because the only Hell's Angel on hand was pacified by LSD.

hours after the action. Most reporters assume the desk sergeant's figures are accurate, for he is the man who makes the entries in the big ledger.

Yet eight different articles on Laconia carried seven different versions of the arrest total. Here is a list I made a week after the riot:

New York Times . . . 'about 50'
Associated Press . . . 'at least 75'
San Francisco Examiner (via U.P.I.) . . . 'at least 100, including five Hell's Angels'.
New York Herald Tribune . . . 29
Life . . . 34
National Observer . . . 34
New York Daily News . . . 'more than 100'
New York Post . . . 'at least 40'

No doubt there is some explanation for this disparity, but since it never emerged, it was not much consolation to anyone who had to make do with the public prints. I was not surprised that the eight articles gave eight different viewpoints on the riot, because no reporter can be on every scene and they get their information from different people. But it would have been reassuring to find a majority agreement on something as basic as the number of arrests; it would have made the rest of the information easier to live with.

Seven weeks after the riot, on 11 August, the Associated Press finally put the correct figure on its wire, but by that time nobody gave a damn, and as far as I know it was never printed. Laconia District Court records show thirty-two arrests. There were no Hell's Angels, no Californians and no person from west of the Adirondacks. The clerk of the court listed: 'Eleven respondents from Massachusetts, ten from Connecticut, four from New York, three from Canada, three from New Jersey and one from New Hampshire.'

Of these, seven drew one-year sentences in the state House of Correction and one got six months. There were ten fines, ranging from $25 to $500. Charges against twelve of the accused were dropped, one was found innocent, and eleven of those found guilty made appeals.

Mayor Lessard was kind enough to have the court send me

these figures. They came as a mild surprise, because during our telephone chat the mayor had said that 'thirty-three rioters had been fined and sentenced' and that 'the bad ones with previous records got thousand-dollar fines and a year in jail'.

He also sent me a packet of photographs taken during the riot, but none showed any sign of the Hell's Angels. Most pictured teenage boys wearing bright sweaters, chinos and loafers. They were faring badly at the hands of riot troopers. The mayor also included photos of himself and the police chief, taken with a Polaroid camera, but they quickly turned yellow and faded away.

We talked on the phone for about an hour one Thursday morning. I was so fascinated that I couldn't hang up. The mayor spoke in a very exotic way. It was obvious that he was a man who marched through life to the rhythms of some drum I would never hear.

I expected a denial of the strange intelligence attributed to him by *The New York Times* . . . but no, he was proud of his insights and eager to be quoted further. I had no sooner mentioned the Hell's Angels than he began to ramble about 'ringleaders, Communists and narcotics'. He was privy to information that four Hell's Angels had been arrested in Connecticut, *en route* to Laconia with a 'carload of drugs, hand weapons and a sawed-off shotgun'. He was not sure whether these four had trained south of the border. 'I'd rather not say where we got the information that they trained in Mexico,' he said. 'It was confidential. It came in the mail. But I turned it over to the F.B.I. right away. They're following up on the Communist angle. We got some pictures of them wearing swastikas.'*

When I asked him how many Hell's Angels had been arrested he said none, or none that admitted it anyway. Not even those four bums in Connecticut would admit to being Angels. At one point somebody in Laconia had seen a car with California plates, but it too had disappeared.

About halfway through our talk I got a strong whiff of the transmogrification factor, but I was hardly prepared for the mayor's special fillip on it. There were plenty of Hell's Angels at the riot, 'but they escaped', he explained, 'behind a wall of fire'.

* No swastikas were visible in any of the photos he sent me, which presumably were the most convincing he could round up.

While he elaborated on this I checked my calendar to make sure I hadn't lost track of the days. If it was Sunday, perhaps he had just come back from church in a high, biblical state of mind. At any moment I expected to hear that the Angels had driven their motorcycles straight into the sea, which had rolled back to let them pass. But no, it wasn't like that. The mayor was not loath to give details of the escape; he wanted law enforcement agencies everywhere to be warned of the Angels' methods. Knowledge is power, he opined.

So Mayor Lessard described for me, in what sounded like sober tones, how the Hell's Angels – prior to the riot – had soaked a major egress road with gasoline. And then, at the height of the violence, just as they were about to be arrested, they roared out of town at great speed . . . and the last one to cross the gasoline soak dropped a match on it. A sheet of flame exploded in the night, making pursuit impossible. Yes, it was the old firewall technique, a legacy of the Boer War. It was highly successful in Laconia. The lawmen were stopped in their tracks by heat so intense that it presumably scrambled the crystals in their short-wave radio transmitters. Had the Hell's Angels been any less clever, they might have been intercepted, by means of a general alert, somewhere between New Hampshire and California.

As it was, they made it back safely, and with plenty of time to shake the cross-country dust out of their clothes for the Bass Lake Run just two weeks later. There was no denying the wizardry of it, and when the clan came together it was a prime topic of conversation. Everybody wanted to congratulate the hardies who'd pulled it off . . . but for some reason nobody spoke up. The only Angel who knew anything more about Laconia than what the others had read in the newspapers was Tiny, whose ex-wife had called him from a Laconia telephone booth at the height of the action. One of the low points of the Bass Lake Run was Tiny's rueful declaration that no Angels had made it to Laconia.

'My old lady was right there,' he told the disappointed outlaws, 'and if any of our people were there she'd have told me. Those guys from Quebec were the ones – them and a bunch called Banditos, from the East. They showed real class. We should get together with those guys.'

This news caused the others to stare balefully at the fire. Finally somebody grunted. 'Shit, that was a bunch of amateurs – if we'd been there they wouldn't of busted it up so easy. Man, fifteen thousand bikes in one town – I tell you it hurts my mind.'

After the first wild stories were scaled down, nobody, even in respectable motorcycle circles, thought the Hell's Angels had anything to do with the Laconia trouble. *Cycle World*, which calls itself 'America's leading motorcycle-enthusiasts' publication', blamed French–Canadian outlaws, refugees from 'the scabby side of motorcycling in the Eastern United States', and 'radical crackpots, some of whom are in public offices in towns around Laconia . . .'.

21

Lies! You're lying! You're all lying against my boys!
– *Ma Barker*

By late summer of 1965 the Angels had become a factor to be reckoned with in the social, intellectual and political life of northern California. They were quoted almost daily in the Press, and no half-bohemian party made the grade unless there were strong rumours – circulated by the host – that the Hell's Angels would also attend. I was vaguely afflicted by this syndrome, since my name was becoming increasingly associated with the Angels and there was a feeling in the air that I could produce them whenever I felt like it. This was never true, but I did what I could to put the outlaws on to as much free booze and action as seemed advisable. At the same time I was loath to be responsible for their behaviour. Their pre-eminence on so many guest lists made it inevitable that a certain amount of looting, assault and rapine would occur if they took the social whirl at full gallop. I recall one party at which I was badgered by children and young mothers because the Angels didn't show up. Most of the guests were respectable Berkeley intellectuals, whose idea of motorcycle outlaws was not consistent with reality. I told the Angels about the party and gave them the address, a quiet residential street in the East Bay, but I hoped they wouldn't come. The setting was guaranteed trouble: heaping tubs of beer, wild music and several dozen young girls looking for excitement while their husbands and varied escorts wanted to talk about 'alienation' and 'a generation in revolt'. Even a half-dozen Angels would have quickly reduced the scene to an intolerable common denominator: Who will get fucked?

It was Bass Lake all over again, but with a different breed of voyeur: this time it was the Bay Area's hip establishment, who adopted the Angels just as eagerly as any crowd of tourists at a scraggy Sierra beer market.* The outlaws were very much the rage. They were big, dirty and titillating . . . unlike the Beatles, who were small, clean and much too popular to be fashionable. As the Beatles drifted Out, they created a vacuum that sucked the Hell's Angels In. And right behind the outlaws came Roth saying: 'They're the Wild Bill Hickoks, the Billy the Kids – they're the last American heroes we have, man.' Roth was so interested in the Angels that he began producing icons to commemorate their existence – plastic replicas of Nazi helmets with swinging slogans ('Christ was a Hype') and Iron Crosses, which he sold on the teenage market from coast to coast.

The only real problem with the Angels' new image was that the outlaws themselves didn't understand it. It puzzled them to be treated as symbolic heroes by people with whom they had almost nothing in common. Yet they were gaining access to a whole reservoir of women, booze, drugs and new action – which they were eager to get their hands on, and symbolism be damned. But they could never get the hang of the role they were expected to play and insisted on ad-libbing the lines. This fouled their channels of communication, which made them nervous . . . and after a brief whirl on the hipster party circuit, all but a few decided it was both cheaper and easier, in the long run, to buy their own booze and hustle a less complicated breed of pussy.

The only really successful connection I made for the Angels was Ken Kesey, a young novelist† then living in the woods near La Honda, south of San Francisco. During 1965 and 1966 Kesey was arrested twice for possession of marijuana and finally had to flee the country to avoid a long prison term. His association with the Hell's Angels was not calculated to calm his relationship with the forces of law and decency, but he pursued it nonetheless, and with overweening zeal.

I met Kesey one afternoon in August at the studios of K.Q.E.D., the educational TV station in San Francisco. We had a few beers at a nearby tavern, but I was forced to leave early because I had a Brazilian drum record to take out to Frenchy at the Box Shop.

* It reminded me of a cartoon in *The Realist* showing the World's Fair Poverty Pavilion.

† *One Flew Over the Cuckoo's Nest*, *Sometimes a Great Notion*.

Kesey said he'd come along, and when we got there he made a great hit with the four or five Angels still on the job. After several hours of eating, drinking and the symbolic sharing of herbs, Kesey invited the Frisco chapter down to La Honda for a party on the coming weekend. He and his band of Pranksters had about six acres, with a deep creek between the house and the highway, and a general overcrowded madness in the private sector.

As it happened, nine marijuana charges against the Kesey menagerie were dropped on Friday; this was duly noted in the Saturday papers, which appeared in La Honda just about the time Kesey was posting a sign on his gate saying THE MERRY PRANKSTERS WELCOME THE HELL'S ANGELS. The sign, in red, white, and blue, was fifteen feet long and three feet high. It had a bad effect on the neighbours. When I got there, in the middle of the afternoon, five San Mateo County sheriffs' cars were parked on the highway in front of Kesey's property. About ten Angels had already arrived and were safely inside the gate; twenty others were said to be *en route*. The pot was boiling nicely.

I had brought my wife and small son along, and we wanted to go down to the beach for a short meal before joining the festivities. Several miles down the road I stopped at the general store in San Gregorio, a crossroads community with no real population but which serves as a centre for the surrounding farms. The store was quiet back around the tool, produce and harness sections, but up front at the bar, things were loud and edgy. The folks were not happy about the goings on up the road. 'That goddamn dope addict,' said a middle-aged farmer. 'First it's marywanna, now it's Hell's Angels. Christ alive, he's just pushin' our faces in the dirt!'

'Beatniks!' said somebody else. 'Not worth a pound of piss.'

There was talk of divvying up the axe handles in the store and 'goin' up there to clean the place out'. But somebody said the cops were already on the job: 'Gonna put 'em in jail for good this time, every damn one of 'em. . . .' So the axe handles stayed in the rack.

By nightfall Kesey's enclave was full of people, music and multi-coloured lights. The police added a nice touch by parking along the highway with their own lights flashing . . . red and orange blips lighting up the trees and the sheer dirt cliff along the road. Earlier that spring the Kesey estate had been raided by seventeen cops and a half-dozen dogs, led by a notorious federal narcotics agent named Willie Wong. Kesey and twelve of his friends were arrested on marijuana charges, but most of these had to be dropped due to peculiarities in the search warrant. Shortly after the raid Agent Wong was transferred out of the district; and the local police made no further attempts to breach the gates. They contented themselves with lurking the highway across the creek and checking out all those coming and going. Local sheriffs' deputies stopped and questioned a steady stream of college professors, vagrants, lawyers, students, psychologists and high-style hippies. There was not much the police could do except run radio checks for unpaid traffic citations, but they did this with unflagging determination. Now and then they would roust an obvious drunk or somebody completely stoned, but during several months of intense vigil their only actual arrests netted less than a half-dozen traffic-fine fugitives.

Meanwhile, the parties grew wilder and louder. There was very little marijuana, but plenty of LSD, which was then legal. The cops stood out on the highway and looked across the creek at a scene that must have tortured the very roots of their understanding. Here were all these people running wild, bellowing, and dancing half-naked to rock-'n'-roll sounds piped out through the trees from massive amplifiers, reeling and stumbling in a maze of psychedelic lights . . . WILD, by God, and with no law to stop them.

Then, with the arrival of the Hell's Angels, the cops finally got a handle – a *raison d'être*, as it were – and they quickly tripled the guard. Kesey had finally gone over the line. A bunch of beatniks and college types eating some kind of invisible drug was a hard thing to deal with, but a gang of rotten thugs on motorcycles was as tangible a menace as the law could hope for.*

The first party, featuring only the Frisco chapter, was a roaring

* Several months later, when Kesey came to trial on the first marijuana charge, one of the conditions attached to his relatively light six months' jail sentence was that he sell his property and leave San Mateo County – permanently. Which he did, but he moved a little farther than the authorities had in mind. On 31 January 1966, Kesey jumped bail and disappeared. A suicide note was found in his abandoned bus on the northern California coast, but not even the police believed he was dead. Results of my own

success. Sometime around midnight, Pete, the drag racer, grinned as he rummaged through a beer tub and said: 'Man, this is nothin' but a goddamn wonderful scene. We didn't know what to expect when we came, but it turned out just fine. This time it's all ha-ha, not thump-thump.'

Most of the Angels were posed and defensive until they got thoroughly drunk, and a few never got over the idea that they were going to be challenged and whipped on at any moment . . . but as a group, they seemed to realize that if they wanted any tension they were going to have to work pretty hard to create it on their own. Kesey's people were too busy getting out of their heads to worry about anything so raw and realistic as the Hell's Angels. Other luminaries wandered through the party (notably, poet Allen Ginsberg and Richard Alpert, the LSD guru), and although the Angels didn't know them, they were put a bit off balance by having to share the spotlight.

This was Ginsberg's first encounter with the Angels, and he quickly became an *aficionada*. Sometime late in the evening, when it became apparent that everyone leaving the party was being grabbed by the police, Ginsberg and I drove out to see what it meant. A Volkswagen which left just ahead of us had been pulled over about a half-mile down the highway, and the occupants were taken out for grilling. Our idea was to arrive on the capture scene with a tape recorder, but I barely got out of first gear before we were pulled over by another sheriff's car. I stepped out with the microphone in my hand to ask what the trouble was. The sight of the mike caused the deputies to stand mute except for the bare essentials. One asked to see my licence while the other tried to ignore Ginsberg, who inquired very pleasantly and repeatedly why everyone who left the party was being seized. The cop stood with his feet apart, hands clasped behind his back and his face frozen in a dumb stare. Ginsberg continued to question him while the other deputy ran a check on my licence. I enjoy listening to that encounter

---

investigations are very hazy, although I managed – after many months of digging – to locate his forwarding address:

c/o Agriculture Attaché
U.S. Embassy
Asunción, Paraguay

on tape. It sounds as if Ginsberg and I are flapping rhetorical questions at each other, with a police radio chattering in the background. Every few moments a different voice comes in with a monosyllabic utterance, but our questions are never answered. For several moments there is no talk at all – only the sound of Ginsberg humming a Near Eastern raga, backed up now and then by the spastic crackling of the Voice from Headquarters. The scene was so ridiculous that even the cops began smiling after a while. Their refusal to speak amounted to an unlikely reversal of roles, starkly emphasized by our amusement.

The deputy who'd been left to deal with us was staring curiously at Ginsberg. Suddenly he asked: 'How long did it take you to grow that beard?'

Ginsberg stopped humming, gave the question some thought, and replied: 'About two years – no, I think it was eighteen months.'

The cop nodded thoughtfully . . . as if he meant to grow one himself, but might not be able to invest all that time; twelve months, okay, but eighteen – well, the chief might wonder.

The conversation lagged again until the radio deputy came back to report that I was clean of outstanding warrants. At this point I said I'd turn off the tape recorder if they'd engage in even the most limited conversation. They agreed, and we talked for a while. It was the Hell's Angels they were watching, they said, not Kesey. Sooner or later the hoodlums would cause bad trouble, and what the hell were they doing there anyway? They were curious about how I'd managed to find out enough to write about them. 'How do you get 'em to talk?' said one. 'You've never been beaten up? They let you hang around? What's with 'em anyway? Are they really as bad as we hear?'

I said the Angels were probably worse than they'd heard, but that they'd never given me trouble. The deputies said they didn't know anything more about the outlaws than what they'd read in the papers.*

* In the summer of 1966 the San Mateo County sheriff, Earl Whitmore – a key figure in the Kesey harassment – was up to his badge in a bookie scandal. A county Grand Jury, on the basis of evidence supplied by the district attorney's office, was preparing charges that Sheriff Whitmore was implicated in a system of payoffs and police protection for local book-makers.

We parted on good terms except for the citation they eventually got around to giving me – for having cracked tail-light lenses. Ginsberg asked why the driver of the Volkswagen had been taken away in a police car. After several minutes the radio came back with an answer: he'd failed to pay a traffic citation several months back, and the original $20 fine had grown, as fines will in California, to a current figure of $57 – which would have to be paid in cash before the fugitive could be released. Neither Ginsberg nor I had $57, so we got the victim's name, thinking to send one of his friends after him when we got back to Kesey's. But it turned out that nobody knew him, and for all I know he is still in the Redwood City jail.

The party continued for two days and nights, but the only other crisis came when the worldly inspiration* for the protagonist of several recent novels stood naked on the private side of the creek and screamed off a long, brutal diatribe against the cops only twenty yards away. He was swaying and yelling in the bright glare of a light from the porch, holding a beer bottle in one hand and shaking his fist at the objects of his scorn: 'You sneaky motherfuckers! What the fuck's wrong with you? Come on over here and see what you get . . . goddamn your shit-filled souls anyway!' Then he would laugh and wave his beer around. 'Don't fuck with me you sons of shitlovers. Come on over. You'll get every fucking thing you deserve.'

Luckily, somebody pulled him back to the party, still naked and yelling. His drunken challenge to the cops might have kicked off a real disaster. In California and most other states the police cannot legally invade private property without a search warrant unless (1) they are reasonably certain a crime is being committed or (2) they are 'invited' by the owner or occupant of the property. His performance could have been interpreted either way if the cops had been in the mood, and at that stage in the evening, a raiding party could not have made it across the bridge without violence. The Angels were in no mood to be rounded up quietly and they were too drunk to care about consequences.

It didn't take long for tales of La Honda to circulate among other Angel chapters. A scouting party from Oakland checked it

* Name deleted at insistence of publisher's lawyers.

out and came back with such glowing reports that La Honda quickly became a mecca for Angels from all over northern California. They would arrive unannounced, usually in groups of five to fifteen, and stay until they got bored or ran out of LSD, which only a few had ever tried prior to the Kesey hookup.

Long before the outlaws discovered La Honda, the free-wheeling acid parties were already cause for alarm among respectable LSD buffs – scientists, psychiatrists and others in the behavioural-science fields who felt the drug should only be taken in 'controlled experiment' situations, featuring carefully screened subjects under constant observation by experienced 'guides'. Such precautions are thought to be insurance against bad trips. Any potential flip-out who leaks through the screening process can be quickly stuffed with tranquillizers the moment he shows signs of blood lust or attempts to wrench off his own head to get a better look inside it.*

The controlled-experiment people felt that public LSD orgies would lead to disaster for their own research. There was little optimism about what might happen when the Angels – worshipping violence, rape and swastikas – found themselves in a crowd of intellectual hipsters, Marxist radicals and pacifist peace marchers. It was a nervous thing to consider even if anybody could be expected to keep a straight head . . . but of course that was out of the question. With everyone drunk, stoned and loaded, there was nobody capable of taking objective notes, no guides to soothe the flip-outs, no rational spectator to put out fires or hide the butcher knives . . . no control at all.

People who regularly attended Kesey's parties were not so worried as those who'd only heard about them. The enclave was public only in the sense that anyone who felt like it could walk through the gate on the bridge. But once inside, a man who didn't speak the language was made to feel very self-conscious. Acid

* There is a minority opinion among acid-eaters that the solemn preparations for a controlled LSD experiment might produce more bad trips than they prevent. Many 'subjects' are so rigidly indoctrinated by what they've read and heard that by the time they finally swallow the capsule, their reactions have already been articulated in their own minds. When the experience deviates from their preconceived notions – or shatters them altogether – they are likely to panic. And panic is always a bad trip, with or without acid.

freaks are not given to voluble hospitality; they stare fixedly at strangers, or look right through them. Many guests were made fearful, and never came back. Those who stayed were mainly the bohemian refugee element, whose sense of interdependence led them to spare each other the focus of their personal hostilities. For that there was always the cops, across the creek, who might come crashing in at any moment.*

But even amongst the Pranksters there was enough uncertainty about the Angels that the first party was noticeably light on LSD. Then, once the threat of violence seemed to fade, there was acid in great profusion. The Angels used it cautiously at first, never bringing their own, but it didn't take them long to cultivate sources on their own turf . . . so that any run to La Honda was preceded by a general mustering of the capsules, which they would take down to Kesey's and distribute, for money or otherwise.

Once the outlaws accepted LSD as a righteous thing, they handled it with the mindless zeal they bring to their other pleasures. Earlier that summer the consensus was that any drug powerful enough to render a man incapable of riding a bike should be left alone . . . but when the general resistance collapsed, after several Kesey parties, the Angels began to eat LSD as often as they could get their hands on it – which was often indeed, due to their numerous contacts in the underground drug market. For several months the only limit on their consumption was a chronic shortage of cash. Given an unlimited supply of the acid, probably half the Hell's Angels then extant would have charred their brains to cinders in less than a month. As it was, their consumption pushed the limits of human toleration. They talked of little else, and many stopped talking altogether. LSD is a guaranteed cure for boredom, a malady no less prevalent among Hell's Angels than any other segment of the Great Society . . . and on afternoons at the El Adobe, when nothing else was happening and there was not much money for beer, somebody like Jimmy or Terry or Skip would show up with

* In retrospect I think the cops' restraint was not entirely rooted in the knowledge that any illegal arrests might cause them embarrassment later, in the courtroom. I'm sure they also felt that if they waited long enough the loonies in Kesey's enclave would destroy each other, thus saving the taxpayers the expense of loading court dockets with complicated trials.

the caps and they would all take a peaceful trip to Somewhere Else.

Contrary to all expectations, most of the Angels became oddly peaceful on acid. With one or two exceptions, they were much easier to get along with then than stone sober and straight on their own turf. The acid dissolved many of their conditioned reflexes. There was little of the sullen craftiness or the readiness to fight that usually pervades their attitude when dealing with strangers. The aggressiveness went out of them; they lost the bristling, suspicious quality of wild animals sensing a snare. It was a strange thing, and I still don't quite understand it. At the time I had an uneasy feeling that it was a lull before the storm, that they weren't really taking enough to get the full effect and that sooner or later the whole scene would be razed by some kind of hellish delayed reaction. Yet there was plenty of evidence that the drug was taking hold. The Angels have no regard for what psychiatrists consider the limits of safe dosage; they doubled and then tripled the recommended maximums, often dropping 800 or 1,000 micrograms in a twelve-hour span. Some went into long fits of crying and wailing, babbling incoherent requests to people nobody else could see. Others fell into catatonic slumps and said nothing for hours at a time, then sprang to life again with tales of travelling to distant lands and seeing incredible sights. One night Magoo wandered off in the woods and became panic-stricken, screaming for help until somebody led him back to the light. On another night Terry the Tramp was convinced that he'd died as a person and come back to life as a rooster which was going to be cooked on the bonfire just as soon as the music stopped. Towards the end of every dance he would rush over to the tape recorder, shouting 'No! No! Don't let it stop!' An outlaw whose name I forget 'skied' down an almost perpendicular two-hundred-foot cliff in full view of the police; everyone cheered as he leaped off the brink and somehow kept his balance while the heels of his boots kicked up huge sprays of dirt. The only outburst of violence involved an Angel who tried to strangle his old lady on Kesey's front steps less than a half-hour after swallowing his first – and last – capsule.

My own acid-eating experience is limited in terms of total consumption, but widely varied as to company and circumstances

... and if I had a choice of repeating any one of the half-dozen bouts I recall, I would choose one of those Hell's Angels parties in La Honda, complete with all the mad lighting, cops on the road, a Ron Boise sculpture looming out of the woods, and all the big speakers vibrating with Dylan's 'Mister Tambourine Man'. It was a very electric atmosphere. If the Angels lent a feeling of menace, they also made it more interesting ... and far more alive than anything likely to come out of a controlled experiment or a politely brittle gathering of well-educated truth-seekers looking for wisdom in a capsule. Dropping acid with the Angels was an adventure; they were too ignorant to know what to expect, and too wild to care. They just swallowed the stuff and hung on ... which is probably just as dangerous as the experts say, but a far, far nuttier trip than sitting in some sterile chamber with a condescending guide and a handful of nervous, would-be hipsters. To my knowledge there are no cases of outlaw motorcyclists running amok on LSD; perhaps the hoodlum psyche is too unfertile to sustain the kind of secret madness that comes to life on acid. Lawmakers calling for a ban on LSD invariably cite crimes by intelligent, middle-upper-class strivers with no history of crime or thuggery. A butcher-knife murder in Brooklyn triggered a U.S. Senate investigation. The alleged killer, a brilliant graduate student said he'd been flying on LSD for three days and couldn't remember what he'd done.* The California State Legislature passed a stiff LSD law after hearing a Los Angeles police official testify that it caused people to perch naked in trees, run screaming through the streets and get down on all fours to munch on grassy lawns. Other LSD cases feature murder, suicide and crazed behaviour of all kinds. A student in Berkeley walked out a third-storey window saying: 'As long as I'm going to take a trip I might as well go to Europe.' The fall killed him instantly.

None of these incidents involve that element of American society usually associated with criminal behaviour. Like price fixing, tax evasion and embezzlement, psychedelic crimes seem to be a vice of the fatter classes. This has nothing to do with the price of LSD, which ranges from $.75 a cap, or cube, up to $5 – the maximum price for a twelve-hour trip of indeterminate intensity.

* In June 1966.

Heroin, by contrast, is definitely a lower-class vice, yet it costs most addicts at least $20 a day, and usually much more.

Conclusions are a bit hazy at this point, and the rash of LSD laws passed in 1965 and 1966 will probably abort any meaningful research on the subject for many years. In the meantime the Kesey Experiment should be noted, pondered and perhaps expanded upon by researchers of a similar persuasion. Even in its abbreviated form, it deflated the conventional wisdom concerning (1) the nature of LSD, (2) the structure and flexibility of the hoodlum personality or (3) both of these.*

One of the best of the La Honda soirées was held on Labour Day weekend of 1965, the first anniversary of the Monterey rape. By this time the Angels' publicity blitz was in high gear and they were dealing constantly with the news media. Reporters and photographers were hanging around the El Adobe nearly every weekend – asking questions, taking photos and hoping for some action to beef up the next day's headlines. The Oakland police assigned a special four-man detail to keep tabs on the Angels at all times. They would stop by the bar now and then, smiling good-naturedly in a torrent of insults, and hang around just long enough to make sure the outlaws knew they were being watched. The Angels enjoyed these visits; they were much happier talking with cops than they were with reporters or even sympathetic strangers, who were frequenting the El Adobe in ever increasing numbers. Despite the outlaws' growing notoriety, the Oakland

* After three or four months of chronic overindulgence on acid, most of the Angels began tapering off. A few suffered terrifying hallucinations and swore off the drug entirely. Some said they were afraid it would drive them crazy or cause them to wreck their bikes. By 1966 only a few were still eating acid with any consistency. One of these told me LSD was the best thing that ever happened to him. 'I haven't had a worry since I took the first cap,' he said. In September 1966 Kesey returned to California unannounced and made a series of brief appearances at 'underground' parties and Press conferences. He said he'd decided, after six months south of the border, to return to America as 'a permanent fugitive and salt in the wounds of J. Edgar Hoover'. Kesey's red panel truck was either too slow, or his driver too inept, to avoid J. Edgar's hounds. As this was written he was free on more than $30,000 bail and awaiting trial on charges that could send him to prison for one to five years. My own feeling is that he should have stayed in Asunción and got a job.

police never put the kind of death-rattle heat on them that the other chapters were getting. Even at the peak of the heat, Barger's chapter had a special relationship with the local law. Barger explained it as a potential common front against the long-rumoured Negro uprising in East Oakland, which both Negroes and Hell's Angels think of as their own turf. The cops, he said, were counting on the Angels to 'keep the niggers in line'.

'They're a lot more scared of the niggers than they are of us,' Sonny said, 'because there's a lot more of 'em.'

The Angels' relationship with Oakland Negroes is just as ambivalent as it is with the cops. Their colour line is strangely gerrymandered, so that individual 'good spades' are on one side and the mass of 'crazy niggers' are on the other. One of the Nomads (formerly the Sacramento chapter) shares an apartment with a Negro artist who makes all the Angel parties without any hint of self-consciousness. The outlaws call him a 'real good cat'.

'He's an artist,' Jimmy told me one night at a party in Oakland. 'I don't know much about art, but they say he's good.'

Charley is another good spade. He's a wiry little Negro who's been riding with the Angels for so long that some of them are embarrassed to explain why he's not a member. 'Hell, I admire the little bastard,' said one, 'but he'll never get in. He thinks he will, but he won't . . . shit, all it takes is two blackballs, and I could tell you who they'd be by just looking around the room.'

I never asked Charley why he didn't ride with the East Bay Dragons, an all-Negro outlaw club like the Rattlers in San Francisco. The Dragons have the same kind of half-made *élan* as the Angels, and a group of them wailing down the highway is every bit as spectacular. They wear multicoloured helmets and their bikes are a flashy mixture of choppers and garbage wagons – all Harley 74s. The Dragons, like the Angels, are mainly in their twenties and more or less unemployed. Also like the Angels, they have a keen taste for the action, violent or otherwise.*

Shortly after I met the Oakland Angels, and long before I knew

* The Rattlers are generally older. The club dates back to the days of the Booze Fighters. 'The Rattlers had a lot of class in the old days,' one of the Oakland Angels lamented. 'But all they do now is sit around their bar and play dominoes.'

the Dragons even existed, I was standing in the doorway of the El Adobe on a dull Friday night, when the parking lot suddenly filled up with about twenty big chrome-flashing bikes ridden by the wildest-looking bunch of Negroes I'd ever seen. They rolled in, gunning their engines, and dismounted with such an easy, swaggering confidence that my first impulse was to drop my beer and run. I had been around the Angels long enough to get the drift of their thinking on 'niggers' . . . and now here they were, a gang of black commandos booming right up to the Hell's Angels command post. I stepped out of the doorway to a spot where I would have a clear sprint to the street when the chain-whipping started.

There were about thirty Angels at the bar that night and most of them hurried outside, still carrying their beers, to see who the visitors were. But nobody looked ready to fight. By the time the Dragons had cut their engines, the Angels were greeting them with friendly jibes about 'calling the cops' and 'having you bastards locked up for scaring hell out of the citizens'. Barger shook hands with Lewis, the Dragons' president, and asked what was happening. 'Where've you guys been hiding?' Sonny said. 'If you came around here more often you might make the papers.' Lewis laughed and introduced Sonny, Terry and Gut to some of the new Dragon members. Most of the black outlaws seemed to know the Angels by their first names. Some went into the bar while others drifted around the parking lot, shaking hands here and there and admiring the bikes. The talk was mainly of motorcycles, and although it was pointedly friendly, it was also a bit reserved. By this time Sonny had introduced me to Lewis and some of the others. 'He's a writer,' Barger said with a smile. 'God only knows what he's writin', but he's good people.' Lewis nodded and shook hands with me. 'How you makin' it?' he said. 'If Sonny says you're okay with him, you're okay with us.' He said it with such a wide smile that I thought he was going to laugh. Then he clapped me on the shoulder in a quick, friendly sort of way, as if to make sure I understood that he'd pegged me for an arch con man, but that he wasn't going to ruin the joke by letting Sonny in on it.

The Dragons stayed about an hour, then boomed off to wherever they were going. The Angels didn't invite them to any parties later on, and I had a feeling that both groups were relieved that the visit had come off so smoothly. The Angels seemed to forget all about the Dragons just as soon as they rolled out of sight. The El Adobe shuffle resumed once again . . . the familiar beery tedium, the honkytonk blare of the juke box, bikes coming and going, balls clacking on the pool table, and the raucous, repetitious chatter of people who spend so much time together that they can only kill the boredom by getting out of their heads. Sonny left early, as he usually does, and as he mounted his black Sportster in the parking lot I remembered the Dragons and asked why they seemed on such friendly terms with the Angels. 'We're not real close,' he replied, 'and we never will be as long as I'm president. But they're different from most niggers. They're our kind of people.'

I never saw the Dragons at the El Adobe again, but other Negroes who came there got a different reception. One weekend night in late August a group of four came in. They were all in their twenties, wearing sports coats without ties, and one was so big that he had to duck through the doorway. He was almost seven feet tall and weighed between 250 and 300. The place was crowded, but the four negroes found some room at the bar and the big one struck up an apparently friendly conversation with Don Mohr, the photographer, who had just been made an honorary Angel. The rest of the outlaws ignored the newcomers, but about thirty minutes after their arrival, Mohr and the black Goliath began snarling at each other. The nature of the dispute was never made clear, but Mohr said later that he'd bought the 'big nigger' two beers in the course of their conversation. 'Then he ordered another one,' Mohr explained, 'and I told him I'd be fucked if I'd pay for it. That's all it took, man. He was lookin' for trouble just by comin' in here. When I told him to buy his own goddamn beer after I paid for the first two rounds he got sarcastic – so I said let's go outside.'

The two were already squared off in the parking lot before the other Angels realized a fight was in the making, but by the time the first blow landed, the combat area was enclosed in a ring of spectators. Mohr went after his huge opponent without any preliminaries he leaped forward and swung at the Negro's head – and that was the end of the fight.

The Negro swung blindly as the others swarmed over him. He was whacked simultaneously in the stomach, the kidneys and on all sides of his head. One of his friends tried to help him, but ran into Tiny's forearm and was knocked unconscious. The other two had enough sense to run. The monster reeled back for a moment, then rushed forward, still swinging, until he was hit from the side and sent sprawling. Three of the outlaws tried to hold him, but he jumped up and bulled into the bar. He didn't look hurt, but he was bleeding from several small cuts, and after being hit so often, from so many different directions, he couldn't get his bearings. He went down again but got up quickly and backed against the jukebox. Until then he'd been a moving, lunging target and only two or three of the Angels had managed a solid shot at him. But now he was brought to bay. For about five seconds nothing happened. The Negro looked desperately for an opening to run through, and he was still looking when Terry's off-the-floor block-buster caught him in the left eye. He fell back on the jukebox, smashing the glass cover, and sank to the floor. For a moment he seemed done, but after a flurry of boots in the ribs he pulled one of his attackers off balance and got back on his feet. He was still straightening up when Andy, one of the frailest and least talkative of the Angels, caught him in the right eye with a frenzied running punch that would have fractured a normal man's skull. When he went down this time Sonny grabbed his collar and jerked him on to his back. A boot heel crashed into his mouth. He was helpless now, his face covered with blood, but the stomping continued. Finally they dragged him outside and dropped him face down in the parking lot.

The first police car arrived just as the beating ended. Two others rolled up from different directions, then came a paddy wagon, and finally an ambulance. The Angels insisted the huge victim had pulled a knife and had to be subdued. The cops looked around with their flashlights, but the knife was not to be found. The Negro was in no condition to deny anything, although he regained consciousness almost immediately and was able to walk to the ambulance. This seemed to satisfy the police, at least for the time being. They took a few notes and warned Sonny that the victim might want to press charges when he came out of shock, but

I had the impression that they considered the case already closed . . natural justice had prevailed.

The beating never came to court, but it whipped the Angels into a very agitated state of mind. There was no doubt in their heads that the niggers would try to get even. And next time it wouldn't be just four of them. Never in hell. Next time it would be massive retaliation. Probably they would strike on a moonless night. . . . they would wait until almost closing time, hoping to catch the Angels drunk and helpless, and then they would make their move. The dreary neon calm of East Fourteenth Street would be shattered without warning by the screeching of primitive bone whistles. Wave after wave of sweaty black bodies would move out of the command post – the Doggie Diner on East Twenty-third – and move silently through the streets to their positions on the attack perimeter, about four hundred yards from the El Adobe. Then, when the bone whistles sounded, the first wave of niggers would run like the devil across East Fourteenth, ignoring the red light, and fall on the Angels with savage home-made weapons.

Every time I talked to the Angels in the weeks after the Big Nigger incident they warned me that the cork was ready to blow. 'We're pretty sure it's gonna be Saturday night,' Sonny would tell me. 'We got the word from a fink.' I assured him that I wanted to be there when the attack came, and I did. Several months earlier I would have laughed the whole thing off as some kind of twisted, adolescent delusion . . . but after spending most of that summer in the drunk-bloody, whore-walloping taverns of East Oakland, I had changed my ideas about reality and the human animal.

One weekend night in late summer I got out of my car in the El Adobe lot. Somebody called my name in a high-pitched whisper and I nodded to the handful of Angels standing near the doorway. I heard the whisper again, but none of the people I could see had said anything. Then I realized somebody was on the roof. I looked up and saw Sonny's head peering over the concrete ledge. 'Around back,' he hissed. 'There's a ladder.'

Behind the building, in a jumble of garbage cans, I found a twenty-foot ladder leading up to the roof. I climbed up to find Sonny and Zorro lying in a corner, almost invisible in a maze of peeling tar paper. Sonny had an AR-16, the newest U.S. army rifle, and Zorro had an M-1 carbine. Piled between them on the roof was a stack of ammunition in boxes and clips, a flashlight and a Thermos bottle of coffee. They were waiting for the niggers, they said. This was the night.

It wasn't – but the Angels kept armed guards on the roof of the El Adobe for nearly a month until they were sure the niggers were completely intimidated. One afternoon at the height of the tension Barger and five others rode their bikes out to a target range in Almeda. They carried their rifles strapped over their backs and took a route through the middle of Oakland. The police telephone hummed with reports of a heavily armed Hell's Angel patrol moving south through the centre of town. But there was nothing the cops could do. The outlaws had their unloaded guns in plain sight and were observing the speed limit. They felt they needed some target practice . . . and if their appearance had a bad effect on the public, well, that was the public's problem, not theirs.

Most of the Angels know better than to carry weapons openly, but some of their homes resemble private arsenals – knives, revolvers, automatic rifles and even a home-made armoured car with a machine-gun turret on top. They don't like to talk about their weaponry . . . it's their only insurance policy against that day when the Main Cop decides on a showdown, and the Angels are absolutely certain that day is coming.

*

> No, I wouldn't call them 'racists'. Not really. Maybe deep down they are. There ain't no Negro Angels, you notice. But the Angels ain't *for* anybody, and that makes them anti-Negro and just about anything else. – ***San Bernardino County police inspector***

*

In the language of politics and public relations the Angels 'peaked' in the fall of 1965. The Labour Day Run to Kesey's was a letdown of sorts, because towns all over the country were braced for the invasion, waiting to be raped and pillaged. The National Guard was called out at such far-flung points as Parker, Arizona, and Claremont, Indiana. Canadian police set up a special border watch near Vancouver, British Columbia; and in Ketchum, Idaho, the locals mounted a machine-gun on the roof of a Main Street drugstore. 'We're ready for those punks,' said the sheriff. 'We'll put half of 'em in jail and the other half in the graveyard.'

The Angels' jaunt to La Honda was a sad anticlimax for the Press. The outlaws did a lot of strange, high-speed travelling, but it was not in the realm of the five W's. One of my memories of that weekend is Terry the Tramp's keynote speech delivered to the police on the highway. He got hold of a microphone tied up to some powerful speakers and used the opportunity to unburden his mind . . . addressing the police in a very direct way, speaking of morals and music and madness, and finishing on a high, white note which the San Mateo sheriff's department will not soon forget:

'Remember this,' he screamed into the mike. 'Just remember that while you're standing out there on that cold road, doin' your righteous duty and watchin' all us sex fiends and dope addicts in here havin' a good time . . . just think about that little old *wife of yours* back home with some dirty old Hell's Angel crawlin' up *between her thighs*!' Then a burst of wild laughter, clearly audible on the road. 'What do you think about that, you worthless fuzz? You gettin' hungry? We'll bring you some chili if we have any left over . . . but don't hurry home, let your wife enjoy herself.'

It was hard to know, in the triumphant chaos of that Labour Day, that the Angels were on the verge of blowing one of the best connections they'd ever had. Busting up country towns was old stuff, and the cops were getting tense about it. The hippie drug scene was a brand new dimension – a different gig, as it were – but as the Vietnam war became more and more a public issue the Angels were put in a bind.

For several months they'd been drifting towards political involvement, but the picture was hazy and one of the most confusing elements was their geographical proximity to Berkeley, the citadel of West Coast radicalism. Berkeley is right next door to Oakland, with nothing between them but a line on the map and a few street signs, but in many ways they are as different as Manhattan and the Bronx. Berkeley is a college town and, like Manhattan, a magnet for intellectual transients. Oakland is a magnet for people who want hour-wage jobs and cheap housing, who can't afford to live in Berkeley, San Francisco or any of the middle-class Bay Area suburbs.* It is a noisy, ugly, mean-spirited place, with the sort of charm that Chicago had for Sandburg. It is also a natural environment for hoodlums, brawlers, teenage gangs and racial tensions.

The Hell's Angels massive publicity – coming hard on the heels of the widely publicized student rebellion in Berkeley – was interpreted in liberal–radical–intellectual circles as the signal for a natural alliance. Beyond that, the Angels' aggressive, anti-social stance – their *alienation*, as it were – had a tremendous appeal for the more aesthetic Berkeley temperament. Students who could barely get the nerve up to sign a petition or to shoplift a candy bar were fascinated by the tales of the Hell's Angels ripping up towns and taking whatever they wanted. Most important, the Angels had a reputation for defying police, for successfully bucking authority, and to the frustrated student radical this was a powerful image indeed. The Angels didn't masturbate, they raped. They didn't come on with theories and songs and quotations, but with noise and muscle and sheer balls.

The honeymoon lasted about three months and came to a jangled end on 16 October, when the Hell's Angels attacked a Get Out of Vietnam demonstration at the Oakland–Berkeley border. The existential heroes who had passed the joint with Berkeley liberals at Kesey's parties suddenly turned into venomous beasts rushing on the same liberals with flailing fists and shouts of 'Traitors', 'Communists', 'Beatniks'! When push came to shove, the Hell's Angels lined up solidly with the cops, the Pentagon and the John Birch Society. And there was no joy that day in Berkeley, for Casey had apparently gone mad.

The attack was an awful shock to those who had seen the Hell's Angels as pioneers of the human spirit, but to anyone who knew them it was entirely logical. The Angels' collective viewpoint has always been fascistic. They insist and seem to believe that the swastika fetish is no more than an anti-social joke, a guaranteed gimmick to bug the squares, the taxpayers – all those they spitefully refer to as 'citizens'. What they really mean is the Middle Class, the Bourgeoisie, the Burghers – but the Angels don't know these terms

* Oakland's official population is nearly four hundred thousand, but it is the centre of a vastly urban sprawl called the East Bay, with a population of about two million – more than twice the size of San Francisco.

and they're suspicious of anyone who tries to explain them. If they wanted to be artful about bugging the squares they would drop the swastika and decorate their bikes with the hammer and sickle. That would really raise hell on the freeways ... hundreds of Communist thugs roaming the countryside on big motorcycles, looking for trouble.

The first clash came on a Saturday afternoon, at the midway point of a protest march from the Berkeley campus to the Oakland Army Terminal, a shipping point for men and material bound for the Far East. Some fifteen thousand demonstrators moved down Telegraph Avenue, one of the main streets of Berkeley, and came face to face – at the city limits – with a four-hundred man wall of Oakland police wearing helmets and holding riot sticks at port arms. They were deployed in a flying wedge formation, with Police Chief Toothman in the central, ball-carrier's position, giving orders over many walkie-talkies. It was obvious that the march was not going to cross the Oakland line without a fight. I approached the confrontation from the Oakland side – but even with a tape recorder, camera and Press credentials, it took almost thirty minutes to get through the no-man's-land of the police wall. Most people – even some legitimate journalists – were turned back.

So it is still beyond my understanding how a dozen Hell's Angels, obviously intent on causing trouble, managed to filter through and attack the leaders of the protest march as they came forward to confer with Chief Toothman. Tiny led the charge, swinging at anyone unlucky enough to be in his way. The Angels were quickly subdued by Berkeley police, but not before they managed to punch a few people, tear up some signs and rip microphone wires off the march leader's sound truck. This was the infamous struggle that resulted in the cop's broken leg.

It was all a misunderstanding, the hipster commandos said, explaining the attack: the Angels were duped by the cops, their heads had been turned by secret Right Wing money, and they would certainly adjust their allegiance just as soon as they knew the score.

But the score was a lot more complicated than the hipsters seemed to think. Another Vietnam protest was scheduled for mid-November, and in the meantime there were numerous meetings between the anti-war brain trust and the Hell's Angels. Barger would sit in his living-room and listen patiently to everything the Vietnam Day Committee had to say, then brush it all aside. The Berkeley people argued long and well, but they never seemed to realize they were talking on a different frequency. It didn't matter how many beards, busts or acid caps they could muster; Sonny considered them all chickenshit – and that was that.

The Angels, like all other motorcycle outlaws, are rigidly anti-Communist. Their political views are limited to the same kind of retrograde patriotism that motivates the John Birch Society, the Ku Klux Klan and the American Nazi Party. They are blind to the irony of their role . . . knight errants of a faith from which they have already been excommunicated. The Angels will be among the first to be locked up or croaked if the politicians they think they agree with ever come to power.

During the weeks preceding the second march on the Oakland Army Terminal, Allen Ginsberg spent much of his time trying to persuade Barger and his people not to attack the marchers. The outlaws had never encountered anyone quite like Ginsberg: they considered him otherworldly. 'That goddamn Ginsberg is gonna fuck us *all* up,' said Terry. 'For a guy that ain't straight at all, he's about the straightest sonofabitch I've ever seen. Man, you shoulda been there when he told Sonny he loved him. . . . Sonny didn't know *what* the hell to say.'

The Angels never really understood what Ginsberg meant, but his unnerving frankness and the fact that Kesey liked him gave them second thoughts about attacking a march that he obviously considered a Right thing. Shortly before the November march, Ginsberg published this speech in the *Berkeley Barb*:

To the Angels

by Allen Ginsberg

These are the thoughts – anxieties – of anxious marchers
  That the Angels will attack them
    for kicks, or to get publicity, to take the heat off themselves
      or to get the goodwill of police & press &/or right wing Money
  That a conscious deal has been made with Oakland police
    or an unconscious rapport, tacit understanding
      mutual sympathy

that Oakland will lay off persecuting the Angels
if the Angels attack & break up the March &
make it a riot.

Is any of this true, or is it the paranoia of the less stable-minded
marchers?
As long as Angels are ambiguous and don't give open reassurance
that they can be trusted to be tranquil,
The anxious souls, the naturally violent, the insecure, the hysterics
among the marchers have an excuse for policy of
self-defence thru violence,
a rationalization for their own inner violence.

That leaves the Marchers with choice of defending themselves thru
force on account of fear & threat
unleashing the more irrational minority of rebels
or at best, defending themselves, coolly under control
BUT CRITICIZED FOR BEING LAWLESS

or not defending selves, and possibly abandoned by police
(for we have no clear assurance from Oakland police
that they will sincerely try to maintain order and guard our
lawful right to march)
if you attack, & having innocent pacifists, youths
& old ladies busted up
AND CRITICIZED AS IRRESPONSIBLE COWARDS
By you, by Press, by Public & by Violence loving leftists
& rightists.

As it stands the VDC adopted policy of pacifism for marchers, WHO
SIMPLY WILL NOT FIGHT. And will try to make the march a
HAPPY SPECTACLE.

*

Do Angels have any questions for Vietnam Day Committee?
any suspicions that might be cleared up now?
What's the main complaint?

What do the Angels plan to do Nov. 20? Do they really have a plan?
Let's now make a plan that will leave everybody secure.

Because the Fearheads around the VDC public meetings believe the
Image of Angels as 'They like to bust people up for kicks'
and naturally you get a bad rep. that way

especially if you've finally found a group you can beat up
with some social approval, temporarily,
& compliance of the cops.

You don't want to 'change' you want to be yourselves,
& if that includes sadism, or forced hostility,
here's a situation where you can get away with it.

BUT NOBODY WANTS TO REJECT THE SOULS OF THE
HELL'S ANGELS
or make them change –
WE JUST DON'T WANT TO GET BEAT UP

*

The protest march is trying to point out
that the terror in Vietnam is making
same terror here inside our country
loosing publicly the same cruel psychology that'll
give approval to busting yellow head gooks in Vietnam
This is infecting peaceful human relations here
allowing for public mass persecution of people
who disagree with

the
growth of mass hostility   mass hypocrisy   mass conflict

The mass of marchers are not POLITICAL, they're
PSYCHOLOGICAL HEADS
who don't want the country to drift into the habit of blind violence
& unconscious cruelty & egoism NOT COMMUNICATION – with
outside world or lonely minorities in America
such as yourselves
and ourselves
AND the negroes
AND the teaheads
AND the Communists
AND the Beatniks
AND the Birchers
AND even the so called Squares

I am afraid that once
the people who hate us peace
Marchers & let you beat us up, – afraid of us Pacifists –
will then, still having this

fear and hate at heart, turn it on you
afraid of you, too,
or ask you to turn it on other minorities
the negroes?
Ultimately on you and each other.
(This was the pattern of Brown Shirts in Germany
who were used by hate politicians,
& then creamed in Concentration Camps.
I think.)

*

I said we were not politicians mostly. And you say you're indifferent to politics. But you're getting hung on politics and taking Geopolitical positions promoting bomb Vietnam.

*

What ELSE, besides this politics, will take the heat
off the Hell's Angels?

*

That heat's on everybody, *not* just you
To go to war, to be drafted,
To make money on war jobs & economy, to be destroyed
by Bomb, to get busted
for pot –

To take the heat off, you've got
to take the heat off
INSIDE YOURSELVES –
Find Peace means stop hating yourself
stop hating people who hate you
stop reflecting HEAT
THERE ARE PEOPLE WHO ARE NOT HEAT
THE MOST OF PEACE MARCHERS ARE NOT HEAT
They want you to join them to relieve
the heat on you & on all of us.

Take the heat – Anxiety Paranoia –
off us, AND off the police, off all the fearful –
REASSURE, and act clearly in such a way
as to reassure –
by being kind not
cruel –
and it'll be remembered and responded to.

Forcing self, others and police into a corner
  increases heat.
Beating up on Vietnam won't take the heat off –
 even if whole country joined Hell's Angels
 – world will apply heat & world be destroyed –
  (almost happened thru Hitler)

Yes time to take the heat symbolism off the Swastika
 and give the swastika back to the Indians & Peaceful Mystics
  & Calcutta Ganja Smokers
Can you imagine doing the same for the Hammer and Sickle?
 I've seen Jewish Stars, & there is M13, & LSD
  & Negro Crescent
   to make HAPPY on yr. backs.

*

I called Beatnick or Vietnick not want a way that is not common for all – recognizable & acceptable to all – want a way we can all live together without heat & rejection.

My desire to share, not
MONOPOLIZE the images, because I don't want to be ALONE
in Earth.
I don't want unnecessary suffering for me, or anybody. – you,
the police, the Vietnamese, the entire human universe.

*

What is the way out of the heat
for you? If stop threat to take over
others, then people let you alone.
Have you stopped threatening the Marcher people
yet?
If you threat, you must WANT heat.
We're trying
to take it off you, & off us, & off the
cops, & off the U.S. & off China & off Vietnam.

The heat is human, emotional, not a law
of nature.

*

How many Angels really dig your political position,
aside from its tactics as heat relief?

How many hate the marchers? really want to bug them?
Is it you & Tiny's personal goof, or really what you all *want*?
If you dig POT why don't you dig that the whole generation who don't dig the heat war also dig pot and consciousness & spontaneity & hair & they are your natural brothers.
rather than the moralistic rigid types
who have fixed warlike negative image of America?
The great image – which all can buy – is your own ideal Image –
WHITMAN's free soul, camarado, also of Open Road!
I asking you be Camarado, friend, kind, lover, because vast majority
of peace marchers
actually respect & venerate your lonesomeness
& struggle & would rather be peaceful intimates
with you than fearful enraged frightened paranoid enemies
hitting each other.
That probably goes for the police too who have human bodies under
uniform.

There are some rigid souls – who believe the universe is evil –
frightened of sex & pot & motorcycles & PEACE even it it was
all peaceful and tranquil –
afraid of life, not realizing its harmless emptiness –
These are the people we should be
working on – making love to them –
blowing our minds and theirs –
softening them, enlarging their consciousness
and our own too in the process –
not fighting each other

All separate identities are bankrupt –
Square, beat, Jews, negros, Hell's Angels, Communist & American.

Hell's Angels & Tiny's Intervention has probably had good effect –
forced the leaders & marchers to look inside
themselves to measure
how much their march is blind aggression
put-on motivated by rage &
confused desire to find someone to BLAME
& fight & Scream

OR

How much the march will be a free expression
of calm people who have controlled
their own hatreds

and are showing the American people
    how to control their own fear & hatred
and once and for all be done with the pressure
    building up to annihilate the planet
and take our part ENDING THE HEAT on earth.

– Delivered as a speech at San Jose State College, Monday, 15 November 1965, before students and representatives of Bay Area Hell's Angels

Despite Ginsberg's pleas, Sonny told me a week before the march that he was going to meet it with 'the biggest bunch of outlaw bikes anybody ever saw in California'. Allen and his friends meant well, he said, but they just didn't know what was happening. So it came as a real surprise when, on 19 November – the day before the march – the Angels called a Press conference to announce that they would not man the barricades. The explanation, in the form of a mimeographed Press release, said: 'Although we have stated our intention to counterdemonstrate at this despicable, un-American activity, we believe that in the interest of public safety and the protection of the good name of Oakland, we should not justify the V.D.C. by our presence . . . because our patriotic concern for what these people are doing to our great nation may provoke us to violent acts ... [and that] any physical encounter would only produce sympathy for this mob of traitors.'

The highlight of the Press conference was the reading, by Barger, of a telegram he had already sent to His Excellency, the President of the United States:

PRESIDENT LYNDON B. JOHNSON
1600 Penn Ave.
Washington D.C.

Dear Mr President:

On behalf of myself and my associates I volunteer a group of loyal americans for behind the lines duty in Viet Nam. We feel that a crack group of trained gorrillas [*sic*] would demoralize the Viet Cong and advance the cause of freedom. We are available for training and duty immediately.

Sincerely
RALPH BARGER JR
Oakland, California
President of Hell's Angels

For reasons never divulged, Mr Johnson was slow to capitalize on Barger's offer, and the Angels never went to Vietnam. But they didn't bust up the 20 November protest march either, and some people said this meant the outlaws were coming around.

*

> We don't have a police problem in this community – we have a people problem. – *Former Oakland police chief*

*

It was about this time that my long-standing *rapport* with the Angels began to deteriorate. All the humour went out of the act when they began to believe their own Press clippings, and it was no longer much fun to drink with them. Even the names lost their magic. Instead of Bagmaster, Scuzzy and Hupe, it was Luther Young, E. O. Sturm and Normal Scarlet III. There was no more mystery; overexposure had reduced the menace to an all-too-common denominator, and as the group portrait became more understandable it also became less appealing.

For nine months I had lived in a world that had seemed, at first, like something original. It was obvious from the beginning that the menace bore little resemblance to its publicized image, but there was a certain pleasure in sharing the Angels' amusement at the stir they'd created. Later, as they attracted more and more attention, the mystique was stretched so thin that it finally became transparent. One afternoon as I sat in the El Adobe and watched an Angel sell a handful of barbiturate pills to a brace of pimply punks no more than sixteen I realized that the roots of this act were not in any time-honoured American myth but right beneath my feet in a new kind of society that is only beginning to take shape. To see the Hell's Angels as caretakers of the old 'individualist' tradition 'that made this country great' is only a painless way to get around seeing them for what they really are – not some romantic leftover, but the first wave of a future that nothing in our history has prepared us to cope with. The Angels are prototypes. Their lack of education has not only rendered them completely useless in a highly technical economy, but it has also given them the leisure to cultivate a powerful resentment . . . and to translate it into a destructive cult which the mass media insist on portraying as a sort of isolated oddity, a temporary phenomenon that will shortly become extinct now that it's been called to the attention of the police.

This is a reassuring viewpoint and it would be even more so if the police shared it. Unfortunately, they don't. Cops who know the Angels only from Press accounts are sometimes afraid of them, but familiarity seems to breed contempt, and cops who know the Angels from experience usually dismiss them as an overrated threat. On the other hand, at least ninety per cent of the dozens of cops I talked to all over California were seriously worried about what they referred to as 'the rising tide of lawlessness', or 'the dangerous trend towards lack of respect for law and order'. To them the Hell's Angels are only a symptom of a much more threatening thing . . . the Rising Tide.

'Mainly it's the teenagers,' said a young patrolman in Santa Cruz. 'Five years ago it was only a matter of talking to them, telling them in a friendly kind of way just what they could or couldn't get away with. They were just as wild, I guess, but you knew they would listen to reason.' He shrugged, fingering the ·38 Special cartridges that circled his waist. 'But now, goddamnit, it's different. You never know when some kid's going to swing on you, or pull a gun, or maybe just take off running. The badge doesn't mean a damn thing to them. They've lost all respect for it, all fear. Hell, I'd rather bust a dozen Hell's Angels every day of the week than have to break up one fight at a big high school beer party. With the motorcycle crowd you at least know what you're up against, but these kids are capable of anything. I mean it, they give me the creeps. I used to understand them, but not any more.'

The trends and problems of law enforcement have never interested the Angels, however, and even after their temporary *détente* with the Oakland police, they still viewed cops very simply as the enemy. Nor do they take much interest in their emotional or ideological connection to other rebellious elements. To them all comparisons are either presumptuous or insulting. 'There's only two kinds of people in the world,' Magoo explained one night. 'Angels, and people who wish they were Angels.'

Yet not even Magoo really believes that. When the party swings right, with plenty of beer and broads, being an Angel is a pretty good way to go. But on some of those lonely afternoons when you're fighting a toothache and trying to scrape up a few dollars to pay a traffic fine and the landlord has changed the lock on your door until you pay the back rent . . . then it's no fun being an Angel. It's hard to laugh when your teeth are so rotten that they hurt all the time and no dentist will touch you unless the bill is paid in advance. So it helps to believe, when the body rots start to hurt, that the pain is a small price to pay for the higher rewards of being a righteous Angel.

This wavering paradox is a pillar of the outlaw stance. A man who has blown all his options can't afford the luxury of changing his ways. He has to capitalize on whatever he has left, and he can't afford to admit – no matter how often he's reminded of it – that every day of his life takes him farther down a blind alley. Most Angels understand where they are, but not why, and they are well enough grounded in the eternal verities to know that very few of the toads in this world are Charming Princes in disguise. The others are simply toads, and no matter how many magic maidens they kiss or rape, they are going to stay that way.... Toads don't make laws or change any basic structures, but one or two rooty insights can work powerful changes in the way they get through life. A toad who believes he got a raw deal before he even knew who was dealing will usually be sympathetic to the mean, vindictive ignorance that colours the Hell's Angels' view of humanity. There is not much mental distance between a feeling of having been screwed and the ethic of total retaliation, or at least the kind of random revenge that comes with outraging the public decency.

The outlaw stance is patently anti-social, although most Angels, as individuals, are naturally social creatures. The contradiction is deeprooted and has parallels on every level of American society. Sociologists call it 'alienation', or 'anomie'. It is a sense of being cut off, or left out of whatever society one was presumably meant to be a part of. In a strongly motivated society the victims of anomie are usually extreme cases, isolated from each other by differing viewpoints or personal quirks too private for any broad explanation.

But in a society with no central motivation, so far adrift and puzzled with itself that its President [Eisenhower] feels called upon to appoint a Committee of National Goals, a sense of alienation is likely to be very popular – especially among people young enough to shrug off the guilt they're supposed to feel for deviating from a goal or purpose they never understood in the first place. Let the old people wallow in the shame of having failed. The laws they made to preserve a myth are no longer pertinent; the so-called American Way begins to seem like a dyke made of cheap cement, with many more leaks than the law has fingers to plug. America has been breeding mass anomie since the end of the Second World War. It is not a political thing, but the sense of new realities, of urgency, anger and sometimes desperation in a society where even the highest authorities seem to be grasping at straws.

In the terms of our Great Society the Hell's Angels and their ilk are losers – dropouts, failures and malcontents. They are rejects looking for a way to get even with a world in which they are only a problem. The Hell's Angels are not visionaries, but diehards, and if they are the forerunners or the vanguard of anything it is not the 'moral revolution' in vogue on college campuses, but a fast-growing legion of young employables whose untapped energy will inevitably find the same kind of destructive outlet that 'outlaws' like the Hell's Angels have been finding for years. The difference between the student radicals and the Hell's Angels is that the students are rebelling against the past, while the Angels are fighting the future. Their only common ground is their disdain for the present, or the *status quo*.

It goes without saying that some of the student radicals, in Berkeley and on dozens of other campuses, are as wild and aggressive as any Hell's Angels – and that not all the Angels are cruel thugs and potential Nazis. This was especially true before the Angels got all their publicity. As recently as early 1965 there were less than a half-dozen Angels who gave a hoot in hell what was happening on the Berkeley campus. If they'd been seriously interested in Red-baiting, they would have made an appearance at some of the free-speech rallies. But they didn't show up. Not even to swagger through the crowds and get their pictures in the papers. Nor – at about the same time – did they harass CORE's picket lines in Jack London Square, in the middle of downtown Oakland!

Even in the spring and early summer of 1965, when they were beginning to realize the extent of their infamy, they ignored several golden opportunities to tangle with both civil rights and Get Out of Vietnam demonstrators. They simply didn't care. Or at least not enough of them cared . . . and not all of them care even now.

But the burden of fame made the Hell's Angels very conscious of their image; they began reading the newspapers like politicians, looking for mention of things they had said or done. And as they dealt more and more with the Press, they were inevitably asked to comment on the issues of the day. ('Tell me, Sonny, do the Hell's Angels have any position on the war in Vietnam?' . . . 'How do you feel about the civil rights movement, Tiny?') The answers made good copy and it was not long before the Angels discovered they could call a Press conference,* complete with TV cameras, for the purpose of delivering various screeds and pronouncements. The news media loved it, and although many of the items on the Angels were rendered with considerable humour, the outlaws never noticed. They got a great boot out of seeing themselves on TV, and by the time things had come to this pass, there was no question of any ideological deviation within the club. Barger and the other officers spoke for the whole organization, and anybody who didn't agree could hang up his colours. None did, of course, even though Barger and perhaps two or three others were the only Angels with any kind of political awareness. But if Sonny had a beef with some pinko demonstrators, then by God, they all had a beef. And that was the way it went. Yet there were shreds of evidence, towards the end of 1965, that the La Honda atmosphere was having a gradual effect. One afternoon several weeks before the political crisis Terry was sitting in the El Adobe, sipping a beer and talking thoughtfully about the difference between the Angels and the hipster-radical types he'd been partying with: 'You know, sometimes I think we ain't makin' it,' he said. 'These other people at least get somethin' goin' for 'em. They're fuck-ups too, but they're constructive. We're too goddamn negative. Our whole

* At one Press conference in Oakland, held at the downtown office of the Angels' bondswoman, I counted forty-two reporters on hand and thirteen microphones massed in front of Barger while he spoke – and five TV cameras.

bit is destructive. I can't see any way out for us if we can't find some other kind of scene besides tearin' things up.'

Six months earlier the Angels' only real problem had been keeping out of jail, but now they were *engagé* and had to sit through meetings with other people who were *engagé*. A few of the outlaws thrived on the new gig, but for most it was only a drag. And to those who could look back on a decade or more of hostile isolation, it seemed like the end of an era.

*

> No more self-defeating device could be discovered than the one society has developed in dealing with the criminal. It proclaims his career in such loud and dramatic forms that both he and the community accept the judgement as a fixed description. He becomes conscious of himself as a criminal, and the community expects him to live up to his reputation, and will not credit him if he does not live up to it.
> – *Frank Tannenbaum*, Crime and the Community

*

Far from being freaks, the Hell's Angels are a logical product of the culture that now claims to be shocked at their existence. The generation represented by the editors of *Time* has lived so long in a world full of celluloid outlaws hustling toothpaste and hair oil that it is no longer capable of confronting the real thing. For twenty years they have sat with their children and watched yesterday's outlaws raise hell with yesterday's world . . . and now they are bringing up children who think Jesse James is a television character. This is the generation that went to war for Mom, God, and Apple Butter, the American Way of Life. When they came back, they crowned Eisenhower and then retired to the giddy comfort of their TV parlours, to cultivate the subtleties of American history as seen by Hollywood.

To them the appearance of the Hell's Angels must have seemed like a wonderful publicity stunt. In a nation of frightened dullards there is a sorry shortage of outlaws, and those few who make the grade are always welcome: Frank Sinatra, Alexander King, Elizabeth Taylor, Raoul Duke . . . they have that extra 'something'.

Charles Starkweather had something extra too, but he couldn't get an agent, and instead of taking his vitality to Hollywood, he freaked out in Wyoming and killed a dozen people for reasons he couldn't explain. So the state put him to death. There were other outlaws who missed the brass ring in the fifties. Lenny Bruce was one; he was never quite right for television. Bruce had tremendous promise until about 1961, when the people who'd been getting such a kick out of him suddenly realized he was serious. Just like Starkweather was serious . . . and like the Hell's Angels are serious.

Soon after the *Post* article appeared, the Associated Press put this item on the wire, with a Detroit dateline: 'A gang of seven teenage terrorists – 13, 14 and 15 years old – has been broken up, police said yesterday. Police said the boys perpetrated arson, armed robbery, burglary and cruelty to animals. The gang usually wore hoods, made of pillowcases. They called themselves "The Bylaws" and named Jews, Negroes and Frats (well-dressed students) as hate objects.'

Several months earlier the United Press International wire carried this item, from Dallas, headed: MOB BLOCKS RESCUE.

Firemen attempting to reach a burning home in south Dallas Thursday night were blocked by a group of 60 yelling, heckling youths who refused to move out of the street.

The firemen called police. Several carloads of police, using dogs, finally dispersed the young hecklers, whom they described as 'wild punks'.

The youths threatened and fought with police.

Firemen who then were able to make their way into the burning house found the limp form of Patrick Chambers, too. But it was too late. The child was pronounced dead on arrival at a hospital.

His mother, Mrs Geneva Chambers, 31, and a neighbour, Mrs Jessie Jones, 27, were hospitalized in shock.

'If your police want trouble, they've come to the right place and we'll take care of you, too,' a fire department spokesman quoted one of the youths as saying.

Firemen said when they tried to revive the baby on the lawn, several youths ran up and 'tried to stomp on the dead baby'.

A woman and two men, part of the growing crowd of 400 persons, were arrested.

Police said the woman scratched and slapped a policeman. The men jumped on policemen trying to prevent the woman from attacking the officer.

*

> If you publish that I'll come and get you and I'll kill you. I don't care what happens. I'll be ruined. This is all I've got to live for. – *Daniel Burros, an organizer for the American Nazi Party, to a* New York Times *reporter who dug up evidence that Burros himself was Jewish*

> As you were, I was
> As I am, you will be. – *H. Himmler (quotation scrawled on a wall at a Hell's Angels party)*

*

Now, looking for labels, it is hard to call the Hell's Angels anything but mutants. They are urban outlaws with a rural ethic and a new improvised style of self-preservation. Their image of themselves derives mainly from celluloid, from the Western movies and two-fisted TV shows that have taught them most of what they know about the society they live in. Very few read books, and in most cases their formal education ended at fifteen or sixteen. What little they know of history has come from the mass media, beginning with comics . . . so if they see themselves in terms of the past, it's because they can't grasp the terms of the present, much less the future. They are the sons of poor men and drifters, losers and the sons of losers. Their backgrounds are overwhelmingly ordinary. As people, they are like millions of other people. But in their collective identity they have a peculiar fascination so obvious that even the Press has recognized it, although not without cynicism. In its ritual flirtation with reality the Press has viewed the Angels with a mixture of awe, humour and terror – justified, as always, by a slavish dedication to the public appetite, which most journalists find so puzzling and contemptible that they have long since abandoned the task of understanding it to a handful of poll-takers and 'experts'.

The widespread appeal of the Angels is worth pondering. Unlike most other rebels, the Angels have given up hope that the world is going to change for them. They assume, on good evidence, that the people who run the social machinery have little use for outlaw motorcyclists, and they are reconciled to being losers. But instead of losing quietly, one by one, they have banded together with a mindless kind of loyalty and moved outside the framework, for good or ill. They may not have an answer, but at least they are still on their feet. One night about halfway through one of their weekly meetings I thought of Joe Hill on his way to face a Utah firing squad and saying his final words: 'Don't mourn. Organize.' It is safe to say that no Hell's Angel has ever heard of Joe Hill or would know a Wobbly from a bushmaster, but there is something very similar about the attitudes. The Industrial Workers of the World had serious blueprints for society, while the Hell's Angels mean only to defy the social machinery. There is no talk among the Angels of 'building a better world', yet their reactions to the world they live in are rooted in the same kind of anarchic, para-legal sense of conviction that brought the armed wrath of the Establishment down on the Wobblies. There is the same kind of suicidal loyalty, the same kind of in-group rituals and nicknames, and above all the same feeling of constant warfare with an unjust world. The Wobblies were losers, and so are the Angels . . . and if every loser in this country today rode a motorcycle the whole highway system would have to be modified.

There is an important difference between the words 'loser' and 'outlaw'. One is passive and the other is active, and the main reasons the Angels are such good copy is that they are acting out the day-dreams of millions of losers who don't wear any defiant insignia and who don't know how to be outlaws. The streets of every city are thronged with men who would pay all the money they could get their hands on to be transformed – even for a day – into hairy, hard-fisted brutes who walk over cops, extort free drinks from terrified bartenders and then thunder out of town on big motorcycles after raping the banker's daughter. Even people who think the Angels should all be put to sleep find it easy to identify with them. They command a fascination, however reluctant, that borders on psychic masturbation.

The Angels don't like being called losers, but they have learned to live with it. 'Yeah, I guess I am,' said one. 'But you're looking at one loser who's going to make a hell of a scene on the way out.'

22

He who makes a beast of himself gets rid of the pain of being a man. – *Dr Johnson*

The neighbourhood suddenly exploded with excited, morbid crowds. Hysterical women surged forward in a frenzy, screeching in almost sexual ecstasy, scratching and fighting the agents and police in their attempt to reach the body. One fat-breasted woman with stringy red hair broke through the cordon and dipped her handkerchief in the blood, clutched it to her sweaty dress and waddled off down the street. . . . – *From an account of the death of John Dillinger*

TOWARDS Christmas the action slowed down and the Angels dropped out of the headlines. Tiny lost his job, Sonny got involved in a long jury trial on the attempted-murder charge.* and the El Adobe was demolished by the wrecker's ball. The Angels drifted from one bar to another, but they found it harder to establish a hangout than to maintain one. In San Francisco it was just as slow. Frenchy spent three months in General Hospital when a can of gasoline blew up on him, and Puff went to jail after a fracas with two cops who raided an Angel birthday party. Winter is always slow for the outlaws. Many have to go to work to stay eligible for next summer's unemployment insurance, it is too cold for big outdoor parties, and the constant rain makes riding an uncomfortable hazard.

It seemed like a good time to get some work done, so I dropped off the circuit. Terry came by now and then to keep me posted. One day he showed up with a broken arm, saying he'd wrecked his bike, his old lady had left him and the niggers had blown up his house. I'd heard about the house from Barger's wife, Elsie, who

* Which ended with a hung jury and eventual reduction of the charge to 'assault with a deadly weapon' – to which Barger pleaded guilty and served six months in jail.

was handling the communications post at their home in Oakland. During one of the sporadic flare-ups between the Angels and Oakland Negroes somebody had thrown a homemade bomb through the window of the house Terry was renting in East Oakland. The fire destroyed the house and all of Marilyn's paintings. She was a pretty little girl about nineteen, with long blonde hair and a respectable family in one of the valley towns. She'd been living with Terry for nearly six months, covering the walls with her artwork, but she had no stomach for bombs. The divorce was effected soon after they moved to another dwelling. 'I came back one night and she was gone,' said Terry. 'All she left was a note: "Dear Terry, Fuck it." And that was that.'

Nothing else happened until January, when Mother Miles got snuffed. He was riding his bike through Berkeley when a truck came out of a side street and hit him head on, breaking both legs and fracturing his skull. He hung in a coma for six days, then died on a Sunday morning, less than twenty-four hours before his thirtieth birthday – leaving a wife, two children and his righteous girl friend, Ann.

Miles had been president of the Sacramento chapter. His influence was so great that in 1965 he moved the whole club down to Oakland, claiming the police had made life intolerable for them by constant harassment. The outlaws simply picked up and moved, not questioning Miles's wisdom. His real name was James, but the Angels called him Mother.

'I guess it was because he was kind of motherly,' said Gut. 'Miles was great, great people. He took care of everybody. He worried. You could always depend on him.'

I knew Miles in a distant kind of way. He didn't trust writers, but there was nothing mean about him, and once he decided I wasn't going to get him locked up somehow, he was friendly. He had the build of a pot-bellied stevedore, with a round face and a wide, flaring beard. I never thought of him as a hoodlum. He had the usual Hell's Angel police record: drunk, disorderly, fighting, vagrancy, loitering, petty larceny and a handful of ominous 'suspicion of' charges that had never gone to trial. But he wasn't plagued by the same demons that motivate some of the others. He wasn't happy with the world, but he didn't brood about it, and his appetite for revenge didn't extend beyond specific wrongs done to the Angels or to him personally. You could drink with Miles without wondering when he was going to swing on somebody or lift your money off the bar. He wasn't that way. Booze seemed to make him more genial. Like most of the Angels' leaders, he had a quick mind and a quality of self-control which the others relied on.

When I heard he'd been killed I called Sonny to ask about the funeral, but by the time I finally got hold of him the details were already on the radio and in the newspapers. Miles's mother was arranging for the funeral in Sacramento. The outlaw caravan would form at Barger's house at eleven on Thursday morning. The Angels have gone to plenty of funerals for their own people, but until this one they had never tried to run the procession for ninety miles along a major highway. There was also a chance that the Sacramento police would try to keep them out of town.

The word went out on Monday and Tuesday by telephone. This was not going to be any Jay Gatsby funeral; the Angels wanted a full-dress rally. Miles's status was not the point; the death of any Angel requires a show of strength by the others. It is a form of affirmation – not for the dead, but the living. There are no set penalties for not showing up, because none are necessary. In the cheap loneliness that is the overriding fact of every outlaw's life, a funeral is a bleak reminder that the tribe is smaller by one. The circle is one link smaller, the enemy jacks up the odds just a little bit more, and defenders of the faith need something to take off the chill. A funeral is a time for counting the loyal, for seeing how many are left. There is no question about skipping work, going without sleep or riding for hours in a cold wind to be there on time.

Early Thursday morning the bikes began arriving in Oakland. Most of the outlaws were already in the Bay Area, or at least within fifty or sixty miles, but a handful of Satan's Slaves rode all of Wednesday night, five hundred miles from Los Angeles, to join the main caravan. Others came from Fresno and San Jose and Santa Rosa. There were Hangmen, Misfits, Presidents, Nightriders, Crossmen and some with no colours at all. A hard-faced little man whom nobody spoke to wore an olive-drab bombardier's jacket with just the word 'Loner' on the back, written in small, blue-inked letters that looked like a signature.

I was crossing the Bay Bridge when a dozen Gypsy Jokers came roaring past, ignoring the speed limit as they split up to go around me on both sides of the car. Seconds later they disappeared up ahead in the fog. The morning was cold and bridge traffic was slow except for motorcycles. Down in the Bay there were freighters lined up, waiting for open piers.

The procession rolled at exactly eleven – a hundred and fifty bikes and about twenty cars. A few miles north of Oakland, at the Carquinez Bridge, the outlaws picked up a police escort assigned to keep them under control. A Highway Patrol car led the caravan all the way to Sacramento. The lead Angels rode two abreast in the right lane, holding a steady sixty-five miles an hour. At the head, with Barger, was the scruffy Praetorian Guard: Magoo, Tommy, Jimmy, Skip, Tiny, Zorro, Terry and Charger Charley the Child Molester. The spectacle disrupted traffic all along the way. It looked like something from another world. Here was the 'scum of the earth', the 'lowest form of animals', an army of unwashed gang rapists . . . being escorted towards the state capitol by a Highway Patrol car with a flashing yellow light. The steady pace of the procession made it unnaturally solemn. Not even Senator Murphy could have mistaken it for a dangerous run. There were the same bearded faces; the same earring emblems, swastikas and grinning death's-heads flapping in the wind – but this time there were no party clothes, no hamming it up for the squares. They were still playing the role, but all the humour was missing. The only trouble *en route* came when the procession was halted after a filling-station owner complained that somebody had stolen fourteen quarts of oil at the last gas stop. Barger quickly took up a collection to pay the man off, muttering that whoever stole the oil was due for a chain-whipping later on. The Angels assured each other that it must have been a punk in one of the cars at the rear of the caravan, some shithead without any class.

In Sacramento there was no sign of harassment. Hundreds of curious spectators lined the route between the funeral home and the cemetery. Inside the chapel a handful of Jim Miles's childhood friends and relatives waited with his body, a hired minister and three nervous attendants. They knew what was coming – Mother Miles's 'people', hundreds of thugs, wild brawlers and bizarre-looking girls in tight Levis, scarves and waist-length platinum-coloured wigs. Miles's mother, a heavy middle-aged woman in a black suit, wept openly at a front pew, facing the open casket.

At one-thirty the outlaw caravan arrived. The slow rumble of motorcycle engines rattled glass in the mortuary windows. Police tried to keep traffic moving as TV cameras followed Barger and perhaps a hundred others towards the door of the chapel. Many outlaws waited outside during the service. They stood in quiet groups, leaning against the bikes and killing time with lazy conversation. There was hardly any talk about Miles. In one group a pint of whiskey made the rounds. Some of the outlaws talked to bystanders, trying to explain what was happening. 'Yeah, the guy was one of our leaders,' said an Angel to an elderly man in a baseball cap. 'He was good people. Some punk ran a stop sign and snuffed him. We came to bury him with the colours.'

Inside the pine-panelled chapel the minister was telling his weird congregation that 'the wages of sin is death'. He looked like a Norman Rockwell druggist and was obviously repelled by the whole scene. Not all the pews were full, but standing room in the rear was crowded all the way back to the door. The minister talked about 'sin' and 'justification', pausing now and then as if he expected a rebuttal from the crowd. 'It's not my business to pass judgement on anybody,' he continued. 'Nor is it my business to eulogize anybody. But it *is* my business to speak out a warning that *it will happen to you*! I don't know what philosophy some of you have about death, but I know the Scriptures tell us that God takes no pleasure in the death of the wicked. . . . Jesus didn't die for an animal, he died for a man. . . . What I say about Jim won't change anything, but I can preach the gospel to you and I have a responsibility to warn you that you will all have to *answer to God*!'

The crowd was shifting and sweating. The chapel was so hot that it seemed like the Devil was waiting in one of the anterooms, ready to claim the wicked just as soon as the sermon was over.

'How many of you,' asked the minister, 'how many of you asked yourselves on the way up here, "*Who is next?*"'

At this point several Angels in the pews rose and walked out, cursing quietly at a way of life they had long ago left behind. The minister ignored these mutinous signs and launched into a story about a Philippian jailer. 'Holy shit!' mumbled Tiny. He'd been standing quietly in the rear for about thirty minutes, pouring sweat and eyeing the minister as if he meant to hunt him down later in the day and extract all his teeth. Tiny's departure caused five or six others to leave. The minister sensed he was losing his audience, so he brought the Philippian story to a quick end.

There was no music as the crowd filed out. I passed by the casket and was shocked to see Mother Miles clean-shaven, lying peacefully on his back in a blue suit, white shirt and a wide maroon tie. His Hell's Angels jacket, covered with exotic emblems, was mounted on a stand at the foot of the casket. Behind it were thirteen wreaths, some bearing the names of other outlaw clubs.

I barely recognized Miles. He looked younger than twenty-nine and very ordinary. But his face was calm, as though he were not at all surprised to find himself there in a box. He wouldn't have liked the clothes he was wearing, but since the Angels weren't paying for the funeral, the best they could do was make sure the colours went into the casket before it was sealed. Barger stayed behind with the pallbearers to make sure the thing was done right.

After the funeral more than two hundred motorcycles followed the hearse to the cemetery. Behind the Angels rode all the other clubs, including a half-dozen East Bay Dragons – and, according to a radio commentator, 'dozens of teen-age riders who looked so solemn that you'd think Robin Hood had just died'.

The Hell's Angels knew better. Not all of them had read about Robin Hood, but they understood that the parallel was complimentary. Perhaps the younger outlaws believed it, but there is room in their margin for one or two friendly illusions. Those who are almost thirty, or more than that, have been living too long with their own scurvy image to think of themselves as heroes. They understand that heroes are always 'good guys', and they have seen enough cowboy movies to know that good guys win in the end. The myth didn't seem to include Miles, who was 'one of the best'. But all he got in the end was two broken legs, a smashed head and a tongue-lashing from the preacher. Only his Hell's Angels identity kept him from going to the grave as anonymously as any ribbon clerk. As it was, his funeral got nationwide Press coverage: *Life* had a picture of the procession entering the cemetery, TV newscasts gave the funeral a solemn priority, and the *Chronicle* heading said: HELL'S ANGELS BURY THEIR OWN – BLACK JACKETS AND AN ODD DIGNITY. Mother Miles would have been pleased.

Moments after the burial the caravan was escorted out of town by a phalanx of police cars. with sirens howling. The brief truce was ended. At the city limits the Angels screwed it on and roared back to Richmond, across the Bay from San Francisco, where they held an all-night wake that kept police on edge until long after dawn. On Sunday night there was a meeting in Oakland to confirm Miles's successor. Big Al. It was a quiet affair, but without the grimness of the funeral. The banshee's wail that had seemed so loud on Thursday was already fading away. After the meeting there was a beer party at the Sinner's Club, and by the time the place closed they had already set the date for the next run. The Angels would gather in Bakersfield, on the first day of spring.

*

All my life my heart has sought a thing I cannot name. – *Remembered line from a long-forgotten poem*

*

Months later, when I rarely saw the Angels, I still had the legacy of the big machine – four hundred pounds of chrome and deep red noise to take out on the Coast Highway and cut loose at three in the morning, when all the cops were lurking over on 101. My first crash had wrecked the bike completely and it took several months to have it rebuilt. After that I decided to ride it differently: I would stop pushing my luck on curves, always wear a helmet and try to keep within range of the nearest speed limit ... my insurance had already been cancelled and my driver's licence was hanging by a thread.

So it was always at night, like a werewolf, that I would take the thing out for an honest run down the coast. I would start in Golden Gate Park, thinking only to run a few long curves to clear my head ... but in a matter of minutes I'd be out at the beach with the sound of the engine in my ears, the surf booming up on the sea wall and a fine empty road stretching all the way down to Santa Cruz . . . not even a gas station in the whole seventy miles; the only public light along the way is an all-night diner down around Rockaway Beach.

There was no helmet on those nights, no speed limit, and no cooling it down on the curves. The momentary freedom of the park was like the one unlucky drink that shoves a wavering alcoholic off the wagon. I would come out of the park near the soccer field and pause for a moment at the stop sign wondering if I knew anyone parked out there on the midnight humping strip.

Then into first gear, forgetting the cars and letting the beast wind out . . . thirty-five, forty-five . . . then into second and wailing through the light at Lincoln Way, not worried about green or red signals, but only some other werewolf loony who might be pulling out, too slowly, to start his own run. Not many of these . . . and with three lanes in a wide curve, a bike coming hard has plenty of room to get around almost anything . . . then into third, the boomer gear, pushing seventy-five and the beginning of a windscream in the ears, a pressure on the eyeballs like diving into water off a high board.

Bent forward, far back on the seat, and a rigid grip on the handlebars as the bike starts jumping and wavering in the wind. Tail-lights far up ahead coming closer, faster, and suddenly – zaaapppp – going past and leaning down for a curve near the zoo, where the road swings out to sea.

The dunes are flatter here, and on windy days sand blows across the highway, piling up in thick drifts as deadly as any oil-slick . . . instant loss of control, a crashing, cartwheeling slide and maybe one of those two-inch notices in the paper the next-day: 'An unidentified motorcyclist was killed last night when he failed to negotiate a turn on Highway 1.'

Indeed . . . but no sand this time, so the lever goes up into fourth, and now there's no sound except wind. Screw it all the way over, reach through the handlebars to raise the headlight beam, the needle leans down on a hundred, and wind-burned eyeballs strain to see down the centreline, trying to provide a margin for the reflexes.

But with the throttle screwed on, there is only the barest margin and no room at all for mistakes. It has to be done right . . . and that's when the strange music starts, when you stretch your luck so far that fear becomes exhilaration and vibrates along your arms. You can barely see at a hundred; the tears blow back so fast that they vaporize before they get to your ears. The only sounds are wind and a dull roar floating back from the mufflers. You watch the white line and try to lean with it . . . howling through a turn to the right, then to the left and down the long hill to Pacifica . . . letting off now, watching for cops, but only until the next dark stretch and another few seconds on the edge. . . . The Edge. . . . There is no honest way to explain it because the only people who really know where it is are the ones who have gone over. The others – the iiving – are those who pushed their control as far as they felt they could handle it, and then pulled back, or slowed down, or did whatever they had to when it came time to choose between Now and Later.

But the edge is still Out there. Or maybe it's In. The association of motorcycles with LSD is no accident of publicity. They are both a means to an end, to the place of definitions.

Postscript

ON Labour Day 1966, I pushed my luck a little too far and got badly stomped by four or five Angels who seemed to feel I was taking advantage of them. A minor disagreement suddenly became very serious.

None of those who did me were among the group I considered my friends – but they were Angels, and that was enough to cause many of the others to participate after one of the brethren teed off on me. The first blow was launched with no hint of warning and I thought for a moment that it was just one of those drunken accidents that a man has to live with in this league. But within seconds I was clubbed from behind by the Angel I'd been talking to just a moment earlier. Then I was swarmed in a general flail. As I went down I caught a glimpse of Tiny, standing on the rim of the action. His was the only familiar face I could see . . . and if there is any one person a non-Angel does *not* want to see among his attackers, that person is Tiny. I yelled to him for help – but more out of desperation than hope.

Yet it was Tiny who pulled me out of the stomp circle before the others managed to fracture my skull or explode my groin. Even while the heavy boots were punching into my ribs and jolting my head back and forth I could hear Tiny somewhere above me, saying 'Come on, come on, that's enough'. I suppose he helped more than I realized, but if he had done nothing else I owe him a huge favour for preventing one of the outlaws from crashing a huge rock down on my head. I could see the vicious swine trying to get at me with the stone held in a two-handed Godzilla grip above his head. Tiny kept him mercifully out of range . . . and then, during a lull in the boot action, he pulled me to my feet and hurried me off towards the highway.

Nobody followed. The attack ended with the same inexplicable suddenness that it had begun. There was no vocal aftermath, then or later. I didn't expect one – no more than I'd expect a pack of sharks to explain their feeding frenzy.

I got in my car and sped off, spitting blood on the dashboard and weaving erratically across both lanes of the midnight highway until my one good eye finally came into focus. I hadn't gone very far when I realized Magoo was asleep in the back seat. I pulled off the road and woke him up. He was jolted at the sight of my bloody face. 'Jesus Christ!' he muttered. 'Who's after us? You shoulda woke me up!'

'Never mind,' I said. 'You better get out. I'm leaving.' He nodded blankly, then lurched out to meet the enemy. I left him standing in the gravel beside the road.

My next stop was the hospital in Santa Rosa, nearly fifty miles south of the Angel encampment. The emergency-ward waiting-room was full of wounded Gypsy Jokers. The most serious case was a broken jaw, the result of a clash earlier that evening with a pipe-wielding Hell's Angel.

The Jokers told me they were on their way north to wipe the Angels out. 'It'll be a goddamn slaughter,' said one.

I agreed and wished them luck. I wanted no part of it – not even with a shotgun. I was tired, swollen and whipped. My face looked like it had been jammed into the spokes of a speeding Harley, and the only thing keeping me awake was the spastic pain of a broken rib.

It had been a bad trip . . . fast and wild in some moments, slow and dirty in others, but on balance it looked like a bummer. On my way back to San Francisco, I tried to compose a fitting epitaph. I wanted something original, but there was no escaping the echo of Mistah Kurtz's comment from the heart of the darkness: 'The horror! The horror! . . . Exterminate all the brutes!' It seemed appropriate, if not entirely just . . . but after getting such a concentrated jolt of reality I was not much concerned about justice.